I CAN SEE THE SHORE

Praise for I Can See the Shore

I've known the Dawsons for several years and rejoice in their great faith in God amid severe trials. In spite of the obstacles of primitive conditions, sickness, and death, they have persevered for the souls of the Yanomamö Indians in the rainforest of southern Venezuela. This book is a gripping life story of the triumph of missions with all its mega-challenges.

—Dr. George Sweeting
Chancellor Emeritus
Moody Bible Institute, Chicago

I Can See the Shore *depicts a life lived among the Yanomamö with gusto and good humor, while personal sorrows are overcome with grace and transcendence. Mike Dawson not only tells his own remarkable story, but also translates the experiences of Yanomamö shamans, warriors, and childhood friends as they struggle with illness and warfare and confront choices about how to live as Yanomamö in a modern age.*

—Amy Wray
Filmmaker
Yanomamö Homecoming
National Geographic Television

It's rare that a single book makes you laugh and cry. I laughed at Mike's jungle exploits and cried with him over his daughter's death. Very few people have the opportunity to grow up on both sides of the cultural fence as Mike and I have. Reading this book will highlight the Gospel as a multicultural message.

—Steve Saint
itecusa.org

I Can See the Shore

Growing Up Yanomamö Today

Michael Dawson

Foreword by Paul C. Dye
New Tribes Mission Aviation

Grace Acres Press
P.O. Box 22
Larkspur, CO 80118
888-700-GRACE (4722)
(303) 681-9995
(303) 681-9996 fax
www.GraceAcresPress.com

Illustrations by Heather Dawson, Stephen Dawson, Karin Henley, and James Meyers.

Cover photo of Michael in Matowäteli, 2004, by Rick Johnson.
Cover design by Granite Creative.

Library of Congress Cataloging-in-Publication Data:

Dawson, Mike, 1955–
I Can See the Shore : growing up Yanomamö today / by Mike Dawson
p. cm.
ISBN: 978-1-60265-030-5
1. Yanomamö Indians—Venezuela—Amazonas—Social life and customs. 2. Yanomamö Indians—Venezuela—Amazonas—Social conditions. 3. Yanomamö Indians—Missions—Venezuela—Amazonas. 4. Dawson, Mike, 1955–. 5. Dawson, Mike, 1955– —Family. 6. Missionaries—Venezuela—Amazonas—Biography. 7. Amazonas (Venezuela)—Social life and customs. 8. Amazonas (Venezuela)—Social conditions. 9. Amazonas (Venezuela)—Biography. I. Title.
F2520.1.Y3D395 2010
987'.640049892—dc22 2010017864

Printed in Canada

13 12 11 10 01 02 03 04 05 06 07 08 09 10

DEDICATION

This book is dedicated to the memory of
Mikeila Reneé Dawson
3-23-2000 to 1-12-2006
Jehovah es mi Pastor;
Nada me faltará.
Psalm 23:1

A Bible verse she loved.
Our ray of light
Our spark of joy
Dwells now
With the Shepherd above.

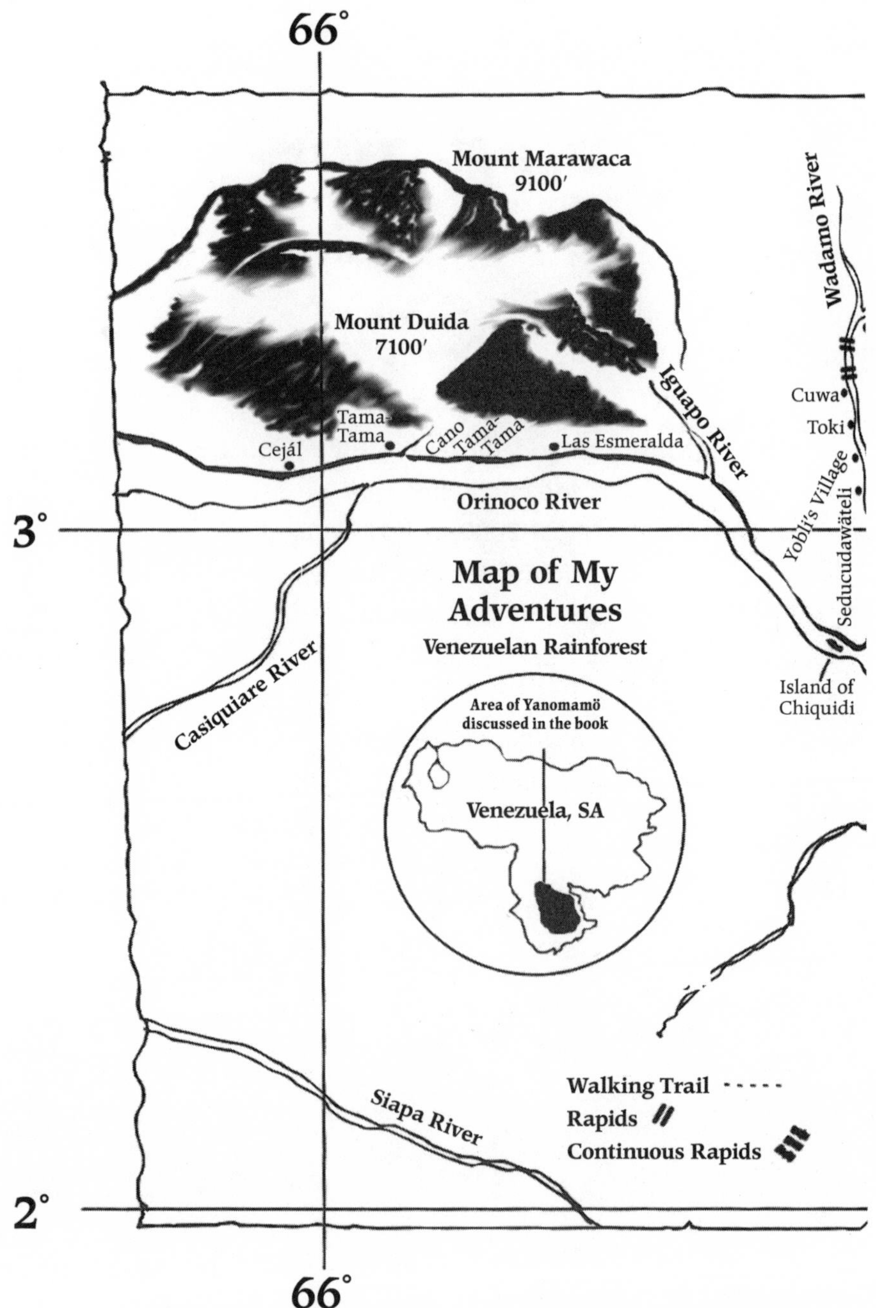
66°
Mount Marawaca
9100′
Wadamo River
Mount Duida
7100′
Iguapo River
Cuwa
Toki
Tama-
Tama
Cano
Tama-
Tama
Las Esmeralda
Cejál
Yobli's Village
Orinoco River
3°
Seducudawäteli
Map of My
Adventures
Venezuelan Rainforest
Island of
Chiquidi
Casiquiare River
Area of Yanomamö
discussed in the book
Venezuela, SA
Walking Trail
Rapids
Continuous Rapids
Siapa River
2°
66°

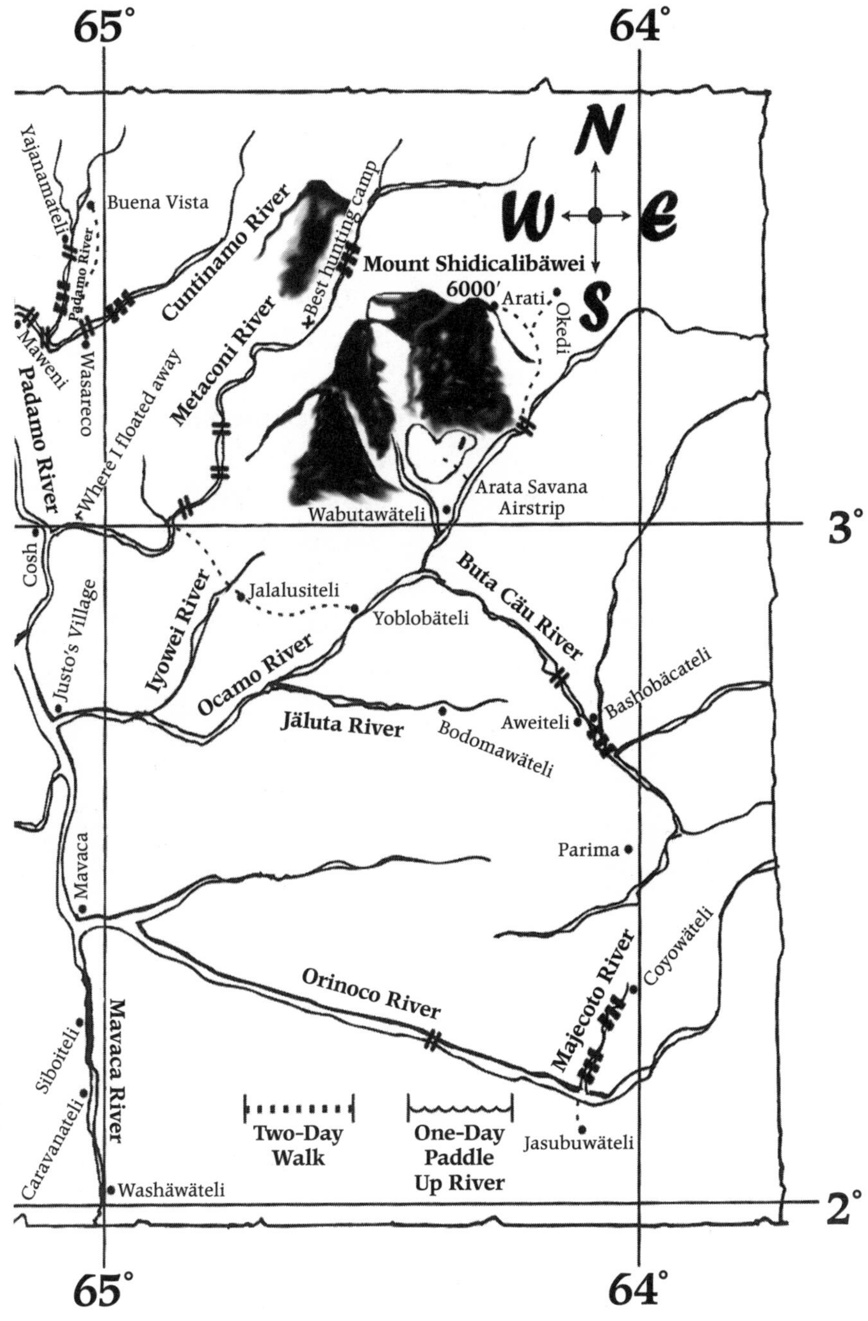

65°
64°
N
W
E
S
Yajanamateli
Buena Vista
Padamo River
Cuntinamo River
Best hunting camp
Mount Shidicalibäwei
6000′
Arati
Okedi
Maweni
Wasareco
Metaconi River
Where I floated away
Padamo River
Arata Savana
Airstrip
Wabutawäteli
3°
Cosh
Buta Cäu River
Jalalusiteli
Iyowei River
Justo's Village
Yoblobäteli
Ocamo River
Bashobäcateli
Aweiteli
Jäluta River
Bodomawäteli
Parima
Mavaca
Coyowäteli
Majecoto River
Orinoco River
Siboiteli
Mavaca River
Caravanateli
Two-Day
Walk
One-Day
Paddle
Up River
Jasubuwäteli
Washäwäteli
2°
65°
64°

I believe, help thou my unbelief.
I take the finite risk of trusting like a child.
I believe, help Thou my unbelief,
I walk into the unknown trusting all the while.
I long so much to feel the warmth
that others seem to know. But should I never
feel a thing, I claim Him even so.
I believe, help thou my unbelief,
I walk into the unknown trusting like a child.
I walk into the unknown trusting.

—Bill Gaither

About the Author

Born in a small missionary base, TamaTama, on the Orinoco River, Michael is the fifth of ten children of Joe and Millie Dawson, who were among the first missionaries to the Yanomamö tribe. His first language was Yanomamö and he learned English when he was seven years old.

After high school, Mike worked in remote villages along the upper Orinoco River system to determine the understandability of a translation of the New Testament. He returned to the United States for Bible School in 1976 and finished missionary training in 1979. He married Reneé Pintor in 1980 and left for Venezuela in 1981, discipling new Yanomamö believers and traveling with them to show how to evangelize their own people. Mike and Reneé had three boys: Joshua, Ryan, and Stephen.

In June 1992, Mike and Reneé both contracted cerebral malaria and were evacuated to Caracas. Reneé did not recover; she is buried in the village of Coshilowäteli. Her headstone reads: "She lives in our hearts as a penetrating reminder that not only is Christ worth living for, He is worth dying for." Because of the delay in Reneé's treatment, Mike dreamed of having an airplane based in the jungle to handle medical emergencies.

Mike and his boys continued working with the Yanomamö. In October 1994, he married Keila Cornieles, with whom he had two daughters, Mikeila and Mia. On January 12, 2006, Mikeila went to be with the Lord. Again, the need to have an airplane based in the jungle was forcefully brought home.

Michael is executive producer of *Yai Wanonabälewä: The Enemy God* (www.theenemygod.com), a feature-length movie based on the true story of how the Gospel of Jesus Christ has affected the life of a Yanomamö shaman and his village.

Acknowledgments

Again, this book has been a joint effort with many of my family. Thanks to my sisters for the poems. Thanks to my sons, Josh and Stephen Dawson; to my nieces, Heather Dawson and Karin Henley; and my friend Jim Meyers for the artwork. Thanks to Pastor Von and Rick Johnson for the beautiful photos of the Yanomamö they were gracious enough to let me use. Thanks to Faith, Sharon, Mom, and Gary for refreshing my memory of stories from long ago.

Huge thanks to Bautista (Shoefoot) for the hours he spent explaining the initiation process the Yanomamö witch doctors go through and the role of the *oca* in their warfare. Although I had observed their initiations, and had heard about and even known *oca* at different times, I still needed his expertise to understand these things sufficiently so that I could describe it in a way that makes sense.

Thanks also to the many of you who encouraged me with your notes and your prayers while this book was being born. My prayer with this book is that God will use it for His glory. While putting the words on paper, I was reminded over and over how much God loves us as individuals and how He controls every detail of our lives. It also came home to me again what a great privilege it is to be able to serve Him!

Contents

Foreword

I met Joe and Millie Dawson in Venezuela when I was sixteen, back in 1957. I will never forget Joe telling me that when they arrived in Venezuela in 1953, they would have climbed right back on the airliner and gone back home if they had had the money to do so. God's enemy tried to stop them from reaching the lost right from the start.

In 1943, five men, attempting to make a friendly contact with a primitive tribe, were speared and clubbed to death in the jungles of Bolivia, South America. Three of these men were married. All three of the wives continued serving the Lord in Bolivia after the death of their husbands; they were not there just because of their husbands' convictions. This was always a tremendous example to me. One of these wives was my mother.

When I was eight or nine years old, I was standing beside my mother after church one Sunday morning while we were on furlough, when a concerned member of the church came up to my mom. He said, "Dorothy, I understand that you are planning to return to Bolivia."

"Yes!" she said.

"How are you going to explain taking your three children back down there to God?" Boy! *Who does he think he is, talking to my mom like that,* I thought. I will never forget my mom's answer.

"Sir," she said, getting his attention, "I would rather explain to God why I took them back down there with me than to explain to Him why I didn't." I was so proud of my mother! She never had it easy raising her three children without her husband, but she had learned to trust God and find Him to be her sufficiency, even in very difficult situations and places. She had decided to continue to trust God.

I will always be grateful for my mother's example and to the faithfulness of God, who gave us the privilege to be a part of His great wonderful plan. We have had the joy of seeing many set free, who had been held by Satan in spiritual darkness and in the bondage of the fear of death. They received everlasting life when they believed the Good News that God's Son, Jesus Christ, satisfied the wrath of God, which we all deserve because of our sin, on their behalf at Calvary. He shed His blood and gave His life as full payment. Then, thanks be to God, Jesus rose again to give them and us a wonderful hope.

I am also thankful that Joe and Millie didn't have the money to go back home. They also have been a great example of commitment and dedication to the Lord, both to me and to their children. They are utterly convinced that the lost need to have a chance to hear the Good News of the Gospel of Jesus Christ, which is the power of God unto salvation to everyone who believes it. You see, the reason they are still there, in 2010, is because they also have learned to depend on and trust in the faithfulness of God and have found Him to be sufficient.

As you read this book and listen to Michael Dawson share his heart with you, you will be challenged, as I was, to trust, depend, obey, and serve our wonderful Savior.

Thank you, Michael.

—Paul C. Dye
New Tribes Mission Aviation
Flight Instructor, Latin America and
Phillipines Area Coordinator

Preface

I enjoyed writing *Growing Up Yanomamö.* In the original manuscript, I had included information about our daughter Mikeila's early days and weeks in the hospital. To be honest, it was sitting in the waiting room of the University of Virginia Hospital, waiting for a little girl who was more dead than alive, that I began writing *Growing Up Yanomamö.* I started writing about all we were going through with her, then went from there to just writing stories of my childhood with the intention of having something to share with her and her brothers when she was older. However, after my editor read it, she recommended I tell the story in two books.

"Leave the part about Keila and Mikeila for a second book," she told me.

What second book? was my first thought. I had no intention of trying to do another one. So I left the manuscript intact. Later on, I asked a good friend to read the manuscript for me and was surprised when she told me the same thing about needing to tell the story with two books. So I took all the parts dealing with Keila and Mikeila out of the first book, but still was not convinced I would ever produce another book.

I have decided to do a second book for two reasons. First, my initial reluctance changed after Mikeila went to be with the Lord. I decided I would tell her story and try to share the impact that her short little life has had on my own. In a way, it has been hard writing about her, but in another way, it has been a healing process for me. The second reason has been the number of e-mails and letters asking about a second book. I am humbled and flattered at the same time by the many people who have written telling me how much they enjoyed *Growing Up Yanomamö* and asking when the second book was coming.

Along with my memories and thoughts of Mikeila, I have included a few more stories from my youth and more stories dealing with the culture of the fascinating Yanomamö. My desire is that you might grow to know and love the Yanomamö as much as I do.

A pastor friend of mine gave me a book on heaven called *Heaven*. It is great! In this book, the author, Randy Alcorn, tells of a young lady who stepped into the cold ocean to try to become the first female swimmer to swim from Catalina Island to the mainland of California. She had already swum the English Channel both ways. The fog hung so thick and low over the ocean that throughout most of the swim she could barely see the accompanying boats escorting her on her way. Finally, she had had enough and asked to be taken up. Her mom, riding in one of the boats beside her, told her to keep swimming, she was already close, so she kept on, but after more than fifteen hours in the water, she had had enough. She begged to be taken aboard. When she recovered her breath, she was dismayed to find out she was only half a mile from shore. The next day at a news conference, she stated, "I would have kept swimming if I could have seen the shore. All I could see was the fog."

There have been so many times that all I could see was the fog. How I desperately wanted and needed to see the shore! But when faced with hard times, when I wonder if I can go on, I am reminded that "We walk by faith, not by sight" (2 Cor. 5:7). How my heart yearns for the day when my faith shall be sight and I shall see Jesus! But until that glorious day:

PREFACE

Seeing then that we have a great high priest, that is passed into the heavens, Jesus the Son of God, let us hold fast *our* profession. For we have not an high priest which cannot be touched with the feeling of our infirmities; but was in all points tempted like as *we are, yet* without sin. [16]Let us therefore come boldly unto the throne of grace, that we may obtain mercy, and find grace to help in time of need (Heb. 4:14–16).

PART ONE

Mikeila

Hair like sunshine
Smile so bright
Laughing eyes so blue
Carefree spirit
Unafraid . . .
This is how we remember you.

And in our hearts
The memories live
And they will never die
You left a part of you behind
Deep inside our lives.

O sweet little angel
Our hearts, they miss you so
We wish that we could understand
Just why you had to go . . .

—Sharon Dawson

1

A Time to Weep

January 13, 2006

My head was reeling as I sat on the American Airlines jet staring at the large flakes of snow falling faster and faster, looking more like chunks of snow than flakes. I kept looking at my watch, mentally adding and subtracting flight times to Dallas and connection time and my heart sank further as I realized again that there just was no way we were going to make our connection to Caracas, Venezuela. My eyes blurred as I pictured my beautiful, blonde-haired, blue-eyed little girl, who had been so alive only the day before yesterday as I boarded the Missionary Aviation Fellowship (MAF) plane to fly out to Puerto Ayacucho to head back for our annual advisory board meeting. She had wrapped her long arms around my neck and had given me a wet kiss.

"I wub you Daddy," she had whispered loudly in my ear. Ever since she had been a tiny baby, I had tried to get her to say, "I love you, Daddy." But she had never been able to say it until just a few weeks earlier, when she had finally learned it from her three-year-old sister. So hearing her say that brought tears of joy to my eyes as I held her tight.

I hugged her in return and we rubbed noses as we have done ever since she was just a tiny little baby. "I love you too, honey! Be good for Mommy while I'm gone and I'll hurry back. I'll bring you a good surprise when I come back."

"OK, Daddy," she nodded, but her blue eyes were filled with tears. She hated when I had to leave and I hated to leave her. She has had so much medical trouble that has driven me to my knees so many times that I just hated to leave her. I hugged her again and handed her off to her mother, who smiled bravely. My wife, Keila, hated my leaving as well, and I sure hated to leave them, but this was important.

That was two days ago. Now, the only thing I could think about was getting home. My world had changed in two days. Mikeila was dead. What could we have done differently? That question haunted me. My mind kept going back to her birth and short life.

How do you condense a little girl's life down to a few brief sentences? Even a short, just-under-six-year life like the one of our little Mikeila? There are so many memories and fragments of glimpses of her in my mind. She was so full of life and had me wrapped around her little finger.

When Mikeila was born, she spent the first six weeks in the hospital more dead than alive, and finally had to be put on ECMO (an extracorporeal membrane oxygenator) because her lungs had totally collapsed. At the time, in 2000, the relatively new ECMO heart-lung bypass technology was the most advanced form of life support available for lung failure, but also the most invasive; in short, they took all Mikeila's blood outside her body to be oxygenated. This allowed time for her lungs to be treated and to recover. One of the downsides of this treatment was the fact that an anticoagulant drug, heparin, had to be given as well, to prevent the blood clotting when it passed through the ECMO system. While she was on the heparin, the danger of her bleeding out was really high. Because of her rough start, even after she was released from the hospital, we had periodic check-ups for her. These were every six months until she was a year and a half old, and then they went to once a year. How she hated having to go to the doctor's office for her check-ups.

Because of the ECMO, we had been told that two areas of special concern for her were her eyes and ears, and sure enough, at about one year old, her eyes began to cross—so much so that it actually hurt my eyes to look at her. We asked Dr. Boyle, her head doctor at the University of Virginia Hospital, if he could recommend a really good eye doctor. We were hoping we could get her problem taken care of without surgery. In a very short time (and I don't know how he did it), Dr. Boyle called us to let us know he had gotten her an appointment with Dr. Carter, one of the best children's eye doctors on the East Coast. We had been told there was a long waiting list of people trying to get in to see him, but thanks to Dr. Boyle, we were able to get right in.

On our first visit, Dr. Carter looked at her history. Knowing we were working overseas, he tried to come up with a method whereby we could do a lot of the therapy that she would need by ourselves. He suggested that we try eye patches and glasses. Mikeila looked like a little pirate in her eye patch, but she seemed to understand the importance of it and left it alone. When we picked up her first pair of glasses, though, they were so tiny that we never thought she would or could ever keep them on. And if she did by chance keep them on, how in the world could a nine-month-old baby deal with a pair of glasses? But again, she surprised us. She not only kept them on, but seemed to really enjoy them. She was so comical with her glasses pushed down on her tiny button nose and looking over them at us. Unfortunately, in spite of the patches and glasses, her eyes continued to deteriorate.

At her year-and-a-half check-up, her eye doctor was not pleased with how much her eyes still continued to cross. He told us he felt she needed eye surgery to correct it. We had no idea where we were going to get the money for this, but decided we were living our lives by faith, so by faith we would trust the Lord for this money as well.

Mikeila seemed to have a sixth sense about what was going to happen, and as soon as we turned down the road toward Charlottesville and the hospital, she let us know in no uncertain terms that she was not happy. After having gone through so much with her, and hating to see her in fear, we stayed with her right up until we turned her over to the nurse at the operating-room door. We waited with bated breath, praying for the doctor to come out and call us and let us know the surgery was over and had been a success. I don't remember how long the surgery actually took, but it seemed to go on forever. Finally, the doors opened and the doctor came out and let us know we could go in and sit with her until she woke up. Keila sat on one side of her and I sat on the other, each holding a little hand until she finally began to wake up. Her little eyes were bloodshot and every so often she would catch her breath, so I could tell she was not happy. We were not yet sure how successful the surgery had been, but the doctor told us he felt really good about it. We took her out of the hospital and were extra careful in bundling her into her car seat to take her home.

One of the areas we had been concerned about in Mikeila's development was that, in spite of her being a year and a half old, she was not walking yet. She would only pull herself along the furniture or she would crawl everywhere. We already had tests scheduled to see what could be causing this. Imagine our surprise when, the day after her eye surgery, she stood up and literally took off running. She started running that day and to be honest, she never slowed down. She was such a bundle of energy!

Another concern was that we had been told she had suffered quite a bit of brain damage due to lack of oxygen during those frantic moments of her birth. After looking at her MRI, the doctor had told us we would need to watch her, as there was a possibility of seizures, for one thing; also, the section of her brain that showed the most damage was the area that allowed her to sense or feel fear or inhibition.

"She won't fear anything," he had told us. This truth came home to me in a real way one afternoon when Keila and Mikeila came out to the hangar where I was working and Keila then had to go back inside. Mikeila wanted to stay with me; since I wasn't really busy, I told Keila to leave her with me, that I would watch her. Then I turned back to what I was doing. She was there with me for a while, getting into everything as a three-year-old will do, when the next thing I knew, Mikeila was no longer standing beside me. It had literally been only seconds since she had been there, so *how far could she have gone?* I asked myself, not really concerned. I stepped over to our house to make sure she had not just walked home. Keila answered my call with a negative, Mikeila was not with her. *Now* I was just a bit concerned. My first thought went to the river a little more than a hundred yards away. I started for the port, not really believing she could have gone that far, but something gave me a sense of urgency. I literally ran the last fifty yards or so. I skidded to a stop at the top of the tall river bank and looked down.

My heart stopped! There was three-year-old Mikeila, up to her little chest in the swiftly flowing river. How in the world she had not already been swept off her feet by the current was more than I will ever know. My feet barely touched the clay bank as I madly dashed down to wade out into the river to grab her. With trembling voice and shaking hands, I held her little body to mine and hugged her to me.

"Oh, Mikeila, you scared your daddy," I told her. She laughed. Her little face was overjoyed to be having so much fun in the water. I carried her up the bank. By that time Keila had joined us. We looked at each other thinking the same thing: "This is what the doctor was talking about." All we could do was shake our heads. We were both deeply disturbed by this incident, but Mikeila had no idea of the fright she had just given us.

Then there was the time we were over at my dad's and mom's house having coffee when a little kid came to the door. She stood there shyly for a few minutes and then said, "I thought you might want to know that Mikeila is up a tree."

Figuring she was just talking about the little shrubby guava trees that grow everywhere, that the little kids are always climbing to get the delicious fruit, I was not very concerned. "Which tree is she climbing now?" I asked, figuring she would point to one of the near guava trees.

"She is up in the top of the tree by Gary's house," she told us. I jumped up. That was different. Those were tall jungle trees.

I led the mad scramble out of the house. Looking up to the top of the trees over by Gary's house, I was horrified to see our tiny little girl way at the very top of the tree squealing in delight. We stared. The fear in my heart was a physical force weighing me down. The family gathered around me with all their faces reflecting the panic I felt. I could not move. I was grateful to see one of my Yanomamö friends run to the tree and almost leap up into the branches, to begin climbing furiously toward our little girl up at the top of the tree, who was still laughing and squealing. She was standing on a small branch and holding onto another branch above her head with no idea of the danger she was in, nor of the fear for her that had us all gripped in speechless dread.

We watched as Vicente climbed toward her. He was climbing as fast as he could, which was considerably fast, but seemed to be only crawling toward her. A cicada droned on endlessly and I heard our macaw voicing his opinion in his coarse squawky voice, but our eyes were on the little blonde girl laughing at the world as she gazed about her, having no idea she was the subject of so much attention. She was just enjoying being able to see so far. Vicente appeared to be barely moving, so desperately did

I want him to get to her before she slipped and fell, but finally he reached her. When he got close enough, he stretched up and grabbed her ankle. It was only then that I realized I was holding my breath.

Well, there were going to be *many* times I would be holding my breath over this little girl. Along with her not being afraid of anything, when she was eleven months old, she began to have violent seizures, and her doctors put her on medications to control them. But her seizures continued, increasing in both frequency and duration. We met with her doctors again, and together decided to take her off her seizure medications. Once she was weaned off the drugs, her seizures tapered off, and we went for more than a year with no seizures. Just about the time we began to breathe normally again, she went into one that about scared us to death. After that, she experienced about one major seizure every six months.

So, on the 10th of January 2006, while packing to leave, I felt good even though I hated to leave my family. Mikeila's seizures were fairly well spaced out, and she had just had a seizure a week earlier. Though this was certainly not something we enjoyed, I felt I could now leave without too much worry, knowing that she would be OK while I was gone. I hugged her goodbye and she wrapped her long arms around my neck and hugged me back. The memory of that hug was still with me the next day as I checked in for my flight to San Juan, Puerto Rico.

After checking in and going to my gate, I called my oldest son, Josh, to let him know I had already checked in. He told me he had received an e-mail from Stephen, another of my sons who was in the jungle, saying that Mikeila was sick. Stephen, my then-seventeen-year-old son, was still in the jungle with Keila and the girls (Mikeila and three-year-old Mia). I asked Josh to e-mail Stephen to see what was wrong, to find out if it was just a cold or something like that, or if it was something that I should head back home for. I told Josh I would call back in about an hour to see if he had more news for me. After about an hour, I walked back to the bank of phones and called Josh again.

"Dad, I just received another e-mail from Stephen and he says Mikeila is doing a bit better, and Keila says there is no reason for you to come home." I breathed a sigh of relief, not because she was saying I did not have to turn back, but because Mikeila was doing better. I thanked Josh and told him I would call him from Puerto Rico as soon as the plane landed over there, and asked him to write Stephen again and let them know what we were doing.

I walked back to my gate and sat down by the window, watching the big plane taxi into the gate. I continued watching as the jetway went out and bumped into the plane and then watched without really seeing as the carts and workers swarmed around the jet in their choreographed jobs. I bowed my head and began to pray for Mikeila.

"God," I prayed, "please touch little Mikeila. I hate her to be sick when I am not there to help. You have done so many miracles with this little girl, please do one more for us now. Give Keila and Stephen strength as they are having to deal with this by themselves."

I continued to pray, and then went back to gazing out the window without really paying much attention. Suddenly I did see something that caught my attention. I had not realized I had been praying that long. I never saw the suitcases going in, but now there was a suitcase coming *down* the conveyor belt out of the plane. It sure looked like mine!

I jumped up and ran over to the counter. "Excuse me, I just saw a suitcase coming off the plane that looked like mine. What's going on?"

The lady turned to me and asked me for my name. After I told her, she said. "I am sorry, sir, but we called you repeatedly and since you did not answer, we had to remove your luggage. The plane is loaded and leaving."

"Señorita? I was sitting right there and I never heard the gate called. All the people I was sitting with are still there and I never heard my name." She looked at me as though I were drunk or something.

"I am sorry, we called," was all she would say.

That flight was the last one of the day with that airline, so the lady tried to get me on another airline's flight, but there were no seats available. While she was checking the next day's flights, I suddenly had a thought. What if this was God's way of telling me He wanted me to head home? I quickly bowed my head. "Lord," I prayed silently, "if You want me to head home, please don't let there be any flights. If I can't find a flight by 10:00 a.m. tomorrow morning, I will take that as from You that I just need to get home. If I get a flight, I will also take that as from You to continue on. Please help Mikeila to feel better and give Keila strength."

Just then the lady looked up with a smile, and said, "I can get you on the first American Airlines flight out of here tomorrow morning with a connecting flight on to Chicago O'Hare getting there at 2:00 p.m. tomorrow afternoon."

Well, that took care of that problem; now what do I do? According to my passport, I had left the country. What does it take now to make it so I can head on back to my hotel? I asked the lady what my next step was, and she told me I had to go down to a small room and get the exit stamp in my passport voided; then they would allow me to leave. Sounded easy enough—but according to my watch, by the time I had the exit stamp voided, I would have been halfway to Chicago. Such is life. I had missed the flight, so there was no one to blame but myself. I finally got back to my hotel and the manager was kind enough to find me a room.

The first thing I did was call Josh to tell him what had happened, and he told me that, according to the last e-mail from Stephen, Mikeila was continuing to improve. "Praise God!" I breathed.

The next morning I left the hotel at 3:00 a.m., and before 6:00 a.m., I was flying out over the Caribbean, winging my way toward the USA. Watching the sunrise from 35,000 feet is a rare treat and filled my heart with gratitude for a God who created such glory and beauty. I again breathed a prayer for Mikeila. While still concerned about her, I felt calmer having heard that she was doing better.

True to the American Airlines lady's word, we landed and were parked at our gate by 2:00 p.m.. I rushed down to grab my bag, and, as soon as I had it in hand, called Josh. I was thankful to hear he was just coming down the airport terminal road, and by the time I got outside, he drove by and picked me up. We drove straight to the house of a good friend, Mike Lesperance, where our mission advisory committee members were holding our annual meeting. I was almost a day late, but I figured better late than never.

As soon as Josh dropped me off at Mike's home, he drove back to his house to change his clothes and head on over to work. However, we had barely gotten into the first issue facing our mission, when I was surprised to see Josh walking back into the Lesperance house. From the look on his face, I knew something was dreadfully wrong.

"Dad, I just received another e-mail from Stephen and he says Mikeila is not doing well. They're trying to call for the plane to evacuate her out." His face showed his concern. "The e-mail was written this morning, so I'm assuming Keila and Mikeila are probably in Puerto Ayacucho by now."

To be honest, my heart froze at this news. I wondered what my first action should be. One of the men handed me a phone and I dialed the home of the MAF program manager's home. He answered the phone himself and I quickly asked him what the news was from Cosh–Coshilowäteli, the village where we lived.

"Mike, I have not heard from Cosh. I don't know anything about an emergency. But I do know our plane did not go to Cosh today."

Well, that made me feel better. If anyone would know about an emergency, it would be MAF. But I had to know for sure, so I called our office in Puerto Ayacucho.

As soon as Gail Alford answered the phone, I knew something was wrong. "Mike, we have been trying to call you, hold on a minute, here is Jim." She passed the phone to a family friend whom I have known all my life.

"Mike," his voice caught. "Mike, I am so sorry, we have been trying to get in touch with you. I just spoke with Jerald, he is driving over to where you are right now, Mike. I don't know how to tell you, I am so sorry. Mikeila did not make it. She passed away in Cosh this afternoon. I am so sorry, Mike." He broke down and started crying. I don't know how, but I somehow kept breathing. I thanked him, and told him I would be calling back with plans. I hung up. From the look on my face, our advisory committee knew something was wrong.

"Mikeila did not make it. I have to head back to Cosh. I need to see if I can get a flight." Ron Ballinger picked up his phone and walked into the next room. In minutes, he not only had me on a flight, but also had seats for my sons Joshua and Ryan as well. We were still in shock. Josh came up and gave me a big hug and whispered that we should call Ryan. Ryan, my second-oldest son, was up in Wisconsin at Nicolet Bible Institute, about six hours from where we were outside of Chicago. He, of course, did not know anything was happening.

One of the hardest things I have ever had to do was get on the phone and call Ryan. He had always had a special bond with Mikeila and I knew I was going to break his heart with my phone call. He took the call and was so quiet on the other end that I got worried.

"Are you OK, Ry?" I asked. I was anxious for him. I could barely hear his answer. "Ron has gotten us tickets for tomorrow; we have to be at the O'Hare airport by 8:00 a.m.," I told him. "Are you going to be able to make it?"

"I'm leaving as soon as I can get going," he told me.

I was worried because I did not want him driving all night by himself in his state of mind. "Ry, you have to let the school know. Explain to the school what has happened, and I'm sure they will allow someone to drive down with you. Do you want me to call them?" I asked him.

"No, I'll call them as soon as I hang up. How is Keila doing, Dad? I'm really concerned for her," he told me. He hung up with a promise to call as soon as he finished making arrangements.

In a very few minutes, my phone rang. "OK, Dad. I just spoke with the dean of students and it's OK for Jenny to drive down with me. I'll also see if Ben Pierce can drive down and drive back with her. I will call you as soon as we are on the road. Are you OK, Dad?"

What could I say? I knew I would never be OK again. This hole in my heart would never go away. There was such a huge part of my life missing now. But life goes on. Knowing he would have his own hole to deal with, I assured him we would get through this. How, I did not know.

The morning had dawned with the sky black and low. They were calling for snow. I hardly even thought about it until, as we were waiting at the gate for our flight, it started to snow. I knew that our connection in Dallas, Texas, was really tight, and the agent had allowed us the tickets only because there wasn't much else available on such short notice. Right on time, the big jet pulled into the jetway and we began to board. By the time we were on the plane, however, it was snowing in earnest. Looking out the window, I noticed that the wings were already covered. I knew the pilots would never take off with that much snow on the wings. Glancing at my watch, I began to get really worried. More than anything else, I was worried about Keila being by herself in the jungle. I was thankful that Stephen was there with her and our youngest daughter, Mia, but I knew he would need me as much as Keila would. This had to be hitting both of them so hard. And little Mia wouldn't know what was going on. I glanced at my watch again.

My heart was full of memories and once again I had to blink back the tears. My two oldest sons, Josh and Ryan, were sitting on either side of me, lost in their own thoughts as we struggled with a reality that had not sunk in yet. Our beautiful little Mikeila was gone. Noticing the tears running down my cheeks, my boys gripped my hands tighter, letting me know they were there and I could count on them.

"Ladies and gentlemen, I am sorry to have to tell you we still are not cleared to take off. The snow is falling so heavily that we are going to need another pass from the snow removal machines. I appreciate your patience," came the captain's voice one more time. I glanced at my watch again. More time to subtract and add, but however the numbers were added or subtracted, it still equated that we were not going to make that connection. I looked down the cabin to see where the flight attendant was and quickly unfastened my seatbelt. Getting up, I walked back to the one who seemed to be in charge.

"I am sorry, miss, but I really need to speak with the captain."

In the post-9/11 environment, this was not something a flight attendant wants to hear. I saw her take a deep breath and finally she asked what I needed. "I am sure he is awfully busy with preflight stuff," I was informed.

I blinked back my tears, and told her, "I have to make it to Caracas today in order to make a further connecting flight up to the last city in Venezuela before heading into the jungle. There is only one flight a day from Dallas to Caracas and I am afraid we have already missed it. If I could get off and get a flight to Miami, perhaps I could catch a later flight today on to Caracas," I explained to her.

She led me forward and knocked on the cockpit door. Speaking softly to the captain, she explained that I wanted to get off. He came out of the cockpit and asked me for more details. In spite of how difficult it was to talk about it, I explained to him that our little girl had just passed away, and my wife was in the jungle with our three-year-old daughter and my teenaged son, and my two older boys and I were trying to get home. Telling him, I again finished with, "If I can at least get to Miami, perhaps I could get a later flight to Caracas. There are many flights to Caracas from Miami, so I could possibly catch a later one today, whereas there is only the one flight a day from Dallas, and I am afraid we are going to miss that one. The connecting flight to Puerto Ayacucho from Caracas is tomorrow morning, so I could still make that one." He listened, frowning, as he also looked at his watch calculating times and schedules. He nodded his head and re-entered the cockpit, and I heard him talking to his dispatcher on the radio.

After a minute he came back out and told me the news: "You would have to go standby from here and I'm afraid there's already quite a list, since so many flights have been delayed and canceled. However, I have also spoken to the people de-icing the plane and they think I can push back in less than ten minutes. I would suggest you stay on this plane and I will do all in my power to help you make your Dallas flight. As a matter of fact, as soon as we're airborne, I will call Dallas and ask them if they can hold the flight for you."

I nodded, thanked him, and walked back to my seat. Sure enough, in just a few minutes I felt the big jet jerk and slowly push back. Snow continued to come down, but with no one ahead of us on the taxiway we made good time out to the end of the active runway. It seemed that in no time the big jet was straining down the runway and lifting off into the snow-laden sky.

They say life is a journey. Well, that is true, and as anyone can tell you, journeys have starting places and rest stops and ending places. Mikeila's journey started with Keila and me meeting and falling in love, but it's a long story and starts in a different time and place—in reality, a different life.

My first wife, Reneé, and I had maintained a house in Ciudad Bolívar (CB for short) for when we were out of the jungle buying our supplies or doing the seemingly endless amounts of tedious paperwork that most missionaries have to do. Getting all the way over to CB from where we were working in the jungle took a long time. First we took the Cessna 206 for the two-hour flight out, then from there went by car for anywhere from 10 to 12 hours, depending on road conditions. Once we got there, we basically had about three or four weeks in CB to get all our stuff bought and get ready to head back to the jungle. Our boys traveled well, but after spending all that time getting out of the jungle, the last thing they wanted to do was get back in a car and go grocery shopping all day. Right down the street from where we had our house, there lived a long-legged tomboy who was always eager to babysit our boys—and since, like I said, she was a tomboy, they much preferred to have her stay with them, as she was always ready to go outside to climb a tree or chase lizards. They became fast friends.

Eventually we decided to stop making the long trip to Ciudad Bolívar and rented our house to some other missionaries who were over there, and we began to do most of our supply-buying in Puerto Ayacucho. After Reneé died, though, I had to go over and take care of some house matters. The couple that was renting it decided they would like to purchase it, but I needed to go over and sign some papers. I put it off as long as I could, but a bit more than a year after Reneé passed away, I finally just had to go and take care of it. I was still deeply mourning the loss of Reneé, and hated to do anything that would remind me yet again that she was gone, but just had to force myself to go. The boys were happy to be doing something different; I hadn't realized how hard that year and a half had been on the boys.

It had been more than four years since we had been to CB and there were many changes. Possibly the biggest change was in our tomboy babysitter, Keila. She was no longer gangly and awkward, but had morphed into a beautiful young lady. The boys had no problem at all picking up where they had left off with her, and she was very good about coming to get them to take them to the park and making sure they had what they needed. I, however, had a very hard time not staring. She was beautiful! But the wound of Reneé's death was still much too new and raw and I noticed this beauty as one would notice a beautiful flower or bird . . . and that was it. My boys had other ideas, and kept dropping hints that here was someone whom we could possibly take home with us. I only smiled and assured them that what they were suggesting was quite impossible. They dropped the subject and so did I.

A missionary couple we knew, Jim and Jeannie Berryhill, had offered to move to Puerto Ayacucho and take over our mission office there, so during the time we were in Ciudad Bolívar, the boys and I stayed with them. We were excited to have them join our team and we talked many hours into the night. Keila was practically living with them, so the boys spent a lot of time with her again. They really enjoyed her company.

Knowing how lost I was without Reneé, and figuring that since I had also been so sick with malaria, our home church suggested that the boys and I come back to the USA and spend a year there to recuperate and regain our equilibrium. I had resisted, but finally decided that was good advice. So I planned our trip to leave the jungle, go to Ciudad Bolívar, and from there head on up to Caracas and back to the States. The Berryhills took us to the airport there in CB, and Keila went with all of us to say goodbye to the boys. As she and the boys stood there talking, I came up to say my own goodbyes. I figured I would possibly never see her again, as I had no plans whatsoever of returning to Ciudad Bolívar. I thanked her for taking time to be with the boys and making sure they were enjoying themselves.

She smiled. "I love your boys, Michael. You don't have to thank me. I enjoyed myself as much as they did." I had thanked her in Spanish, but she answered me in perfect English. She had learned English as a small kid playing with missionary kids—the MKs, as they're called. Most everyone calls me Mike, but Reneé had always called me Michael, so it took me aback a bit to hear Keila call me Michael. I looked into her eyes and again was struck by her beauty. I swallowed hard, said goodbye, and was glad to head into the boarding area. The boys, possibly aware of my discomfort, said again, "Dad, she would probably want to come home with us. We like her, Dad." I ignored them, lost in my own thoughts.

I enjoyed our time in the USA except for the many people who took it upon themselves to set me up with dates with various girls. I was able to refuse most of them, but some I just could not get out of. To be honest, most of the dates were stiff and uncomfortable. I'm sure it was my fault, as my heart was still hurting so much over the loss of my beautiful Reneé that I just couldn't see past that to a future. I hoped that would change for me, and I knew I needed someone, as I felt I was spiraling out of control in one huge free-fall. That was such a difficult time: the boys needed help adjusting to going to public schools—and to everything else in the United States!—and I needed help with just about everything that happens in day-to-day life, from making the boys' lunches to getting them to bed on time. To put it bluntly, we were just a very needy, hurting family.

Finally I could take it no longer. I was tired of the forced, strained dates; tired of trying to change my whole life to live in the United States when I knew there was so much that I could do and that really needed to be done with the Yanomamö. It had been six months since I left Venezuela and almost two years since Reneé died, and though I hadn't fully recovered, I knew I was well on the way to getting my feet back under me in respect to adjusting to life without Reneé. She had brought so much to my life and now she was gone. I knew that for some reason, God had allowed it. While I did not understand why, I was finally comfortable with the fact that God *was* in control. I could rest in that. I did not *need* to know why. I also realized that I needed to get on with my life and let the past be gone. A really good friend suggested that I go and see a movie (at the time, a new hit) called *Sleepless in Seattle.* Normally I never go to movies; I just don't have time for that kind of nonsense. But this time I was curious enough that I went. I'm not saying it was a mistake (I cried through the entire movie), but I left there more determined than ever to head home to the jungle and get on with my life. As much as I loved Reneé, she was gone. Living in the past was not only not fair to the boys, it was unfair to me and to the work both Reneé and I had loved.

I told the boys we were going to be heading back to the field and they yelled out their excitement. Although they were quite young yet, they had already made such lifelong friends with the Yanomamö that it immediately made their day to hear we were heading back. This was in early December, and we planned on being back in Venezuela by the first week in January. As soon as I purchased our tickets, I called our mission office in Puerto Ayacucho to let them know when we were coming and also to ask them to make arrangements for our trip up to the jungle with MAF. I was surprised to hear a young lady's voice, instead of Jim Berryhill's voice that I had expected.

"Hello, this is the Berryhill residence," she said.

"Hello, I would like to talk with Jim," I answered.

"I am sorry. He and Jeannie are gone for the week." I wracked my brain trying to figure out who I was talking with. Her next question gave her away: "May I help you, Michael?" I knew who I was talking to then!—but what was she doing in Puerto Ayacucho?

2

A Time to Love

Arise my love, my lovely one come;
The winter is past, the rains are gone;
The flowers appear, it is the season of song.
My beautiful one, arise and come with me . . .

. . . Arise my love and come with me.
Before the dawn breaks and the shadows flee,
you ravish my heart with just one glance.
My beautiful one, arise and come with me . . .

—Michael Card

Well, we were back. Our flights to Caracas and then on to Puerto Ayacucho went off without a hitch, and I felt truly ready to get back upriver and get to work. As we walked into the terminal, I looked around trying to spot someone from our office. I have to be honest and tell you that I was especially looking for a certain young lady who called me "Michael." But there was no one there to meet us. Not until later did I realize that after the young lady told me that the Berryhills were gone, I had thanked her and just hung up. They didn't know we were coming in, which meant that MAF didn't know we were coming in, nor did anyone else. The boys and I caught a cab over to the MAF hangar and I spoke with the program manager about a flight.

He was surprised to see us, but said, "Hey, you're in luck. We have a flight going up right now. If you are ready to head up today, let's go!"

That was great news. We dropped our bags off to be weighed and someone drove us back over to the terminal to wait for the MAF plane to taxi over. The whole time I kept looking around wishing someone would come out from our office, but I never even thought of calling to let anyone know we had gotten in. I wondered if Keila was still in Puerto Ayacucho. I had no idea what she could possibly be doing over here and how long she was going to be in town, but there was no one I could ask without exposing myself to a lot of teasing. That I wanted to see her was something I would not even admit to myself, but I kept looking around. I was also wondering how I could ask about her in a way to avoid incriminating myself.

Finally, the perfect solution crossed my mind. "Hey, boys, would you-all like to call the Berryhills and say hi to Keila before we head into the jungle?" I immediately had their attention.

"Yes, but isn't she in Ciudad Bolívar?" Josh asked.

"No, I think she's at Berryhills' here in town," I told him.

"Yes, let's call her. Maybe she can come out and visit before we fly up to Cosh," the boys said, putting into motion the very plan I had wanted.

My great plan failed, however. We did make the call, but when I asked about Keila—for the boys, of course—we were told she was up at another jungle base helping out for a couple of weeks. I told Jim Berryhill that we had been offered a flight upriver and we were heading right on up. I also told him I had a shipment coming in from the United States in a couple of weeks and I would head back out to take care of it when I heard it had left Caracas. By that time, the MAF plane had arrived at the terminal; we climbed aboard and headed on up to Cosh and our life there.

About three weeks later, I received a radio call from Jim saying that our container had left Caracas. The boys and I flew out to Puerto Ayacucho so we could unpack our stuff and separate the supplies that we were going to fly up immediately from the materials that could just come up by barge. I had given our whole house, with all the furniture and appliances, to my dad and mom, as I just could not stand to live in the house that I had built for Reneé. She had made it our home and now she was gone, so I figured it would be easier to build a new house rather than try and adjust to that one without Reneé. Plus, Dad and Mom really needed a new house anyway, and this was one of the nicer homes in the village. It was rammed earth with big thick walls and a shingle roof, so I was very happy that my parents accepted the house. I had given it to them before I left for the USA, so in this container that was coming down I had a new fridge, stove, washer and dryer, and the myriad of other things needed to set up house. Now all I needed was a house to put the stuff in. But I figured that would come.

We got out to Puerto Ayacucho and I went on down to try and find out any news about the container. When I got back to the apartment that we were staying in, I found some very excited boys. The reason for their excitement was that they had a guest: Keila. I realized how glad I was to see her, and not just as a babysitter, either. If anything, she was even more beautiful. She had long dark hair and large eyes that were full of laughter and life. Again, I found myself almost staring. I reminded myself that this was impossible, I was much too old to even be harboring thoughts about this young lady. But here she was, smiling and chatting with the boys. They obviously thought a lot of her, and she of them. She was familiar to them and they were comfortable. I made an excuse and got out of there.

The next day our container arrived and I spent all day unloading and repacking stuff to take back up to the jungle with me. The boys were there helping, and because Keila lived just across the street, she came over with the Berryhills and was soon helping me unpack and repack stuff. I enjoyed showing off the new appliances, figuring, what could it hurt to show her how together I had it with my new stove, fridge, washer and dryer, and all the other stuff? She did not seem that impressed, however, so I dropped it. While appearing to ignore her, I couldn't help but continue to notice how well she interacted with my boys. They loved the attention she was giving them and I was grateful that she was spending time with them. What I didn't understand at the time was that she was better at the game than I was! She had already decided I was the man for her, and had already enlisted my boys as willing conspirators in her strategy.

We spent three or four days getting the loads ready for the barge. I had already selected the few items I was going to have flown up, which was not that much because it cost an awful lot to fly stuff into the jungle. Most of the stuff was going up by barge. The night before we were to head upriver, the three boys were talking with Keila. The conversation was just out of earshot, so I had no idea what they were talking about. After she left to head back across the street, the boys came over and we started going over all the stuff we still had to do before we left in the morning.

"Hey, Dad. Keila said she will just come over after we leave and clean the apartment, so we don't have to worry about that," Josh said.

I looked up. "Josh, that would not be right to leave a big mess for her," I told him. "We can clean this place."

"She said that's what you would say," Josh said, but he didn't press the matter. A bit later, they asked for permission to walk over to the Berryhills', which I granted. About fifteen minutes later, Keila came back in with the boys.

"Michael, there is no reason you all have to get up so early to clean. I don't mind coming over and cleaning up," she smiled. I did not know what to say, so I agreed, first making sure she understood that I was going to pay her. She tried to argue, but dropped it. I didn't know it then, but I had already lost the first battle—and I didn't even know I was in a war yet!

When the Berryhills drove us to the airport the next morning, Keila went along with the boys. While sitting in the waiting area, I heard the boys invite Keila up to visit. The next thing I knew, they were at my side asking if it would be all right if Keila came up for a visit.

"Well, that's a great idea, but this flight is full," I said, hoping to distract them. Secretly I hoped they would keep pressing, but again, I was afraid of opening myself up to teasing.

"Hey, Dad, what about the flight that's coming up next week?" they wanted to know.

"I don't have a problem with it. When we get to Cosh, we can make sure it's OK with Faith and Sharon, as she would have to stay with them," I told them. The boys ran back to tell Keila it was all set up.

It was with more anticipation than I had felt in a long time for anything that I found myself waiting for the airplane to come in the following week. Finally the day came, and I heard the sound of the airplane in the distance. I still would not admit to anyone that I was interested, as I felt that this could never be. She was coming up to visit the boys and that was it.

The plane landed and we walked over to start unloading it. I busied myself getting stuff out of the belly pod of the plane, trying to act as disinterested as possible with the lone passenger who had arrived. I knew the Yanomamö would be especially suspicious of any single female coming in, and I had to make sure I didn't give them any reason to talk. I straightened up from the pod and there she was, looking if anything more beautiful than I had remembered her. Her long dark hair was tied up in a ponytail. I said hi, and went right to work helping to unload the plane, trying to act as aloof as I could. I felt like everyone was watching me.

Well, I was correct. The Yanomamö were suspicious and my pretense of acting uninterested was not fooling them in the least. I heard one of the men ask Joshua, "Is this your dad's new wife?"

"Shio [shut up]! Don't talk like that. You will make everyone start talking about me!" I demanded. Everyone laughed and I flushed, further giving myself away.

The next two weeks passed quickly. Keila and I began to spend a lot of time playing a game she had brought up with her, Jenga, where the object of the game is to withdraw as many blocks of wood as possible without making the tower fall over. Well, I might not have a good mind for table and board games (I always used to dislike playing cards and games), but I sure had a steady hand in pulling out those little blocks of wood. Of course, Keila says now that she just let me win, but who's going to believe her? But I know one thing: all of a sudden I had a fascination for that game that would not quit! Not only did I find myself playing, but we stayed up talking late after the boys were in bed. Keila shared a lot of the same dreams I did of reaching a people for the Lord. Her parents had worked with the Pemon Indians in Eastern Venezuela before the government made them leave the area, and Keila was still very interested in becoming a missionary.

The two weeks she had for a visit went way too fast and her time was over. Her flight was coming in the next day to pick her up and take her back out to Puerto Ayacucho. "Will I see you again?" I asked. We were playing Jenga for the last time and most of the family had gone to bed.

"That is up to you," she told me with a smile.

"Well, if it were up to me, I would just have you stay," I told her, finally putting out in the open the subject that we had both been skating around.

"Like I said, that is up to you," she told me again.

I looked her in the eyes and held my breath as I asked her, "Are you saying what I think you are saying?"

She nodded.

"Well, why don't you come back up in a couple of weeks for another visit so we can talk more?" I asked her.

She nodded again, and I was very happy.

"This is a big night for us. May I kiss you?" I asked her.

"Sure, but then you would have to marry me!" she laughed. "I have always said, the man who kisses me has to marry me," she explained. "I am not someone who believes you go from person to person, kissing and trying and then finally finding the right one. With me, you don't kiss me unless you are the right one!"

Not only beautiful, but she has the right morals as well, I thought to myself. To her I said, "OK, if that is a proposal, I accept. I will marry you."

She blushed. "No, I am not proposing, I am only warning you!"

Regardless, I took it as a proposal, got my kiss, and began to make plans. I was even able to convince her it was her idea, I thought, but now, looking back, I wonder if maybe she didn't just make me think she thought that. Oh well, whoever's idea it was, it was a good one. While the next months were a whirlwind of activity, we were married in the United States on the 4th of October 1994. Life was good again.

3

A Time to Be Born

July 1999

Keila fairly glowed as she told me her news. She was pregnant! We were both ecstatic. We had been married for almost five years and had about given up on her having children. We were happy with the three boys, but Keila's heart yearned for a baby. God granted our requests and now all we had to do was wait for the big day. There were some complications with paperwork, however. Although I am a U.S. citizen, I had not been born on U.S. soil, which, according to the U.S. embassy, meant I could not give citizenship. Keila was a Venezuelan, so the embassy told us if we wanted the baby to have U.S. citizenship, it had to be born on U.S. soil. We made plans to head stateside when Keila was seven and one-half months pregnant.

Because we didn't have insurance, we opted to go with a midwife birth instead of an in-hospital birth, to cut costs. Some friends had recommended a midwife in Charlottesville, Virginia, and after going in and checking out the midwife and the birthing center, we felt like it was ideal.

The boys had all been born in Venezuela and the doctors there don't go in much for making the birth of a baby a family affair, which was fine with me. I was much happier out pacing the lobby than doing all the fancy breathing and coaching that Americans go for. But there we were getting ready to have a baby in the United States, and guess what? The midwife *did* go in for all that stuff! We got in from Venezuela too late to go to special classes and whatnot, but there were a bunch of books that we had to study. I started reading the books to Keila. Although she speaks perfect English, she still has a difficult time reading and writing it. I wanted to skip all the parts where it talks about all the terrible things that can go wrong (and believe me, there are a lot of things that can go wrong), but Keila made me read the books without skipping anything. Before I knew it, I was retaining water and had a backache!

Anyway, finally it was time to head to the midwife's facility. We thought Keila was in hard labor, or should I say, she thought she was. I was only the driver. When I was awakened, I immediately ran out to the car and started to drive—not that I panic easily, you understand, I was just quite singleminded. Husbands, after all, have the easiest part of the birthing program (at least that is what my wife tells me), so the least I could do was take my easy part seriously.

I tried to be bighearted and lighthearted as we started the twenty-mile drive back to the house where we were staying. "Hey, honey, just look at it like a good practice run," I grinned at Keila. She was so uncomfortable that I tried to cheer her up. "Next time it will be for real."

She looked at me and frowned, the dead winter landscape mirrored in her large eyes. "I just wish we would have stayed in Venezuela. This winter stuff is too depressing. I just want this over with."

I patted her on the hand. "That's OK, honey. False labor can happen to anyone. Let's just try to not let it happen at 2:00 a.m.

again. I mean, I love to drive and would drive anywhere for you, but 2:00 a.m. would get old quickly, if you know what I mean."

My attempts at humor went unheeded and Keila stayed quiet the rest of the ride home. Mentally, I agreed with her: The quicker this baby came, the better, but her due date was still two weeks away, so there was no need for concern.

How excited we all were when we found out Keila was pregnant. Back then the only thing we had to worry about was trying to find a name we all could agree on. Keila finally came up with the name Mikeila Reneé and we immediately agreed. She had put our two names together and made Mikeila. Mi from Mike, ke from both our names, and the ila from Keila, equaling Mikeila, and she gave the middle name Reneé to honor the boys' mother. A most beautiful name for what we were sure was going to be a most beautiful baby.

The jet broke through the clouds and the sun was shining fiercely. Gone were the snow and clouds that had trapped us down below, but my heart was still choked with the pain of my loss. I leaned back in my seat and closed my eyes, letting my mind drift back to thinking of my beautiful little girl. Her birth had been so traumatic. It all came rushing back like a flood. We had come so close to losing her at birth.

She was born on the 23rd of March 2000, but we started this whole thing on the 22nd when Keila went into hard labor. We cheerfully loaded the infant seat into the car, thinking we would be returning home the next day with our little bundle of joy. We had had a couple of practice runs when Keila had false labor, but this time we knew it was the real thing. We arrived at the birthing center at about 8:00 a.m., but Keila did not have a good labor. It went on and on: By 3:30 the following morning, she was no nearer to having the baby than when we arrived.

The midwife recommended that we go to the hospital, just to make sure everything was all right. We arrived at the hospital about 5:00 a.m. on the 23rd. Keila continued in hard labor. They were monitoring the baby's heartbeat and it was obvious even to me that the baby was in a lot of distress—and I know nothing. They kept telling Keila to breathe slowly and yet her body was being wracked by great big wails of pain. By 7:30 it was obvious that things were not good. I ran to try and find a doctor and the nurse told me he had been called. By 8:30 I ran out and found him in his office, apparently totally unconcerned; he told me they were keeping their eyes on things. At a little before 10:30, when Keila's water finally broke, it was obvious that something was dreadfully wrong. I ran back out and found the doctor again, but it seemed to me that the doctors and midwife were having some kind of a power play and we were caught in the middle, I think because we didn't have insurance. They made poor Keila continue to fight through the labor pains, despite the fact that she was losing ground now. Her eyes were dull with pain and exhaustion and it was all I could do to keep her focused. When the nurse came back in, I asked what we had to do to just have the baby taken C-section. I also told them how concerned I was that the baby might have aspirated meconium. When the doctor came back in, I again voiced my concern and he told me that all they would have to do was suction the baby's airway well before she took her first breath. This is fairly normal, I was told. Well, it did not seem fairly normal to me! It looked scary and traumatic, and I wanted to be a long way away from there!

At 11:30, things really began going badly, so they finally moved into high gear to quickly get Keila ready for a C-section.

I had assured them we would pay the bill, and I guess there wasn't much left to prove with the midwife, so while they got Keila ready, with my own heart pounding, I scrubbed up. I don't do hospitals, or blood, or anything, and I just felt bad about the way things were going. I remember crying out to God to spare my Keila. They rushed her into the operating room. I sat on a stool near her head and held her hand. I listened to the doctors and nurses talking, though actually they might as well have been speaking a foreign language for all I understood. All I knew was something was hideously, horribly wrong! As they grabbed the baby out, I heard them say, "It's a girl!" And something about not making her breathe yet, that she needed suction. I watched as they frantically worked over her, trying to get the suction going to get her airways clean. The suction machine was not working, and I watched as the nurse took the tube out and reinserted it. Still no good. The nurse kept shouting that she was not getting any suction and needed suction—NOW! The anesthesiologist who was working on Keila asked her if she was OK and whether he could leave for a minute. She nodded. I watched him begin working on the suction machine and then give up in desperation; grabbing a bag respirator, he tried to force oxygen into Mikeila's little lungs with this primitive device.

I watched, praying for something to happen. How I longed to hear that little baby start screaming, but all I heard was the nurse frantically yelling for a respiratory therapist! STAT! It sure did not sound good. Suddenly they realized I was still there, and someone came over and asked me to step out and wait over in the waiting room. I stumbled out, almost too numb to pray. Already my arms were feeling the loss! Your mind does funny things at a time like this. I remember thinking, *Well, I guess we won't need the car seat.* Then I thought, *How in the world do you do a funeral back here?* I have had to see so much death, but most of it has been with the Yanomamö. My heart sank as I thought of trying to figure out where to start. *"God! Help us!"* I prayed.

My heart ached for Keila still in the operating room. As soon as they brought her out, I went in to sit with her. She was still groggy from the anesthesia but kept telling me everything was going to be OK. I was not so sure. I had watched them working over the baby and in the last two or three minutes I was in there, I had not seen her take a breath. I was worried! I looked up as the doctor came by: He told us that the baby was alive, but was very sick and they were sending her to the University of Virginia Hospital. Her lungs were badly burned from meconium aspiration. I asked the doctor when she would leave and if I could see her. He took me down to the intensive care unit and I watched as they continued to work over her.

Five hours later, they felt they had her stabilized to the point where she could make the trip. The helicopter arrived, but something still wasn't right. They continued to work, and finally got her strapped in and all wired up inside her little incubator-type box for the flight. I walked behind them, my heart in my throat, as they pushed her outside to the heliport. I watched as all these people went about their jobs with the calm efficiency that comes from knowing what you are doing. The pilot rapidly preflighted the copter, and as soon as they had the little box strapped in, the huge blades began to turn. With tears in my eyes, I watched the helicopter go out of sight. At that point I didn't think I would see my little girl alive again. How empty were my arms!

Praise the Lord for friends! Darryl Walter, a pastor from Christian Fellowship Church, called to see how we were doing. He immediately offered to come and drive me down to UVA to see what was happening with Mikeila. My niece and nephew brought our three boys over, and while the two oldest stayed with Keila, Stephen and I went with Pastor

Darryl to the other hospital, about eighty miles away. I remember looking at Mikeila as she lay there on that little platform in the neonatal (newborns') intensive care unit (NICU). She was in such fragile shape that they hadn't even washed her off and she was covered with the dried afterbirth all over her body, but she was so beautiful. Slowly, I took in all the tubes and wires sticking out of her little body. I listened numbly as the doctor told me how sick she was—as if the wires and tubes didn't tell me enough!

The next days were a blur as I drove between the two hospitals; Mikeila was in the University of Virginia Hospital (UVA) in Charlottesville and Keila was still in the Warrenton hospital in Warrenton, Virginia, where Mikeila had been born. We were happy, though, to see Mikeila making improvements. On Saturday, the doctor released Keila from the Warrenton hospital so we could go down and be closer to Mikeila. He admonished her about the necessity of taking it easy and not overdoing it. Get plenty of rest, he told her. What a joke! I had the hardest time getting her to move away from Mikeila's side.

On Monday, the doctor told us he thought Mikeila was out of danger. They felt we would be able to take her home in maybe a couple of days. We needed to go back up to the other hospital so they could remove the staples from Keila's incision. Mikeila seemed to be doing so much better, we thought we could leave for a while. We drove to Warrenton and Keila had her stitches out. We drove back toward UVA, confident that in a couple of days we would be taking our baby home. We were full of plans to take her back to our mission station in Venezuela. But when we arrived back at the NICU around 5:30 p.m., we walked into a madhouse. Mikeila's lungs had filled with fluid and the doctors were frantically trying to get her to breathe. We sat outside her unit and watched the nurses and doctors running back and forth. We were told that they had lost her heartbeat and her lungs had failed. In their efforts to get her to breathe, they had actually caused her right lung to collapse. Nothing looked good. All Keila and I could do was watch and pray. Watching was too scary, so we bowed our heads and prayed. Oh, the many times this little girl would drive us to our knees. That evening, though, we came to the point where all we could tell the Lord was, *"She is Yours. You are the ultimate giver and sustainer of life. We give her back to You. You have loaned her to us, and we love her. If we have her for a week, a month, or however many years You choose to give her to us, we will love her and enjoy her. When You take her back, we will accept that as from You, because You do all things well."*

The doctors and nurses were still running frantically around, but Keila and I both felt a peace. It was not a peace that we knew she was going to get better, but a peace that we could trust our heavenly Father with our precious little daughter.

The hospital chaplain came over and sat with us. At that point I don't think any of the NICU staff thought she was going to make it. Seeing that we were praying, he sat there beside us quietly. I think that it was because the entire hospital staff thought there was not much hope for her, he never did say anything to us, but just sat there trying to comfort us with his presence.

They did an emergency procedure right there in the NICU to put her on a special machine, the ECMO. That machine took all her blood and ran it through a special pump, which pumped it through a membrane where it was cleaned of carbon dioxide, then it pumped on through where it picked up oxygen and then back into her little body. This was normally done down in a surgical suite, because it involved placing the ends of the tubes right at the heart, but because of her condition they did it right there.

Finally the head doctor came out and told us she was stable. They were not sure why her lungs had filled with fluid, or even what the fluid was, but at least for the moment she was stable. We could go in and see her if we wanted. We went in not knowing what to expect. What a mess! The machinery took up the whole corner. There were now more tubes and wires than I had ever thought possible attached to our little girl. She was now on a platform more than five feet high, as her blood had to gravity-feed into the pump. We had to stand on little stools to even be able to see her. She had two big hoses leaving her neck filled with her blood, one going to the pump and the other one bringing the oxygenated blood back to her heart. The machine was doing 100 percent of the work of her lungs. Both her lungs, the doctor told us, were collapsed. I cannot even put into words the anxiety and fear that went through my mind as I stood there watching all this. *"Lord,"* I prayed, *"what are You trying to teach me? Please don't let me be so hardheaded! Let me learn in a hurry. It hurts me so to see this little girl suffer like this."*

The next day, the head nurse came in with a form for us to sign. They had to do a bronchoscopy to look down Mikeila's airway to see what had caused her lungs to fill with fluid. One of the doctors had told me the night before that he had seen what he thought was possibly a birth defect. "She has a large hole in her trachea," he said. "We will need to reexamine that to see whether we will have to repair it with surgery."

Now the nurse was asking us to sign the form giving our consent to have the procedure done again. After giving our consent, we stood helplessly by as the doctor inserted his little camera down her windpipe. It was obvious that Mikeila did not like that, and she struggled and tried to get away. She had so many tubes down her throat that she could not even cry out, but you could tell from her screwed-up little face that she desperately hated what they were doing to her. Keila and I hurt with her.

Josh nudged my arm and I opened my eyes to see the flight attendant leaning over me. "Sir, the captain has asked me to let you know they have communicated your situation to Dallas and they are holding the plane. He also asked me to tell you that we have made up almost thirty minutes of the time we lost there on the ground. He is pushing this jet as fast as it can go," she said.

I thanked her and closed my eyes again. I wasn't ready to give up the memories of Mikeila, as painful as they were.

A couple of hours later the doctor who had done the procedure came back in and spoke with Keila and me. "I am not sure," he said, "but that tear in her trachea is from trauma, not a birth defect."

"Trauma?" I said, not understanding. "What does that mean?"

"Well, it means it is man-made," the doctor told me. My mind flashed back to the delivery room up at the first hospital, with the nurse frantically inserting, removing, and reinserting the suction tube at least three or four times while I was standing there.

"Could this have been caused by a suction tube?" I asked him.

He looked at me closely and finally nodded his head.

The next day the nurse asked me to sign another form to allow the doctor to look down Mikeila's airway again.

"How necessary is this?" I asked. "The last time it really set Mikeila back. The ECMO nurses said they had to really turn the pump up and it took her a long time to stabilize, so if this is not that necessary, I would just as soon not sign for it."

"Well, our doctors are not in the habit of doing procedures that are not necessary," the nurse frowned.

I had to push it. "What happens if I refuse to sign?"

"We will get a judge to order you to sign, and if you still refuse, the doctors will get a court order authorizing them to do the procedure, but you would possibly not be here to see it," she told me. It didn't look like I had much choice, so I reluctantly signed that time—and a bunch more times for many different procedures.

I did feel a lot better when the doctor told me that the hole was totally closed up and healed. There is no doubt now that the hole was caused by trauma, he told me; most probably by the intubating procedure. "But now that we have dealt with the cause, we should be able to get the symptoms under control and get your little girl better," the doctor told me optimistically.

In spite of the fact that we could see no improvement, her doctors continued to be optimistic. But day dragged after long day, week after longer week. Finally, by the end of the third week, they told us there must be something they had missed with her heart. They couldn't explain her lack of improvement. She was not only not getting better, she was getting worse. The machine was running at 640, the highest it could run. One hundred percent for a baby the size of Mikeila was 540. The doctors told us that she could not tolerate the machine running that high for very long. Neither her blood vessels nor her brain could endure the increased blood pressure much longer.

I remembered the night Keila and I returned to the Ronald McDonald House about 1:00 a.m. We were so tired and so discouraged. *"God,"* I prayed, *"Please give me something to hang on to. We want to trust, but please help our unbelief!"*

I picked up my Bible and began to read. I had been reading in Psalms. I came to the 118th chapter, the 17th verse: *"I shall not die, but live, and declare the works of the Lord."*

"Thank you, Lord," I cried. *"This is Mikeila's verse."*

In spite of the verse I claimed for her, she continued to weaken daily, and every day when we headed over to the NICU, we were never sure what we would find. We stayed over there hour after long hour, because once we left her, we never were sure we were going to see her alive again. She was so fragile and weak, but her spirit was so strong. She would throw little temper tantrums that would bring the ECMO machine right to a stop. Feisty, we called her. But daily my mind wondered if that day we had just had with her would be our last.

I remembered the many different people we met who had their own little tragedies going on around us. One lady had a daughter in the NICU with us and she and her husband were staying at the Ronald McDonald House just up the hall from Keila and me. We talked with them and discovered that we shared another common bond, our faith in Jesus. One day, knowing we always prayed with Mikeila before leaving for the night, this lady asked if she could pray with us, as she was leaving for her home town the following morning. As she prayed, she claimed verse after verse over little Mikeila. What a wonderful prayer! I could not stop crying.

When she finished, she told us, "You know, I'm not a prophet, but while I was praying, I suddenly had the clearest picture of Mikeila standing and singing praises to the Lord." She must have seen my face, because she said, "No! Not in heaven, here on earth!"

I felt Josh nudge me again, and once again I looked up to see the flight attendant.

"Sir, we are about twenty minutes out. I have spoken with the row of passengers in the first business class seats and they have agreed to switch places with you to make it easier for you to deplane. Could you get your carry-on bags and I will help you switch places."

I nodded and Josh, Ryan, and I stood up and picked up our bags. We moved forward and stepped into the first-class cabin to give the three people room to maneuver back to the seats we had just left. I sank into the vacated seats after saying a heartfelt thank-you to them and rebuckled my seat belt.

"We continue to make up for lost time. We should be landing shortly, and I have asked the people in first class to stay seated so you can be the first ones off the plane," the helpful flight attendant told us. How I wish I had gotten the names of the flight crew on this flight, because they went far beyond the call of duty to make this flight bearable for us. But my mind was too numb with the past to think of anything in the present.

Mikeila continued to get worse. Finally, the doctors decided to try to place a tube in her chest to see if they could get rid of the air trapped outside of her right lung. This pneumothorax was keeping her right lung collapsed, and was what had caused her left lung to collapse as well. They were hesitant to do anything, as they had her blood filled with anticoagulants to keep her blood from clotting in the tubes running to and from the machine. One of the greatest dangers with the ECMO machine is if a patient starts bleeding internally; because of the anticoagulants, they might not be able to stop it. Still, the doctor told us, they had to do something. If they started her bleeding, they would deal with that.

The operation was a success! The nurses told us later they could hear the air come out when the doctor placed the tube. We waited for improvement. This operation was done on Saturday.

Day dragged into day, and finally it was the next Sunday. We brought our boys down to visit. The doctors were going to start tests on Mikeila's heart the next day, as they could not explain her lack of improvement. We wanted the boys to see her before that, because (to be honest) we really were not sure how much longer we had with her. We could only be back at her bedside two at a time. Stephen and I went in first, and then Keila went back with Joshua. When they came out, I took Ryan in for a while, and then got ready to take them all home. Stephen wanted to go in and see Mikeila once more before we left. I said OK. We went back in and just stood there watching her. The machine was still overworking, trying to keep up with the demands her body was putting on it. It was doing 100 percent of the work of putting oxygen in her blood. She was still getting worse, even after all they had done. I noticed Stephen praying for her. My heart went out to him and to our other boys. They had been so excited to finally have a sister.

"Lord," I prayed. *"Please no more heartache for the boys."* With that we left to take the boys home. We returned to the hospital about 10:30 p.m. One look at the nurse's face as we came back into the ward told us something had happened.

I felt the plane's engine rev up, the nose pitch for landing, and felt the tires kiss the runway. As we braked off the active runway, the stewardess was beside us again.

"As soon as the captain turns into our jetway spot, please stand up and walk up to the front of the plane," she told us. "We have someone waiting for you."

She moved forward, and as soon as we felt the plane slow, she waved us up. We grabbed our bags and moved to the front of the plane. As the plane stopped moving we felt the bump of the jetway against the side of the plane. The stewardess immediately had the airplane door open and showed us out. There was another young lady standing there and she motioned us to follow her. Instead of walking up the jetway, she opened a door and led us outside and down some stairs to a waiting van. As soon as we were boarded, she signaled the driver to move and we began to head around the terminal of the Dallas airport—not inside the terminal, but outside. Around we went. The departing flight must have been on the opposite side of the terminal from where we had landed, because it seemed like we drove for a long way, but finally we pulled up beside another jetway with a plane already parked at the gate. The escort lady asked us to get out and watch our step and we followed her up the stairway into the jetway. The airplane's door was open and we walked in and were immediately shown to our seats. It seemed like only minutes later that the plane was pushing back from the jetway. I briefly wondered if our luggage had made it, and just as quickly decided I did not care.

Again, how I wish I would have properly thanked the captain and crew of the American flight we were on from Chicago to Dallas, because I don't know what we would have done without all the special help they offered us that day. They really went above and beyond the call of duty for us. I am still grateful!

Every time I closed my eyes, my mind filled in a picture of my beautiful Mikeila. Her large eyes were so blue, and her smile would light a dark room. She was a study in perpetual motion and any time a song started up, she was quick to start dancing to the music. We just knew she was going to be musical; when she was just months old, any time music started to play, she would start snapping her fingers. Yes, snapping her fingers. With the news I had just gotten hours ago, the memories were painful, but I allowed my mind to once again pick up my memories where I had dropped them.

Keila and I were walking back into the NICU after driving up to Madison, Virginia, to take the boys home. We were tired and discouraged. This was our fifth week here at the hospital. If only our little girl showed any signs of improving, it would be so much easier. The trauma of being in a unit with so many desperately sick babies and watching many of them die was getting to us. How our hearts ached for their parents. By now, due to the nature of what held us there, firm friendships were forming, and also our own hearts were terrified that in the very near future, what was happening to them could very easily happen to us. There were some babies who did get better, and we rejoiced for their parents when they left to go home, but our rejoicing was always tempered with just a tinge of jealousy as well, because our situation showed no signs of improving. Still, we were very happy for them. We just wanted to be happy for ourselves as well. And I might add, we had become awfully attached to that little girl who continued to lie there with all the tubes and machines whirring around her. Her little eyes did light up at Keila's cooing, and they followed Keila all around the little corner where we stood beside her elevated platform.

In the midst of my reverie, I was startled to hear the nurse talking with Keila.

"You won't believe it," she said," but ever since you walked out the door to take your boys home, I have been turning the machine down! I really think she has turned the corner! She is getting better!"

By the time we left the hospital, at about 1:00 a.m., the machine was way down. She continued to be weaned off it. The doctors cautioned us not to be too optimistic, but we knew we were watching a miracle. By 4:00 a.m. on Tuesday, the machine was at idle! She was breathing on her own! She had to stay with the machine at idle for eight hours to make sure she was ready to come off. After that, they clamped the machine off while leaving it attached to her, just to make sure she really was on her own. By that evening, the doctors told us they were calling the surgeons to come and take the machine off. Praise the Lord! What a miracle! I later asked Stephen, "What did you pray when I saw you praying for Mikeila?"

"I just told the Lord she had been sick long enough, and we really wanted to take her home," he said with a smile.

The doctors say we still have a long way to go. I don't care. I finally got to hold our little girl tonight! How soft she is. They have told us it always takes a long time to recover from the effects of the ECMO machine. Children become "orally defensive," they told us. It might take three or four weeks to get her to start eating. Also, it will take at least three weeks to wean her off the medication she has been on. "Yes, sad to say, your daughter is a little druggie," they said.

I remembered looking down at her, now asleep, my heart full to overflowing with thanks to our Lord. *"Thank you, Jesus! You deal with us according to Your mercies, not according to what I deserve!"* My heart was so full of gratitude to all our friends who prayed for us so faithfully, and had their friends pray. We received so many e-mails from people we didn't even know, letting us know they were praying for Mikeila. Thank you all so much.

Psalms 118:17 says: "I shall not die but live, and declare the work of the Lord!" In spite of my pain now, I knew we had seen this verse come true. Little Mikeila continued to declare the work of the Lord every day of her short life. Contrary to what the doctors told us, Mikeila weaned off the medicine in less than a week, and began eating well the day they took the tubes out of her mouth. We took her home and she continued to improve every day.

The jet out of Dallas reached its cruising altitude and once again I leaned back to try and get some sleep. I had not slept much the night before. My mind was just too full: Full of worry for Keila having to deal with this on her own, and worry about our boys. How were they going to take this new tragedy? I could not say. How was I going to get through this? I had no idea.

There had been much to deal with after Reneé died, but the most difficult thing to handle was when the boys got hurt or sick. Josh was eight, Ryan was six, and Stephen was four when their mother died, so they could get into a lot of trouble in a hurry. Mercy, Ryan was the first, with a serious bout of hepatitis. He also seemed to be the most accident-prone, and we ended up at the hospital several times. I remember the time he fell while sliding on a water slide and busted the side of his eye open. We took him to the clinic's emergency room in Puerto Ayacucho and I had to watch a butcher try to stitch up my kid. Closest I have ever come to losing it while watching a guy work. First, I wanted to bust him in the face for being so rough on my kid, and the next thing I knew, I was about to lose my lunch. How that hurt, having to watch Ryan go through that!

Along with the times when he'd hurt himself, there were the trips to check his liver for damage from the hepatitis. This was always painful; he hated to go, and I hated to take him. Ry had such big eyes and they would look at me with so much feeling and pain, it was almost more than I could take. There is something surreal about taking a kid to the hospital. You feel helpless enough that you grasp at any little word the doctor or nurse says, and I guess from experience they have learned not to say too much, so we as parents keep trying to phrase and rephrase the same question over and over to ease our worry and pain.

> Keila was so much calmer about stuff like that than I, and it definitely got better for the boys once she came on board. Well, she was calmer. Ryan would argue she was a bit too calm. One night when he woke us, throwing up and asking for help, she told him, "Go back to bed and call us in the morning."

The five-hour flight to Caracas was finally over. Amazingly enough, in spite of the very quick turnaround time, American Airlines had somehow managed to get our luggage on the Dallas plane. Like I said before, I've always wished I could have thanked that flight crew in person for all they did for us.

We got a taxi over to the hotel where we always stay when we're in the city. The first people I saw while checking in were the husband-and-wife owners of the hotel. I had just left there the day before, and my reservations to stay there again were for the next week, so they were surprised to see me. They had fallen in love with our two little girls from previous visits and the first thing the owner's wife asked me was where their little angels were. It was difficult to tell her, but with tears welling out of my eyes, I told her that Mikeila had died the day before and we were heading back into the jungle for her funeral. The lady hugged me with tears in her own eyes. "We grew to love your girls," she told us. "We are so sorry."

"We know she is in heaven. We miss her terribly already, but I know she is in heaven," I told her.

The next morning found us back at the airport heading to Puerto Ordaz. We had decided not to go to Puerto Ayacucho, as MAF had told us it would be difficult for them to get us into the jungle. New Tribes Mission Aviation had offered to fly us into Cosh from their base in Puerto Ordaz, so we were heading straight there. The flight from Caracas to Puerto Ordaz was uneventful and only an hour long, so by 8:00 a.m. we were in Puerto Ordaz, weighing up to board a Cessna 206 for the more than three-hour flight to Cosh. Again, I stared out the window and let my mind go back.

Mikeila continued to improve and we were encouraged after her first three-month check-up. The doctor approved our return to Venezuela, but did ask that we bring her back for a medical check-up every six months. We were so happy to be allowed to return to our work that we agreed to the schedule. She was doing really well, and her doctors were very impressed with how well she was catching up. We were told, however, that she had suffered brain damage due to lack of oxygen. That had a sinister sound and I asked the doctor if he could give us more details.

"The MRI shows signs of damage. In a child of this age, it is almost impossible to say what is going to happen. She could outgrow it, or she could possibly never walk, talk, or do anything that has to do with fine motor skills," he said.

I looked at my little daughter and my heart sank. We loved this little thing like life itself. What could we do? I would do anything to make everything all right for her, but this was so completely out of my hands.

During the first visits back to the States, she continued to regain the ground she had lost. While still a bit delayed, every check-up showed her closing the gap. We continued to be encouraged in spite of the reconfirmation of brain damage in the following MRIs that the doctor had ordered. Keila and I continued to pray that she would again prove the doctors wrong and grow up to be totally normal.

When she was one year old, we returned to the United States for her check-up and again the doctors were pleased. However, on our way back to Amazonas, we had an incident in Caracas that set the tone for the rest of our time with this beautiful little girl. She had been running a fever and Keila thought it was from teething, so she had given her something to soothe her gums. The next moments are blurred, because all of a sudden Keila told me, "Michael, she's not breathing!" I jumped up and we began to work over her. She was in a pretty violent seizure by that time.

Suddenly I remembered the doctor I had met in Puerto Rico when I had been so sick. He had told me his brother was a pediatrician in Caracas and had given me the phone number. Frantically I searched through my address book until I found his phone number. With trembling hands I dialed his number. Thankfully, the doctor answered the phone himself and I told him we had a little one-year-old girl in a seizure. He directed us to head to a private clinic there in Caracas.

"Just go!" he told me, giving me the address. "I will call ahead and make sure they are waiting for you. I will meet you there."

Meanwhile, Keila had gotten Mikeila bundled up, and we grabbed our stuff and ran out to the street to try to flag down a taxi. Our hearts were pounding wildly with fear and dread. We had no idea what was happening, nor what to do. The doctors at the University Hospital in Charlottesville, Virginia, had told us to expect this, but we had fervently hoped and prayed they would be wrong. Because so much time had gone by with no seizures, we both had silently hoped that the worst was over and she had been healed of this the same way she had been healed of the worst effects of being on the ECMO.

A cab screeched to a halt and we jumped in, giving him the address and urging him to go as fast as he could, as we had an emergency. We continued to work over our little girl in the back seat and the driver, seeing our faces and the unresponsiveness of Mikeila, drove like a madman and we arrived at our destination in record time. Mikeila was by this time very lethargic and I was afraid we were losing her.

We ran in, and found that the doctor had in fact called ahead and they were waiting for us. As they were hooking her up to some kind of solution, the doctor I had called came running in. Thankfully, Keila had had the foresight to grab Mikeila's medical file, and while the doctor was looking it over, we continued to fill him in. By this time they had given her something that brought her out of the seizure, and our precious little girl looked at us with her big blue eyes as if to say, "Well, here we go again."

It was around 10:00 p.m. when we arrived there and the clinic's administration was very hard: "You have to pay to keep her here, or you have to leave." I assured them that we would pay in the morning, but they were not budging. We had to pay right then.

"Everything is closed. I will have to cash a dollar check in the morning, unless you can take a dollar check?" I asked them.

"That is impossible. You have to pay, NOW!" the administrator on duty insisted.

I scurried out, wracking my brain over whom I could call at this late time of the night who might have 2 million bolivares in their house. (At the current exchange rate, that was almost $4,000.) But I just came up with a blank. I walked back to where the doctor was still going over Mikeila's long history. I explained my problem. "We can get the money," I explained, "we just can't get it tonight."

He frowned. "I can't understand why they are being so hard. They know all the banks are closed and who in the world, in this day and age with all the crime, would carry that kind of cash on them?" The doctor said, "Let me go and talk to someone." He walked off and just a few minutes later was back with a big smile. "No problem! They will allow you to stay and you can pay them when the banks open in the morning."

"Thank you, Doctor, I can't tell you how much my wife and I appreciate your help," I told him. He looked down at a now-sleeping Mikeila.

"She is a beautiful baby. I think she is going to be OK when she wakes up. Looking at her history, it is possible that this is going to be an ongoing problem." He looked at us with a frown. "Why was there such a long time before she was taken cesarean?"

"I wish I could tell you," I replied, "but we don't know." He stood there talking for a bit longer. Then, telling us he would see us in the morning, he said his goodbyes.

As he walked away, I thought again what a small world we live in. When I had been so sick in Puerto Rico and a doctor took me from the church to the emergency room—well, that doctor was the brother of the pediatrician who was now taking care of Mikeila. Like I said, a small world!

Normally on these flights, the pilot and I use the time to catch up and fellowship about the work, but this time, out of respect for our grief, he busied himself with his duties and left us to our own thoughts. The engine on the small plane changed tone, meaning we had once again reached cruising altitude. My mind took that fact in and at the same time took me back to another time when I had gotten some disturbing news from Josh.

While driving from Virginia to Boston for a missions conference, we were in rush-hour traffic heading around New York City, when my cell phone rang. Normally, I don't like to handle the phone while driving, especially in heavy traffic, but Keila was occupied dealing with three-month-old Mia, so I picked up the phone, a bit upset at the situation, and said an abrupt hello.

"Well, Dad, the doctor says I have cancer." The words hit me so hard I asked Josh to wait while I pulled over into the next gas station to catch my breath.

This was every parent's nightmare! "What did you say, Josh?"

"Dad," came Josh's voice again, "Dad, I just went to the doctor and he says I have cancer and he wants to have me come in for surgery as soon as possible."

"What kind of cancer, Josh?"

"Testicular cancer," he told me matter-of-factly.

I had thought Ryan's hepatitis was bad! Wow, we had meetings scheduled for a week-long missions conference in Boston at Grace Chapel. This was a very important week, as they had told us they were going to take up an offering to help us purchase a much-needed airplane engine for our plane in Venezuela. Thinking quickly, I asked Josh when the surgery was scheduled and he told me the following Friday. The week started with both services on Sunday morning and a Sunday evening service, then meetings every night of the week, with the most important one being Wednesday night. My brother Gary was also there, so I told Josh I would try and get over to where he was in White Lake, Wisconsin, by his surgery time.

As soon as I arrived in Boston, I met with Ron Ballinger, our contact there at the church, and explained what was happening. Gary was scheduled to fly into Boston later that night with our Yanomamö friend and mentor, Bautista (Shoefoot). We met them and explained what was happening. Gary assured me not to worry, but to take off as soon as I felt we needed to leave. Using a U.S. map, we looked at what was involved in getting from Boston to Wisconsin. Well, first of all, it is a lot of blacktop! Then, to make matters worse, the Weather Channel was calling for a major winter storm in central New York. I decided to stay and do my part at the Wednesday night meeting and leave as soon as the meeting was over. This would leave Gary to handle

Thursday, Friday, Saturday, and the three meetings on the last Sunday by himself.

It worked out well. I took the lion's share of the meetings on Sunday through Wednesday, and even though we were very busy, the days crawled by terribly slowly. I was not ready to deal with having a son who had cancer. The very word gave me chills! There is something somber and unnerving about the word. My mind imagined every possible thing that could go wrong, first with the surgery and then with the follow-up. How my heart ached for my son. I wanted nothing but to be able to be with him and comfort him. It was so difficult to act like nothing was wrong and smile and talk about the work while in my heart, I was worried sick about my oldest son. How Josh had gladdened our hearts when he was born! He was one of those kids who has never met a stranger, but was warm-hearted and had a ready smile for all. He was eight when Reneé, his mother, died, and he suffered terribly missing her. But through it all, he tried to be so brave and I found myself leaning on him as we made it through the first days, then weeks, and finally years. As he matured there in the jungle, he was always quick to take on responsibilities that came with being an MK in the jungle.

As soon as the meeting was over on Wednesday night, Keila bundled up three-year-old Mikeila and her three-month-old sister, Mia, and strapped them into their little car seats and we merged into traffic, heading west. All through the long night, driving through the mountains of northern New York, my thoughts kept returning to those days in the hospital with Reneé. How sore my heart was to have to fly back from Caracas to Puerto Ayacucho to meet my three little boys and tell them they no longer had a mother. As soon as I walked into the room where they were staying in Puerto Ayacucho, Josh's eyes searched my face, and seemed to already know the answer. Ryan and Stephen were younger and were not quite so perceptive. Josh's huge eyes filled with tears in spite of his obvious joy at seeing me walk in. I quietly took them into an inner room and, wrapping my arms around them, I tried to tell them in words that a four-year-old could understand that their mother was not ever going to come home again. Josh was a very mature eight-year-old, and as a matter of fact, had always gravitated to kids about four years older than himself, but in spite of how mature he tried to be, the loss of his mother hit him very hard, as it did the two other boys.

Now I was driving up against a deadline to get there in time to take him to the hospital for cancer surgery. *"God,"* I prayed, *"I need your help. Help me to be strong for Josh."* Ryan and Stephen were still in Cosh and I wondered how they were dealing with this. How I wanted them with me now—but they had offered to stay in the jungle and help with the work there, since both Gary and I were going to be at this conference.

Mikeila, possibly having a bad dream (if three-year-old kids can have bad dreams, and bless her heart, she sure has had enough to give her bad dreams), began to whimper. Hearing her quiet cries, Keila immediately woke from a sound sleep and turned around in her seat to see what the problem was. Keila is a very sound sleeper, and sometimes at night when I have tried to awaken her, I've had to be ready to duck, since many times she wakes up swinging, but never with Mikeila. The slightest little rustle or whimper would have Keila immediately springing up to see what was going on. Keila is such a good mother and loves the boys deeply, but possibly due to those rough first weeks, Mikeila has a hold on her that is almost palpable—actually, on all of us. While Keila was tending to her little needs, my mind drifted back once again to the traumatic time of her birth. I remembered some words I had written down the first time I held her. I was so overawed by this little miracle.

> *It is the 23rd of April today, and I finally got to hold my daughter for the first time. She still has a few wires and tubes, but nothing [like] what she had even as late as this morning. I am holding a little miracle! As I look into her deep baby blue eyes (too early to tell what color they will really be, but I digress), her little eyes stare back at me; you know the look, kinda out of focus. She has no idea of all the turmoil she has caused us this last five weeks. Her little eyes look into mine, and I know I am lost forever to her every whim. The responsibility and enormity of what is waiting for me with this little girl is enough to almost take my breath away.*

Little did we know.

We did make it up to White Lake, Wisconsin, in time to take Joshua in for his surgery, and how my parent's heart ached for him as they took him away on that gurney. I sat by his side in the recovery room and remembered all the good times I had had with my lighthearted little boy, who while I was blinking my eyes had somehow become a man. He was so brave, and if anything, he had helped *me* get over the trauma of his surgery. Now he was sitting beside me on a jet as we fly south to Venezuela to bury his sister, my daughter. All his life he has tried to be brave and now is no different. He is trying to be brave for his brothers and me.

When faced with calamity, my mind races two-forty, trying to sort out this and that, trying to find a way to cope. Part of me is always hoping I'll wake up and find out it has all been a bad dream . . . but this was no dream. My beautiful little Mikeila was gone. All my life, I have lived on the edge. All my life I have watched God do the impossible over and over. But sometimes God has other plans for us. Sometimes He asks that I just trust Him. Just between me and you, honestly, this frightens me. I don't know why, God has always proven Himself trustworthy, but there is something about just walking into the unknown, not knowing where you are going or what you are going to find when you get there, that is frightening—but only for the time it takes you to realize that *not* to trust is so much more terrifying. Working with the Yanomamö has been rewarding and frustrating at the same time and if nothing else, has taught me that God is trustworthy. The challenges are many and the sacrifices have hurt, but God has been faithful. Looking back at my life, most times I feel so privileged. I love my work with the Yanomamö and have no regrets. God has so blessed my life and I know when we get to heaven, we will be reunited with our loved ones, but oh, the holes that are left here. My heart felt as if it would never be whole again. Such a huge hole made by such a little girl.

Thinking about my life and blessings has to include the Yanomamö. So many stories, so much fun and tears with these exuberant people. Since my own heart is heavy with grief, I naturally am thinking along those lines. Working with the Yanomamö has been fun, don't get me wrong. We have laughed until we cried, and at other times we have just cried with them. They deal with so much death!

Part Two

4

Causes and Cures

For the Yanomamö, there are no natural causes of death. Actually, there are almost no natural causes for *anything.* Even your dog dying is the work of an enemy shaman bent on causing you pain. The village *shabolis* (witch doctors) are kept busy guarding the village from attack. The wind is especially suspect, as enemy *shabolis* use it to wreak havoc on villages and gardens. The enemy spirits also use it as their vehicle to move quickly from place to place; thus, any time a storm approaches, the shaman has to get out in the central plaza and, through his own spirits, attempt to divert the storm around his village and their meager food-growing areas.

One day, up in the village of Coyowä, my brother Gary was standing outside his house watching a storm brewing. The thick black clouds and peals of thunder heralded a tropical thunderstorm. These can blow up very quickly, and from a safe place are fascinating to behold. This one looked like it was going to be a good one. Knowing the beliefs of the people, he knew it would be only minutes until the *shabolis* came out and went to battle with the far-away shaman who was sending this storm. Sure enough, here came Sanchez's old father, hurrying out to protect his precious banana trees. The people in Coyo are still primitive now, but back thirty years ago they were *really* rough. This old guy was not wearing anything, just had himself tied up like they do with his little g-string. Oh, he was wearing his paint, which consisted of a broad swath of red onoto across his forehead and some wavy lines starting at the corners of his mouth and extending over his face. He had broad bands running up his torso, too. I'm not sure if his wad of tobacco would count as part of what he was wearing, but he did have the ever-present cud of green tobacco leaves between his lower lip and his teeth. This cud was so huge that you would swear it would keep him from saying a word, but he and all the other men never let it bother them; they chanted, swore, and yelled in spite of their stuffed mouths.

Turning to face the storm, the old man stood with his legs wide apart and his arms held high, with his hands up and palms out as if to hold the storm back by the force of his arms and will.

"Ushu, ushu, ushu!" ("Don't, don't, don't!") he began. But the wind, never mindful of man, began to swirl around him, turning the banana trees' leaves upside down and exposing their lighter undersides.

"Haa clashi!" he screamed, making a chopping motion with his arm in a downward swipe. This was to cut the wind off from its source, the spirit that was blowing it. Sweat glistened on his wrinkled body as he raised his arm for another chop.

While the old man continued to rant and chop the wind, it continued to build up to a full-size gale. Gary moved under his porch to get away from the rain that had blown in with the blustery weather. His view of the old shaman was unhindered by the roof and Gary became aware that the old guy had moved over closer to the plantain trees he was trying to protect. He kept up his loud *"Clashi!"* and continued chopping violently at the base of the wind in the spirit world, but by now his sweat had been washed away by the torrents of rain that was causing his body paint to streak in insane lines down his naked torso. The stronger the wind blew, the more the battle in the spirit world intensified, with the old shaman answering blasts of lighting and the crash of thunder with chants and dances to protect his precious banana trees. To better protect the trees, he had his back to them and was furiously waving his arms as he did battle in the spirit world against a shaman he only knew by reputation.

The wind by this time was blowing full force—and the harder the wind blew, the more determined became the efforts of the lonely bulwark against the storm. From his vantage point, Gary noticed a huge banana tree slowly give up the battle and begin to tilt and then faster begin to fall. Knowing that any warning shout would be impossible to hear over the roar of the wind and the whoosh of the rain—not to mention the fact that the old witch doctor was still in full voice slashing and chopping the wind—Gary took off running as hard as he could toward the old man, afraid he would be crushed if the banana tree with its large stalk of bananas hit him. But before he could get there, the tree fell. With a crash that could be heard above the roar of the wind and the rain, it smashed the pugnacious witch doctor to the ground so hard that his cud of tobacco was slung out of his mouth. Gary, fearing the worst, ran up just in time to see the old man crawl out from under the dripping, heavy leaves of the banana plant. Before Gary could offer him any assistance, the old man turned with as much dignity as could be mustered by a rain-drenched, naked man after being the victim of a perfidious traitor tree. A trickle of blood mixed with rain-soaked paint snaked its way down the wrinkles of the old man's back. Shaking his fist at the rest of the trees still standing in his garden, the old man swore. "See if I ever come out and protect you again, you bunch of unworthy trees! You can all get blown over as far as I am concerned!" he shouted. He bent down and dug in the soggy grass to find his precious wad of tobacco. Finally finding it, he angrily shook the rain and mud off it before placing it back in its spot between his lower lip and teeth. Muttering angrily, he limped on back over to the safety of his hearth, where he continued to vent his rage at the world in general and at the shaman who had sent the storm in particular. Tomorrow he would plot his revenge. This was the code he lived by. Every act had to be answered with a retaliatory act. If this was not done, no one would be safe in his village.

So the shamans each sought to protect their villages. They wage hostilities with shamans in other villages known only through their reputation in the spirit world. The shaman works his black magic openly in the village center, calling his spirits to combat on his behalf against his enemies. The other shamans of the village assist him as he calls on the *naikiliwä* (cannibal) spirits; these are Jaguar spirit, Moon spirit, Hawk spirit, *Shakina* spirit, and a myriad of others that can help him get revenge. They travel through the spirit world to the village that they have determined is the guilty one, and there they seek to wreak similar havoc on the livelihood of that village. If they can catch a small child unaware and steal his soul to eat, even better. The blood lust of the cannibal spirits is such that if they can't find enough from their enemies, they will demand of the *shabolis* that they steal the soul of one of their own little ones. So continues the endless cycle of illusions and delusions.

Most of the time, the witch doctor is fighting against shabolis in villages so far away that his actions don't cause an outright physical war. His wars are fought with shabolis who answer every wrong done with an equal one in return. He does not have to do the painstaking symbolic cleansing ritual, the *unocai,* that all Yanomamö who have killed someone have to undertake. This ritual can last from five to ten days, and is fraught with much danger because the one doing the ritual is unclean. He has to be very careful not to touch even himself, for fear of contaminating himself. Contamination could cause him to develop large sores, possibly go blind, or even (in extreme cases) to die. After his sessions, even though he might have stolen the soul of a child for his bloodthirsty horde, but he continually has to be on his guard against the revenge attacks of his opponent.

Now, the *oca* (lone killers using black magic), in contrast, do cause wars. They go physically against villages that are close and that normally do have some kind of relations with their own villages. Although they do use magic, they physically go against a village to blow their magic powder on some unsuspecting victim. In other words, the weapon they leave their own villages with is not their bow and arrows, but rather a small, apparently insignificant blowgun. With this blowgun, they blow a tiny dart with the head wrapped in cotton and sprinkled with spirit poison. The dart is not expected to hit anything; they just blow it in the general direction of the person they wish to kill. The dart falls far short, but the spirit powder travels on and strikes the person. If successful, their prey should immediately begin to feel the effects of this poison.

First, they gather the ingredients to make the potion they need. These include herbs, leaves, hair, blood of small rodents, teeth of the *aroamö* snake, and some secret ingredients. (By the way, those teeth of the bushmaster snake? They catch it alive and, while holding the snake down with a stick, others force the snake's mouth open and they break the teeth out of the live snake. For the evil charm to work, the teeth have to come from a live snake.) The whole concoction is cooked up until it is a thick substance that they then dry over the coals of the fire. All women and children are told to leave the *shabono* (communal house) while the shamans are busy with this brew. The dry powder is then put in a small pouch along with some darts made specially for their sinister purpose.

Once all is ready, the *oca* leave without fanfare. Normally, they travel in a group limited to around three to five men, a couple of real *oca* and one or two men as their assistants. The helpers go along with their bows and arrows, not to aid in fighting, but to assist the *oca* with daily living in the jungle as they patiently seek to get closer and closer to their enemies so that they might blow their magical poison darts. The men with the bows and arrows are to help with procuring meat and defense; all offensive actions are taken by the *oca.*

Once they are near enough to the enemy village, they lie in wait on main trails or near gardens to find their prey. This is an extremely dangerous time for the *oca* because if discovered, they would be pursued relentlessly and every effort would be expanded to make sure they were killed so they couldn't return.

Finally their patience is rewarded. They see a man out gathering and hunting with his young wife. They follow, quiet as the hunting jaguar, observing and attempting to place themselves in a key spot to get close enough to blow their magic poison on him without giving themselves away. The men with the bows and arrows are not with the *oca,* having stayed behind. This is the fight of the *oca.*

Finally the ambush is set. The two *oca* lie face down in a slight depression covered in *baimi* (underbrush). To be honest, they are in plain sight, but because of their stillness, and with the dirt, mud, and general "ambiance" of the jungle covering them from having lived out in it for so long, their bodies blend in so well with the flora that it would take a very keen eye to detect them.

Perhaps it is because he is out with his young wife, or maybe he is thinking of something else, but whatever the reason, the warrior does not see them and walks right past them to stand looking up into the branches of a fruit tree. The presence of the fruit tree is the reason this place was chosen for the ambush.

Not realizing he is being watched, he stands looking up into the tree to make sure the berries are ripe. Searching on the ground, he picks one up that has fallen. Biting into it, he checks it for taste. Finding it to his satisfaction, he hands a piece to his wife. She also agrees, so he leans his bow and arrows against a nearby tree. Pulling a vine, he skillfully makes a vine hoop for his feet, and, telling his wife to stand a bit to the side, he takes his machete and begins to climb. When he is about twenty feet high, the *oca* raise their heads enough to place their little blowguns into their mouths and blow the magical powder-laden dart at their victim. He immediately begins to get dizzy.

"I am coming down. I can't hold on," he calls down to his wife. His mouth tastes funny and he has a hard time holding on as he lets himself down. By the time he gets to the base of the tree, he is shaking and almost delirious. His wife begins to cry and helps him stand and slowly they begin to make their way home.

There the shamans will do all they can to counteract the effects of the magical potion that has sapped the strength of their warrior. Alas, their efforts are in vain; the young man dies. The oca have already started their *unocaimou* ritual before they get home. But now the tide has turned; it is now their turn to dread going out, it is their turn to live in abject fear, because now they know that the *oca* of the village they attacked are after them and won't be satisfied until they have killed one of theirs . . . and so the cycle continues. *Author's note:* I received this account of the very secret work of the *oca* from Shoefoot and Samuel from Cejal, both of whom had participated in and even led *oca* raids before becoming believers in Jesus Christ.

5

The Power of Suggestion

I have mentioned in previous writings that I never have anything to do with medicine if I can possibly help it. What I have never told anyone is that I am too open to the power of suggestion: Anytime I see someone with some sickness, I am immediately overcome by the same symptoms. This is also why I hate hearing about illness, reading medical papers trying to find out about an illness, or, as I said, just anything to do with sicknesses.

So, anyway, I don't enjoy hearing about, reading about, or in any other way being informed of someone's illness, because I do know that the power of suggestion works. You know, maybe I am not that different from my Yanomamö friends. If life really is a journey, we must pick up a lot of baggage along the way, because I have watched that same power of suggestion act on my friends. I remember the time we were over watching Gary work on a motor. A bunch of the Yanomamö guys were around and we were laughing and joking. We had been talking about one of the local hypochondriacs and Octavio said it was all in his head, this guy just got what everyone else had. Octavio also told us that there were people who could be made sick by just asking them if they felt good. About that time, we were joined by Romero, a visitor from the Ocamo area. Octavio looked at us and smiled, making us conspirators with him, although I had no idea how far he planned to take it. He then turned to Romero and, with a look of real concern on his face, addressed him.

"Romero, are you feeling well? You don't look good." Octavio's eyes were filled with concern and he reached over and touched Romero's forehead to see if he had a fever.

"No, I am not sick, I am well." Romero shrugged off Octavio's hand and his question with a quick smile.

Octavio dropped it, seeming to be absorbed in what Gary was doing in the bowels of the engine he was working on. Catching our eyes about five minutes later, he asked Romero again: "Brother-in-law, are you sure you are well? Your eyes don't look good to me," he said to him again.

"No, no, I'm fine. I'm not sick!" Romero glanced from Octavio to the rest of us and grinned again, but this time I detected a look of uncertainty in his eyes.

About five minutes later Octavio again turned to him. "*Jeriyä* [brother-in-law], you surely do not look good. Perhaps you might want me to take you over to the medicine house . . . " his voice trailed off in concern.

Romero looked up at Octavio. The hurting in his eyes was obvious and he grimaced in pain. "Yes, I do have this throbbing in the back of my head. It has been bothering me for a while. I think I must be getting malaria."

I stared—just minutes earlier he had been the picture of health!

In less time than it takes to tell it, Octavio was leading Romero over to the house of medicine. The poor man could hardly walk. I never did figure out why Octavio took it so far as to make poor Romero sick—just his idea of a practical joke, I guess—but *that* is the power of suggestion. This is what I was raised with, so I suppose I come by it honestly.

Keila even says I displayed all her pregnancy symptoms save one, but we all know how women like to exaggerate about the toils and pain of pregnancies. I mean, just because I might have gained a bit of weight during her pregnancies doesn't mean I had all her symptoms. The gaining weight had nothing to do with her pregnancies anyway, it was all her crazy eating habits and wanting to get up at all hours to eat that did that, but no, to hear her tell the story, I did everything but go into labor.

I thought for a while that the power of suggestion works in dreams as well, because one night shortly after we arrived in the USA for Keila to give birth to our daughter, Mikeila, I was in a sound sleep having a fine adventure involving mountain climbing and rocks, believing that Keila was in an equally sound and refreshing sleep enjoying her own adventure. Little did I know she was lying on her side of the bed wide awake. The baby was moving around so much that she couldn't get comfortable no matter how hard she tried. The later it got, the more irritated she allowed herself to become. Finally the snores of contented sleep coming from my side of the bed were too much for her to overlook. She raised her leg and gave me a vicious kick, her heel catching my leg above the knee and raising a goose egg out on it.

I jumped up and looked around in the darkness, but by that time Keila was pretending to be asleep on her side. I rubbed my leg. Keila rolled over and sleepily asked me what was wrong.

"I don't know, I was having a dream and something woke me up. My leg hurts."

"Go to sleep, it will feel better," she told me.

The next morning my leg still hurt. At breakfast, I commented to my nephew, "Boy, I was having a dream and this huge rock rolled down the hill and crushed my leg. And it still hurts!" Keila started to laugh. She has a laugh that goes on forever and before we knew it, we were all laughing, though I wasn't sure why. I continued to rub my leg.

A little later Keila asked me again about my leg. The concern in her eyes was real and obvious. I told her it was OK, but that I was not sure why it hurt. "That sure was a real dream. My leg is even bruised. Look at it here. I'm glad I didn't wake up with my leg crushed like in the dream!" I told her.

She laughed again. "I have to confess something to you," she told me. "You know when you woke up last night? Well, you were snoring and I could not sleep, so I kicked you on the leg. I did not mean to kick you so hard," she finished quietly.

I stared at her. Of all the nerve! Well, so much for the power of suggestion! I had been the victim of a brutal attack! Growing up with the Yanomamö, I knew about attacks and even brutal attacks, which was what I felt like I had to deal with here. I thought my leg just hurt after dreaming of a rock rolling on me, and now, to find out she had kicked me! She had better be thankful I don't take my Yanomamö upbringing too seriously, because I know how they would handle this. Take the case of Sanchez in Coyowäteli . . .

6

Sanchez Pushed Too Far: Death and the Yanomamö

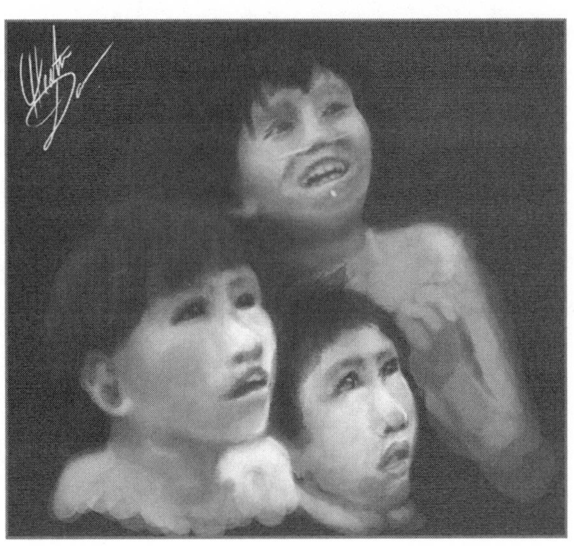

After the fight, Gary walked slowly around the *shabono* of Coyowä, administering what first aid he could. He knew it was woefully inadequate, but he did what he could. Most of the men needed stitches, but since he had nothing to stitch with, they would have to be content with just the antibiotics and bandages he could give them. The fight had been short but brutal. It had started as a lot of Yanomamö fights start, with two little boys playing in the middle of the *shabono*. The larger of the boys had hit the smaller boy and he had run to his mom crying. She had sent him back to avenge himself, but the larger boy pushed him away. This was too much for his short-tempered mom, so she took it upon herself to help her son. She walked over and gave the offending boy a sound slap across his back. His mother, in turn, walked over and slapped her. The first lady hit back, and before they knew it there was hair-pulling and screaming.

The first lady's husband came out; he was an interested observer quick to see the humor in the two ladies battling it out, but he made a grave error. He went from spectator to participant, first by shouting advice and then by stepping in and shoving the other lady away from his wife, causing her to lose her footing in the slippery dirt and fall. By this time, most of the village was around the swirling mass, shouting encouragement and offering counsel. The husband of the wife who had been pushed jumped in and pushed the wife of the man who had pushed his wife. Suddenly, it was no longer a game, as men ran to get clubs. The women, forgetting their fight, ran over and began to yell obscenities at their husbands' opponents and encouragement to their husbands. The fight had split the village down family lines and before it was over, almost every man had a bloody head.

As he doctored them, Gary smiled at the various comments offered up by the men he was doctoring. Most of them took their wounds in stride, and in spite of the tension that still hung in the air over the fight, shouts of laughter were starting to be heard as first one, then another, remembered something funny about his own predicament.

Gary breathed a sigh of relief. For a bit there, he had really been afraid someone was going to get killed, but it seemed like it was over. He glanced over at Sanchez, the charismatic young leader of the village. He would be one of the last guys doctored, and Gary knew he would have to spend a bit more time on him, not only doctoring his wound, but also talking and trying to get the young man to let up a bit. There was a special bond between Gary and Sanchez, and Gary hoped he could get Sanchez to let go of the anger. Of all the men, he was the only one who still lay brooding in his hammock, his handsome face furrowed by a deep frown, his hands clasped in front of his mouth in a show of his deep irritation. His wife sat in her hammock, fanning the fire, her tirade against the ones who had started the fight never ending. The more she talked, the deeper the frown on her husband's face became. She did not seem to notice, but kept talking in her shrill voice that carried over the entire village.

"This is why I have said we need to go home to my village. In my village you would not have a bloody head, but the men would like and respect you," she shrilled. Blood continued to drip down his face and down his chest from the nasty gash on his head. He shook his head as if to clear it, and glared at his wife. Gary was still a couple of hearths away, tending to another man, when he glanced up in time to see Sanchez suddenly spring to his feet. He grabbed his club in one hand and, reaching for his machete with the other, held up the club and deftly cut it shorter with a couple of well-placed swings of his razor-sharp machete.

Realizing what was planned, Gary lunged to put himself near Sanchez so he could grab the club, but he was too slow. Swinging his club down in a short, vicious blow, Sanchez felled his wife where she had been sitting in her hammock. She dropped with a groan, not even finishing the curses she had been yelling at the other women of the village.

But Sanchez was not finished. He ran over to the next hearth and clubbed his neighbor's wife down. Then, while the entire village looked on in disbelief, he ran from hearth to hearth, chasing women down and clubbing them wherever he could catch them. Realizing he had gone berserk, the women who were still able scattered, but he was not deterred. First one, then more and more men began to yell encouragement to him, even herding women who were trying to escape back to the center of the village within reach of Sanchez's club. He chased first one, then another, and clubbed them down.

In spite of the men's efforts to prevent it, a few women escaped the *shabono* and ran down the airstrip, trying to get to Gary's house, hoping to find shelter there with Gary's wife, Marie, but Sanchez was too fast. Quickly he overtook them, smashed them to the ground in mid-stride, knocking them tail over teakettle, and leaving them moaning with bloody heads. By this time the men, realizing why Sanchez was doing this, were all laughing and shouting encouragement. Some were yelling at the women to run faster; others yelled directions to Sanchez. All were laughing uproariously, their hilarity mixing inharmoniously with the screams and moans of the fallen women.

Finally it was over. All the women had bloody heads. Sanchez came back to his hearth with his face still bloody and his big wound gaping, but now instead of a scowl his face had a huge grin. "All the time, the women fuss and get us men worked up and we get our heads pounded, and they don't get anything. This time, I decided I would give the women what we had gotten," he explained to Gary. Although it would mean he would have twice as many people to doctor, Gary tried to keep a straight face.

This was just like him, Gary thought. Sanchez was always impetuous, but his grin was infectious and he and Gary were close friends. How Gary hoped he would listen to the salvation story that Gary so wanted him to understand! But it seemed like Sanchez was more interested in raiding and killing than in listening to anything about a God who loved him. If he was not on a raid, the next best thing was telling about raids he had gone on and about the people he had killed; he almost seemed to enjoy making Gary uncomfortable with the graphic retellings.

On one of their many hunting trips together, while resting, he showed Gary a tree that had died, explaining the near miss he had encountered in this very spot. "I sure thought they had me that time." He said this with an honesty you don't normally find with the overly optimistic Yanomamö. Normally, when they tell a story, they are always the heroes: they outran everyone, they were just too smart, and on and on. But Sanchez never seemed to think he had to put on airs. He told things as he saw them, regardless of whether, in the telling, he came out as the one who had been frightened to death.

"It was close, too close to be honest, I don't see how they did not get me. By the time we got to this place my legs were wobbly. I was so tired and panicked," he smiled. "But they missed. They missed and the poison point they shot at me hit this tree right here." He stood up and pointed to a spot on the tree and sure enough, there was still a short piece of the point sticking out of the wood. "This tree was alive when they shot at me, but the poison point killed it." He pointed again. "I know if that point would have hit me, it would have killed me, I would be gone, and you would have no one to hunt with now!" he told Gary with a large grin.

Without missing a beat, he told Gary of another raid he had gone on.

"I just could not get a good shot," he explained. "So I climbed a tree outside my enemy's village and waited until dawn. The lighter it became, the more exposed I was, but I had gone to a lot of effort, so I held my fire until I was able to get a good shot at my enemy."

"Even while wondering how in the world he could draw his bow and take aim while still holding onto a tree, I searched for the right words to try and tell my friend that God's Word says, 'Thou shalt not kill,'" said Gary.

Not only had Sanchez killed his enemy, but many other deaths would be caused by his reckless act, too, because with the Yanomamö, it never stopped there. Their culture demanded revenge.

The village of Matowä tried to get him even before he got back to his village, and according to Sanchez it was sheer luck that they failed to do so.

"I was running all out. I was so tired I could barely move, and it seemed like I was tripping over everything. Suddenly without warning, I heard a bowstring twang. I twisted away from the sound. With a loud splintering sound my arrow point holder shattered against my back. It felt like someone hit me with his fist right between my shoulder blades. I knew I was hit, and waited for the penetrating pain and blood to start. I almost wet myself," he confessed. "That is how scared I was. But somehow I kept running and I can't tell you how, but I did get away. Hours later, when I finally could stop and rest, I looked for the wound, even still surprised that I felt no pain. I really had thought I was hit in the back. The cord tying the *tola* [arrow point holder] to my back was still around my neck, so I pulled it over my head to feel around on my back for the wound. There was nothing. I was shocked to see that my arrow point holder was shattered and ruined. There, sticking out of a shattered piece of bamboo, was a large, broken-off piece of poison point. That close," he said, holding up his fingers showing a small distance. "That close, and I would have been killed."

Of course, the Matowä villagers' efforts at revenge did not end with the failed attempt on Sanchez; their code demanded that they keep trying. Finally they were successful. While the screams of "raiders" were still echoing across the jungle, mixed in with the wails of the women for their dead, Sanchez grabbed his bow and arrows and took off—not running after the raiders, but rather, betting on a shortcut they did not know, running directly toward their distant village. The way he ran, though shorter, was much higher, and from one vantage point he looked back across the valley and saw the smoke of the funeral pyre rising from his village. It looked close, but he had already been running for a couple of hours. He was silent, a ghost as he ran, his anger being the energy pumping through his body. The danger he was in was real, but only heightened his sense of destiny as he pushed on, his body merging perfectly and soundlessly in his jungle.

Finally arriving at his chosen spot, he lay in ambush outside their village waiting for the raiders to return. He knew he was ahead of them by the lack of commotion coming out of the village. Suddenly he heard someone on the trail. He froze. His body, painted black for war, blended into the shadows perfectly. He was totally camouflaged, and he needed to be, because although his position was a good one for shooting, it was more exposed than he would have liked, but he accepted the risks. The line of raiders came into sight, hurrying down the trail single file. The closer they got to their village, the more they relaxed; now, right outside their village, they let down their guard and were not being as watchful as they should have been with an opponent like Sanchez.

He had his arrow nocked and ready, but he was not interested in shooting just anyone. Even though he figured all to be guilty because of their participation, he wanted to shoot the man who had actually fingered the arrow onto the bowstring, who had felt the pull of the longbow and felt the rush of adrenaline as he released his arrow, knowing it flew true. This was the man Sanchez wanted and he knew who it was!

His grip on his bow tightened as he recognized his enemy. But this was a worthy opponent and presented no good target while in bowshot. Rather than head home in defeat, Sanchez waited until the last man in line had passed him; then, without missing a beat, he fell into step behind him, walking softly. The man never heard the deadly ghost behind him and as they ran into the village amidst the cheers of the women, he ran in with them. Possibly due to the war paint each man was wearing, it was hard to tell who was who; or maybe, because no one could count that high, no one took notice of the extra man running in with arrows drawn, possibly thinking it was just another one of their own celebrating their victory against their enemy.

Sanchez danced around, allowing his steps to bring him closer to his adversary. While the entire village gaped, he pulled his long bow back and let fly an arrow at point-blank range! The village stared in shock at their fallen leader, but before they were able to gather their wits about them, the silent killer was gone!

Gary's prayer for Sanchez to accept the Lord's claims on his life did not come to fruition, at least not while Gary was still working with him and the village of Coyo. But the Lord was working on Sanchez, slowly drawing him to Himself. After Gary and Marie were moved to work in another village, the mission leadership stationed my sister, Sandy, and her husband, Robert Jank, along with others to work in Coyowä. Bobby found himself drawn to the dynamic leader of the village just as Gary had been. A fast friendship was formed, and Sanchez began to grasp the fact that there was a higher authority over him and one day he was going to have to account for the way he spent his life.

One day he became very ill and was close to death. In his fever-induced hallucination, he saw himself being banished from heaven and sent to hell. He thought it was too late for him, but slowly he began to recover with the patient treatment of Bobby and Sandy. Once he was able to get around a bit, he began to seek Bobby out to ask him questions. His near brush with death haunted him and the Spirit kept prodding him. One day he gave in and, with Bobby guiding him, prayed and asked *Yai Bada* (the Yanomamö name for God) to come into his heart and cleanse him of his sin.

The change in Sanchez was real. His normally charismatic—and very likable—personality blossomed and he constantly asked questions about his new life. He also began to display a concern for his people that went beyond the normal Yanomamö style of leadership.

His life was his oldest son, named Pepito. Pepito sat in my house the other day and filled me in on his father's last days. He had gotten sick in another village and sent word for his son to come and help him get home. Pepito hurried to meet him. He was so weak he could barely stumble down the trail. It was possibly falciparum malaria with complications of pneumonia. Getting more and more concerned for his father, Pepito finally talked his dad into allowing him to make a shelter and spend the night. His dad passed away there in that temporary shelter, still almost an entire day away from his village. Pepito was devastated. Eventually they brought his father home for the last time.

Pepito had a huge problem. He did not want to have the village divide up his father's crushed bones to use in their *leajumou* (bone-drinking ceremony), but he was not yet old enough to command much respect in village affairs. His demand that he be allowed to bury his father's bones was met with jeers and ridicule, then anger. He had hoped other Christian leaders in the village would side with him, but they, possibly knowing the mood of the village, did not. He was all alone.

"They drank my father's bones," he told me. "I could not stop them. But I know God knows all about it. I tried. But you know," he continued on, "I wonder sometimes if God, in His mercy, did not take my father when He did. He was really struggling with maintaining his Christian walk and still being able to be the leader of the village. So many times his Christian views were not well received and my dad was starting to be swayed. I believe God took him before he did things that he would have always regretted. My dad really loved God and wanted his life to count for Him." He smiled and wiped the tears from his eyes.

My own eyes were moist as I thought about this man and the impact he was still having on his son. It is very rare to find a Yanomamö who will even speak of someone close to him who has died. Pepito not only spoke candidly about his father, but did so in such an open way that we sat there and talked and reminisced about his father for more than an hour. I told Pepito about the time his father had cracked all the ladies on their heads and he laughed loudly.

"This was so typical of my dad." He smiled. "Everyone loved him, but knew not to push him too far." He smiled again with a faraway look in his eyes. I smiled at him, knowing he was picturing his dad up in heaven now. Knowing I knew what he was thinking, he finished his thought. "Yes, I know I will see my father again. How thankful I am that he heard about God and accepted the price He paid for his salvation."

But death! Nothing has more finality to the Yanomamö. Once someone dies, it is as if they never existed. Everything they owned is destroyed so there will be nothing to stir a memory. Most times, even their house or portion of the *shabono* is pulled down and burned so there will be no possibility that you might look at the house, or a portion of the roof, and remember how the dead person worked on it. Gardens are abandoned, new crops are pulled out of the ground. If the now-dead person had built any little hunting shacks in the jungle, every effort would be made to go out there and burn them as well. Even favorite fruit trees are chopped down. Everything that reminded people of the dead person would be destroyed. It is for this reason that they will not even name a child until after it is older. The chances of the child dying are too great, and they do not want to have a name to try and forget.

I remember the first death I witnessed with the Yanomamö. I stood beside my friend Yacuwä as he cried, and tears streaked down my own face as I began to cry with him. The grief in the small hut was suffocating. I remembered Dad kneeling in the dirt beside the vine hammock of the old man. He almost had to shout to be heard above the wailing.

"Father," he shouted. The old man feebly opened his eyes. "Can you hear me, father?" Dad shouted again. The old man nodded. "Father, when you said you believed on Jesus, were you sure?" Dad was yelling right in the old man's ears. Slowly the old man nodded again.

"Yes," he said, in a voice so low I could barely make out what he was saying. "When you told me about a man who was God that had made a way to save me from the fire, I hung my desires on Him, and they are still hanging on Him."

A short time later the old man died. I stood with Yacuwä as we watched the men build the funeral pyre. Carefully selecting logs that would burn hot and long, they placed them on the bottom. They built up the sides the same way my ancestors had built up the sides of their log cabins. They started a fire in the center of the pyre while they worked. While it was being fanned into a roaring blaze, they built up the sides. By the time the sides were finished, the fire was burning hot.

After the cremation, the bones were carefully gathered by sifting through the ashes, painstakingly finding every bone fragment and placing them in a basket made for that purpose. When they were satisfied that they had gathered every piece of bone, the basket was hung above the hearth of the family of the old man. Runners were sent out to surrounding villages and even to faraway villages where the old man had relatives or the village had allies.

As soon as everyone who had been called arrived, they gathered to grind the bones into a powder. They cried and wailed almost as much doing this as they had when they were actually burning the body.

A four- or five-foot section of a tree had been hollowed out and hardwood poles cut to about six-foot lengths. Both the log and poles were very heavily decorated. Two men were selected. Both had decorated themselves by putting the snow-white down of a large hawk in their hair. On their arms were colorful armbands made from the head feathers of the curassow bird. In between the bands and their arms, they had pushed the long, blood-red tailfeathers of the scarlet macaw sticking up. In their earlobes, one guy had bright toucan feathers, and the other one had the bright indigo blue of the small *moi* bird. Their bodies were painted red with heavy black jagged lines. They emptied the basket of bones into the hollowed-out tree, and then, taking the long poles, they methodically began to grind the bones up accompanied by the wails of the mourners.

The ground-up bones were then placed in large gourds and left near the hearth of the person who had died. That is the point when it begins to get a bit ugly, as the different villages and relatives try to decide how to divide up the powdered bones. Everyone of course wants some, but some of the relatives will be against giving certain people some, claiming that they did not like the deceased for some reason or another. Accusations go back and forth, but finally all the bones are given out.

In the case of this old man, there were already believers in the village when he died, although they were in the minority. Bautista, the old man's oldest son and a very recently converted witch doctor, did not want to have anyone drink his father's bones, but he was only one of many brothers, so he was not strong enough to enforce his wishes. Little gourds full of the ground-up powder went up and down the river to all the villages where the old man had relatives. Then, during the next years, each village or family group hosted a bone-drinking ceremony with their portion of the bones.

This first death I observed was that of a very old man. If the man that had died, or was killed, had had a young son, it would be during the time of drinking the bones that the son would repeatedly be told who was responsible for his father's death, always with the understanding that as soon as he was old enough, he would lead a raid to avenge his father's death.

If he was just a young boy, care would be taken to make sure that enough of the powdery bones were left in a gourd so that he would have his father's bones to drink once he got old enough to participate in the bone-drinking ceremony. Right after that, he would be expected to participate in a raid to avenge his father's death, and also to avenge all the suffering he had had to endure growing up without a father.

The bone-drinking ceremony is possibly the single most important event in the Yanomamö calendar. When their plantains are harvested and hung up to ripen, the men will go on an extended hunt. Everything they kill will be smoked and preserved to take home. During the time the men are out, every evening and all night long the women will sing and dance to assure the men of a successful hunt. This is a time of very loose morals, as any man who has stayed home from going on the hunt will take advantage of as many women as he can.

Then, on or about the day the hunters return, the invited guests begin to arrive. They normally camp out a short distance from the host village and start to make their preparations for their entrance into the village. Much care is taken, as it could be possible that the bone-drinking ceremony is only a ruse to get them to come, and ambushes are not that uncommon.

When the returning hunters are still a short way from their village, they stop to allow each hunter to paint himself up. There is no set pattern or paint scheme; rather, each hunter paints himself as he sees himself. Most of the time they try to represent some spirit or animal. When they are ready, their imminent arrival is heralded by two of the youngest members of their party. Decked out in all their feathered finery, waving bright yellow new palm branches, they burst into the village, dashing madly around the entire circle of the *shabono*, running in opposite directions with great shouts of greeting and encouragement from everyone in the village. As they run around the village, about every thirty yards they stop and do their own shuffling dance, around and back and forth, before taking off again. After running around the entire circumference of the *shabono,* they race back out to meet back up with the main group.

Once the heralds have alerted the entire village to the hunters' arrival, the warriors make their grand entrance. They whirl around in a colorful mass, each one dancing to his own beat and rhythm based on the image of the animal or spirit he is representing. Despite the fact that each is doing his own dance, viewed together it has a certain cohesiveness that is hard to describe but fascinating to watch. When they finish traversing the entire circle of the *shabono,* they return to their own hearths, where they await the arrival of their guests.

With great noise and fanfare, the visiting villages begin to make their entrances. Most of their actions are intended to prove how invincible they are and how strong they would be if attacked. Again, by watching closely you can tell what spirit or animal a dancer is imitating by the way he moves and by the sounds he makes.

After everyone has made their entrances, the gourd of powdery bones is brought out and mixed with a large pot full of ripe plantain drink. This is stirred until the bright yellow of the plantain takes on the dark-brown color of the ashes and bones. Gourds-full are then passed around and, amidst wails and cries, each participant downs a large amount. During this time, alliances are struck to go on raids and try to avenge the person whose bones they are drinking.

During the day, most of the men participate in inhaling a drug called *ebena.* Pretty soon most of the men of the village and their visitors are dancing and chanting with the individual spirits that they can see only when in their drug-induced state. The ones more attuned to the spirits learn new songs or chants from their *jecula* (spirits). They will sing these chants, and the onlookers will do their best to learn the song, so it can be sung later on that night.

During the evenings, the women continue to gather for singing and dancing, with each song getting more and more suggestive. They begin to egg each other on, and soon you will see women leaving their party and each pulling any man she wants to go outside the *shabono* with her. Under the cover of darkness, things that are normally not done are accomplished with little regard for the normal modest behavior of these people. Two, three, or four women will pull one man out and have their way with him. All taboos are off. Later on, in the night, it is the men's turn. Bands of men will go right up to a man's hearth and pull out any women they want. If the woman's husband is angry, he does not show it, but gets his revenge by going and dragging some other woman out of the village for himself. This orgy goes on all night. Most of the time it is a contest between visiting and host villages to see who can get away with more. This is cause for much bragging and leads to many fights later on.

This goes on until it is time for the visiting village to depart. Normally this is when things tend to get out of hand. Pent-up anger over knowing that their wives have been used explodes violently, first with name-calling and quickly escalating into fighting with fists, clubs, machetes, axes, and sometimes going into shooting, although that usually happens only if someone is hurt badly or killed during the fist, machete, axe, or club fights.

Alliances that have been forged over their common grief are suddenly in danger of falling apart. Wise leaders know the best way to get over mutual hostilities is to somehow direct them at a common enemy. Plans are brought forward to go on an avenging raid against an enemy village so that the anger the warriors feel over their women's honor can be directed elsewhere.

There is so much death working with the Yanomamö. I remember going up to the village of Carawana with Antonio, to encourage our good friend and seminar student Juan Carlos, who had lost his son a couple of weeks earlier. His son had also been one of our students. We had been told that the *leajumou* ceremony was going to be held the next week, and we were hoping to get up there before it took place. But we got to Carawana only to find that the hunters had already gotten back from the *jeniomou* (extended hunt), and the village was preparing for a large bone-drinking ceremony the very next day.

As we walked into the village, we saw a large crowd of mourners at the hearth of Juan Carlos. Antonio went straight there. He got down on his knees and hugged Juan Carlos. "Don't cry," he told him. "Your son is in heaven right now." The crowd quieted down to listen to what this visitor was saying. "My friend, Juan Carlos, you and your wife will see your son again." Antonio went on, "The Bible says that when a believer dies, he is already with God. You are sad, that is our lot to be sad since Adam sinned, but we are told not to grieve like those who have no hope. You and your wife have both asked for Christ's salvation, so your eyes will one day see your son again. This is our hope!"

Juan Carlos slowly nodded his head. He got up and came over to us and we all hugged him. He led us to the area next to their hearth, where his son had built a really nice meeting area with some benches so they would have a place for their church services. The crying started up again, and we hung our hammocks quietly as the entire village wailed their grief over the loss of the young man.

"I'll come talk to you later," Juan Carlos told us. We nodded. He returned to the mourners. That night, around 7:00 p.m., he and his wife came back over to where we had our hammocks hung. They sat quietly, listening as each of us talked about our life in Christ and the hope we have. His wife started crying softly as I read the verses where it talks about the living not leaving the dead behind, but that the dead in Christ shall rise first and we shall meet the Lord in the air. I was surprised to hear first Juan Carlos, and then his wife, tell us that they were doing OK, God was making their hearts strong; even though they were sad, they knew their son was in heaven with God.

Juan Carlos also told us, "My friends, I am a believer and yet I am all alone here. All the men in this village, we are related. I have brothers, uncles, cousins, and every one of them claim my son. Now I know we don't have to drink my son's bones for him. But my village will not hear of doing anything else in this matter. I am only one voice. What will drinking my son's bones do to him?" From the intense grief on his face, it was obvious that he was afraid his actions might somehow cause his son to be cast out of heaven or something.

I told him, "My friend, nothing anyone can do can affect your son now. He is gone from this body, his bones are only bones. Your son is in heaven. God will make him a new body." He smiled his thanks.

I wish I could take each of you through the experience in that village. The wailing, the chanting to the demons, the sheer volume of sound all night long made it impossible to sleep. In spite of the fact that Christ died to give life, very few of the Yanomamö have embraced the gospel, so the depths of their despair was something palpable. Early, while it was still dark, the cacophony rose in volume; the morning was split with the sound of shotguns firing, and the wailing increased in intensity as the invited villages began to arrive. Each warrior was painted to represent some animal or spirit. They danced and whirled around the village, their bright colors in sharp contrast to the continued sounds of wailing. It went on and on.

In every Yanomamö funeral, the mourners always carry some piece of the dead person's earthly possessions. Even in this there is a certain pecking order: the most cherished possessions of the dead person are carried by the closest of kin. In this case, the closest was the mother. What a testimony to me when I saw what she was carrying: There, wrapped in the large envelope we had given him, was his Yanomamö New Testament and his song book! In the midst of so much grief, the boy's testimony showed bright and clear.

As I said, in this work with the Yanomamö there have been many occasions to have to say goodbye to friends as they pass from this life to the next one. And as I said, for the Yanomamö death is utterly final, so it has been hard even for the believers to really understand the victory over death that the Bible promises us. But slowly, as they mature in the Word, we are seeing a breakthrough.

A short time ago, our oldest old man here in the village died. Three of the Christian men of the village and I were up in another village for a Yanomamö summit hosted by the New Tribes Mission for the Yanomamö workers in Venezuela and Brazil, so we were not there when the old man died and was cremated. However, they did wait until we were home to dispose of the bones.

He had called his family around him and told them he was in truth going home, as his Father had sent His "beings" to get him. He seemed amazed that no one could see the beings he was trying his hardest to point out, but that was not his real message. He told his sons to really follow the Lord with their whole hearts. "Teach your children, so they might follow after you," he kept stressing. He laid out how he wanted his body to be handled after he was gone. "Don't go and get all the people from other villages," he told them, "just cremate my body and bury the bones. Do not even grind them. Just bury them. Don't let all my relatives from other villages that don't know the Lord come here and try and take my bones," he repeated.

The sons tried to do all he had asked them to do, although with a man as well known and well liked as this old man was, there were people showing up on their own without waiting for an invitation. Nevertheless, it truly was a celebration of life rather than wailing of death down in their house that morning. We all gathered and sang songs while the hole was being dug right there under the old man's hearth for the small box holding the bones that they had asked my son Ryan to build.

After the hole was dug, Alfredo, the old man's grandson, read the precious verses from 1 Thessalonians:

> 13 But I would not have you to be ignorant, brethren, concern-
> ing them which are asleep, that ye sorrow not, even as others
> which have no hope. 14 For if we believe that Jesus died and
> rose again, even so them also which sleep in Jesus will God
> bring with him. 15 For this we say unto you by the word of the
> Lord, that we which are alive *and* remain unto the coming
> of the Lord shall not prevent them which are asleep. 16 For
> the Lord Himself shall descend from heaven with a shout,
> with the voice of the archangel, and with the trump of God:
> and the dead in Christ shall rise first: 17 Then we which are
> alive *and* remain shall be caught up together with them in
> the clouds, to meet the Lord in the air: and so shall we ever
> be with the Lord. 18 Wherefore comfort one another with these
> words.

When he was finished, Timoteo read Hebrews 2:14–15: "Forasmuch then as the children are partakers of flesh and blood, He also Himself likewise took part of the same; that through death He might destroy him that had the power of death, that is, the devil;
15 And deliver them who through fear of death were all their lifetime subject to bondage." What a different scene than I had mentally pictured as to what would happen when this old man died!

He had been the headman, and was a very respected leader in the village. Many times, in their old way, when someone like him dies, it is enough to cause the entire village to move, as no one wants to be reminded of where he lived. As a matter of fact, he was known as "Coshilowäteli" (because he was the headman, he assumed the name of the village). This is the reason they will burn a village down and move, because they don't want to say the name of the village any longer. That's why I wondered how the Christians would handle this death. God really gave the Christians the victory in this area that day.

In Yanomamö culture, personal possessions are never passed on, but are destroyed when they dispose of the bones. So I was surprised to see Octavio, the old man's oldest son, walking around with the old man's spear. This was even more surprising, as one of the old man's names had been "Spear": that would make it even more of an item to be disposed of as quickly as possible. But Octavio walked out in front of everyone, and slowly got their attention. Holding up the spear, he waited until even the old ladies in back had quieted down a bit.

"We are doing things differently here." He told the visitors who had come anyway, "My father became a new person many years ago. He at one time was a fierce warrior, but after he accepted Christ, he changed. He no longer went on raids to kill, but he went on many trips to share his new life in Christ. Now, we are here because my father is not with us any longer. He has gone on ahead. One day, we that have the same new life that he had will meet him again. God's Word says we will meet our loved ones in the air, with Jesus. Well, I believe that. So if my father has just gone on before us, I am not going to destroy his stuff. I am going to keep and cherish this spear of his. When I die, I am asking my son to keep it, because I want to remember my father. I want to remember the great change that God made in his heart. My father loved God! He talked to Him all the time. Now, he can talk to Him face to face. I am very happy for my father. His last years here, he suffered. Well, he is not suffering now. Children," he said turning to the choir, "sing #39 in the song book."

I could not believe it. We had already sung some songs: "I Shall Know Him," "Amazing Grace," and "Sweet Bye and Bye," but this song, #39, was almost too happy! It is a song called "In My Father's House." We all sang it at the top of our voices, and what a sound!

Down through the years we have watched our Yanomamö brothers wrestle with exactly what their own approach should be in handling the death of a family member. It does seem to us that the ones who made a strong, clean break from the bone-drinking ceremony really have grown in the Lord and matured in their faith. The ones that either just could not make up their own minds about it, or did not have the backbone to stand against their village in what to do, have never matured in the Lord, but rather always live defeated Christian lives.

7

Jemoshawä's Initiation

Jemoshawä was small for his age. He looked about ten or twelve years old, but we figured he was probably anywhere from fifteen to eighteen when he came down from the village of Maweni with his family. Because he was my size, we became close friends during the time he was here. His father was Guajaribo (Jungleman, described in the book *Spirit of the Rainforest,* by Mark A. Ritchie), one of the most feared witch doctors on the river. His name only needed to be hissed at any kid to make them obey instantly. His fame as a healer was legendary, but his renown as a "child eater" was also spread far and wide, though it was never discussed openly; it was only whispered during the gossip sessions that inevitably break out whenever more than one Yanomamö get together. Along with his father and mother were his two older brothers and sisters. Jemoshawä was the next to youngest and already it was whispered that his father had plans for him. It was also whispered that he had a special closeness to the spirit world and that the animals would talk with him.

After we became friends, he began to tell Yacuwä and me of the many beings that would come into his dreams. He knew the names of all the *jecula* and could sing the chants of his father's spirits and had even begun to sing his own chants that he had been taught in his dreams. But his large eyes were troubled as he shared this with us, and he confided that the beings coming to him at night were beginning to frighten him.

"I don't want to ever go home," he told us. His solemn face was drawn and his large eyes looked even larger in the soft light of the kerosene lantern flickering on the table. We were sitting in my parents' front room, and even though the three of us were the only ones in the room, he was whispering.

My two older brothers, Steve and Gary, became fast friends with Jemoshawä's brothers, Bali Bali and Seduwä. They were related to Ramon, Pablino Juaquin, and Agusto, also best friends of ours, so it was just natural that the cousins from Maweni would hang out with them. Jemoshawä began to hang around with Yacuwä, Däduwä, and me. We would go out with the older guys as they set out to shoot the long-legged *shoeshoemö* birds in the flooded-out swamp areas. These birds looked ungainly, with their long legs and short wings, but they were ideally made for life in the swamp. We would sneak along the shore behind the older boys as they crept quietly, barely making a sound to get as close to their prey as they could. Then a bowstring would snap, an arrow would whir, and the shrill cry of the *shoeshoemö* would cut the hot, humid afternoon. This was our signal to rush forward as fast as our short legs could churn through the murky water, to try and get to the wounded bird before it could take cover in the tall grass of the swamp. Of course, even if they missed the bird, which was not that often, we still had to wade out into the swamp to retrieve the arrow, but it was not as much fun just going after an arrow as it was to rush out chasing a bird.

Jemoshawä was a quiet boy, but quick to smile. I liked his ready grin and he complemented our group as we hung out fishing and hunting. Soon, however, his family announced that they were heading home. Old Guajaribo was never comfortable in Cosh. He had tolerated it until his brother-in-law, Shoefoot, who had also been one of his students, decided he would give up the power of the *jecula* for a radical idea called Christianity. Everyone knew that the *jecula* gave great power and could give this power to those who allowed the *jecula* to come in and dwell in them. Guajaribo's brother-in-law, Shoefoot (who became Bautista) had shown great promise and quickly became a force to be reckoned with in the spirit world. But, right at the peak of his influence, he had placed his trust in the Supreme Being's Son, Jesus. With his trust in *Yai Bada*, and with the indwelling of *Yai Bada's* Spirit, all the *jecula* were displaced from their home in Shoefoot's chest. Because of this, Guajaribo no longer felt at home in Cosh, and informed his family that he was cutting his visit short. Before this, he had always been able to get any machete, cooking pot, or axe he wanted by making a vague hint at some future catastrophe that he would help someone avoid if they gave them what he wanted, but now, because the people no longer feared him after putting their trust in *Yai Bada's* Son, he was leaving empty-handed. This had really put him in a foul mood. Muttering dire threats against the village in general, and against his brother-in-law in particular, he left the village with his wife and daughters.

We as missionaries did not escape his wrath either, and as he left the village, part of his curses were directed against Dad and even our house. My brothers and I thought it was funny, but there were no smiles on the faces of the listening Yanomamö as Guajaribo called for the spirit of the giant armadillo to come and dig under our house and cave it in. Because of Dad's deep faith in the omnipotence of his God, he did not take Guajaribo's threats seriously, but me? As I was out with my friends, listening to them whisper about the dire consequences of not taking the shaman seriously, I hoped Dad's faith was not misplaced.

Bali Bali and his two brothers decided to stay with their cousins. This further infuriated their father; as he left, not content with all the curses he had already called down, he uttered one more. "I am also leaving behind Jaguar spirit. He will lay in wait outside your village and will ambush you when you go out to hunt. Laugh at me, if you will, but you won't be laughing when your hunters don't return and you find their eaten bodies."

I was overjoyed that Jemoshawä was staying. I really had formed a strong bond of friendship with the quiet, thin boy, and we quickly forgot the curses as we continued to swim and fish and tag after the older boys on the daily *shoeshoemö* hunts. But the rest of the village had not forgotten his curses. People would inspect our house walls for cracks, and—since mud walls are always full of cracks—prophets of doom were quick to point out a supposedly new one. However, the thing that made it the most obvious that the angry witch doctor's threats were being taken seriously was the utter lack of interest in going hunting. This was even affecting our daily search for *shoeshoemös.* The close swamps were quickly hunted out, as the prey learned that when it heard people swimming in the swamp it was time to move on. There were no birds for us to hunt, and we could not convince anyone to head out further.

This kept on until one day Dad had a long talk with a special friend of his, who was one of the best hunters in the village.

"Lobema, why have you not brought me any meat? I am really getting *naiki* [meat-hungry]," Dad told him.

"Pepiwä, I can't go. The *shaboli* has said there will be a jaguar waiting for any hunter foolish enough to go out." Lobema's eyes were full of his worry.

"Well, you have placed your trust in *Yai Bada* and in the power of His Son. Do you think the *shaboli* up the river has as much power as *Yai Bada*?" Dad kept pushing. Looking back, I see Dad was not as interested in the meat we needed as in making the baby Christians really begin to learn that they could trust their newfound Lord and Savior. At the time, though, I hoped Dad was being smart to push someone to leave the village. My friends were very emphatic in their stories of the power of Guajaribo in the spirit world. After listening to Dad, Lobema announced that he was leaving in the morning to go hunting. The entire village could talk of nothing else! This was madness! It was one thing to say you believed that *Yai Bada* loved the Yanomamö, and had died to give them freedom from the spirits and that they no longer needed to fear those spirits, but it was another thing entirely to ignore a curse, especially a curse involving the jaguar. Everyone knew it was the special spirit of Guajaribo and obeyed his every call. Everyone tried to talk Lobema out of going, but he was adamant: He was going hunting! *Yai Bada's* Spirit would protect him!

His wife was horrified. She tried everything to talk him out of going, and stood there teary-eyed the next morning, while the early morning fog still blanketed the trees and the dew lay heavy on the grass, as she watched him arm himself with his bow and arrows and machete and disappear into the trees. She did not expect to ever see him again.

A short time later, the village was startled to hear Lobema yell. Excited calls answered him and when they heard what he was yelling, they became even more excited. Not only had Lobema *not* been eaten by a jaguar, but he had walked right out behind the village and had run up a tapir—some of the best eating you could get in the jungle. Unheard of! Maybe Pepiwä was right. *Yai Bada* could be trusted! It was a turning point in the life of the fledgling church.

A couple of weeks later, Jemoshawä's mother returned to Cosh. She had come down to pick up her three boys and take them home with her. The three did not want to return, but of the three, Jemoshawä wanted to stay even more than his two brothers. It seemed he knew what was waiting for him up in his witch-doctor father's village. In the Yanomamö culture, no male kid is made to do anything against his will; rather, the adults will try and cajole, bribe, or somehow manipulate the kid until he gives in.

Jemoshawä was firm. He was not going home. He was staying with Ramon, his cousin. The next day, Bali Bali, Seduwä, and their mother left the village. Jemoshawä barely watched them leave. He seemed so very relieved that they were gone and he had been left. He seemed relaxed and his normally solemn eyes were bright and flashing with laughter.

The next night people came running into our house all agitated. Jemoshawä had gone out of his head and was running through the jungle. People were trying to catch him before he could hurt himself. Gary and Steve quickly got permission from Dad to go out and help in the search. Grabbing their lights, they ran out with me hot on their heels. I did not have a light, but figured I could stay close enough that I could see where I was going with the light from their flashlights.

Gary, Steve, and Juaquin quickly outdistanced the rest of us, as they actually had the lights. We could hear them following someone in the darkness, but I stopped with Yacuwä and the others because we could not see a thing. We figured once they either caught Jemoshawä or gave up, they would come back through here and we could find our way back out of the jungle with them. Finally we heard them returning. Gary had a very subdued Jemoshawä by the arm. We followed them single file back to our house. As we arrived at the house, all of a sudden Jemoshawä jerked his arm out of Gary's grasp and threw himself to the ground.

"He's burning me up!" he shrieked. He rolled on the ground in a wild attempt to get away from his unseen attacker. Gary grabbed him.

"Who's burning you? You are OK, you're right here! Stop it!" he yelled at Jemoshawä.

Gary's attempts to quiet him had no effect, and it seemed that Jemoshawä's screams only increased in volume. He continued to thrash on the ground. I stood there helplessly, not understanding what was going on. Sensing Yacuwä at my side, I whispered, "What's happening? Who's burning him?"

Yacuwä glanced around to make sure no one was listening. "His father. He wants him to come home. He is supposed to start his training to be a witch doctor."

I could not take my eyes off my screaming friend. In a few short weeks, we had really gotten close. Witch doctor! That was bad! I just could not imagine this soft-spoken, gentle boy becoming a witch doctor. Eventually, he finally started to quiet down. Gary and Steve were still with him and Dad had come up and they were quietly talking to him. He still appeared totally out of it, but at least he was no longer screaming. Finally, Ramon came and led him back to his house.

As soon as I could the next day, when Jemoshawä and I were alone, I asked him what had happened the night before to make him run out into the jungle.

"I didn't run off, Maikiwä," he told me quietly, "but two women came and, grabbing me by the arms, led me away. They were very beautiful and smiled and told me they were taking me to meet some people. I went with them and I did not even know it was nighttime, or that I was running through the jungle. The trail I was on was large and well lit. I never once felt anything catch at me. There were no thorns or vines where we were going. When I heard Ramon tell me what part of the jungle that he, Juaquin, Steve, and Gary had caught me on I could not believe him. Look at my feet, there is not a mark of a thorn there. You know how many thorn trees are out in that area. How could I run through there at night with no light and not get thorns in my feet?" His eyes were huge as he asked this question. I had no answer for him.

The next night was a repeat, and the night after that. Every night for almost two weeks, Jemoshawä would start running. We never knew when it would hit him—or should I say, when *they* would grab him and take off again, if what he had told me was true. The whole village would chase him through the jungle until he was once again caught and brought back. Then the thrashing and screaming about being on fire would start; he would scream that he was being burned up. This happened over and over, until we were all worn out—no one more than poor Jemoshawä. Those couple of weeks really took a toll on him. His skinny face was even more pinched and wan looking, his eyes huge staring out at us. He had such expressive eyes and they mirrored the torture that he was going through every night. We just could not do anything to help him. I tried as best I could to tell him that Jesus could free him from the bondage he was in, and I know Gary and Steve did as well. He would listen, but the spiritual blindness that had him was thicker than we could penetrate. I so wanted him to call out to God for help, but he refused, thinking there was nothing and no one that could help him. Finally he gave up fighting his father. The next day we stood on the river bank and watched them push their little dugout canoe away from the bank and begin the long paddle trip home to their village and the fate that we were afraid was waiting for our friend. Little did we know!

Over the next weeks, months, and years, the stories coming back from Maweni were never good. Contrary to Jemoshawä's promise, he never returned to Cosh. We began to get word about him being chosen by the spirit world. The first reports were that his closeness to this hidden world began to manifest itself again by the many animals that talked openly with him.

After he became a man, he (along with his dad, Guajaribo, and three assistants), after much preparation, went out to gather the different barks, leaves, and seeds they use to make their hallucinogenic drugs. This was time-consuming work, because an initiation requires a tremendous amount of the powder. They took the inner bark and the leaves and carefully dried them over a low fire. Once those materials were dried, they ground them and the seeds up into a fine, gray-green powder, using a piece of hard clay pottery and a flat rock.

A witch doctor will usually have one or two assistants, but Guajaribo was a witch doctor of such fame that he had three assistants working under him. They were very careful as they put their paint and feathers on. The blood-red macaw tailfeathers, more than two feet long, were pushed down between their armbands made of curassow head feathers. The macaw feathers stood straight up, the deep reds contrasting with the black and the white on the armbands. Their paint was put on with equal care: each man put on his paint as dictated to him by his *jecula,* although there seemed to be no rhyme or reason to how the designs were chosen. Everything they put on, from the waving red flame-colored macaw feathers to the designs of their paint schemes, were copied from the *jecula* that appeared to them in daily contacts.

Jemoshawä was equally careful as he put on his feathers. Along with his armbands and macaw feathers, he had the tailfeathers of the *culicaya* parrot pushed through the holes in his earlobes. The iridescent greens shone brightly, contrasting with his dark and solemn eyes.

Women swept the area in front of Guajaribo's hearth and removed all dog feces and litter. This was the communal area, from the inside to the outside, beyond the last supporting post of the roof, with the full sweep of the roof cantilevered out over it to give shelter from the sun and rain. It is in this area that all important activities take place, such as the bone-drinking ceremonies, the taking of drugs, chanting to the demons, and trading sessions.

The opening to the village directly across from where the training session was going to take place had been closed up. Jemoshawä came out and assumed the position he would maintain during his entire initiation. He was sitting with his legs apart, his hands braced behind him. Out from his outstretched legs, the witch doctors made a trail across the village center, the sides of the trail radiating out from each leg of the initiate. Once the trail had been made, great care was taken to clean it thoroughly. No one but the *shaboli cäbä* (witch doctors) could use the trail now, and great care was taken by all the rest in the village to avoid it, even though they had to circle all the way around the entire village to get to someone just on the other side of the trail.

It was time to start. At a signal from Guajaribo, men came out and ceremonially opened the blocked opening to the outside so that the trail ran straight out from Jemoshawä across the village and on outside. From the village to the jungle, every blade of grass, any sticks, and all the leaves were cleared away, leaving a wide, clean trail. All comings and goings of the shamans were made via this trail, so that by the time the initiation was finished, it was even more defined. The wide-open trail from the jungle, ending at Jemoshawä, was supposed to attract the *jecula* and bring them down; the *jecula* used this trail to come to him. These would not be adult *jecula*, but rather adolescent and child *jecula* that would mature with Jemoshawä. These *jecula* would stay with him for life and leave him only when he died.

One of the assistants loaded the blow tube with the powdered drug. One end was inserted in Jemoshawä's nostril and the assistant blew it into his nose with as much force as he could put behind his blasts. The blow tube was reloaded and inserted up Jemoshawä's other nostril. Again he was hit with another blast.

Jemoshawä groaned and grabbed his head; the blasts of the powder had hit him directly in the back of his head. The other assistant helped him resume his pose and again the blow tube was loaded and the contents blown up Jemoshawä's nose. Time and time again this was repeated. He was no longer a pretty sight. He had a dark-green slime running out of each nostril and down his chest. He had also thrown up on himself and it was beginning to dry on him. Initiates were not allowed to clean this residue off themselves, as this was believed to be the deposits of the *jecula*. By this time, Jemoshawä was almost comatose. Guajaribo bent and squatted down beside his son. Grabbing Jemoshawä's face, he tilted it so Jemoshawä was facing the trail.

"Look, my son, this is the trail of the *jecula*. This is the trail they will use to come and build their home in you. This is the only place you need to look now. Do not take your eyes off this trail, here will come Jaguar spirit, Moon spirit, Spider Monkey spirit, *Malashi* spirit, Toucan spirit, and all the rest you need to make you a powerful *shaboli*. They will come in ever-increasing numbers, but we need to show you how to select with care. Many spirits are bad and will harm you or destroy you, but my *jecula* will help you choose only the good ones."

Jemoshawä could barely nod. He was so drugged by this time that he was there only in body. Nevertheless, at a signal from Guajaribo, another two blasts were blown up his nostrils.

Then it was the head witch doctor's turn for drugs. One of the assistants loaded the blow tube and Guajaribo took the end and placed it in his own nostril. He took the blast of drugs gladly and impatiently waited for the tube to be reloaded. This was familiar ground for him, and he enjoyed the sensation that he knew was coming. He gladly traded the brief sharp pain in the back of his head for the euphoric feeling he knew was coming. He stood and made a few dance steps back and forth. Placing his lips together, he blew through them, producing the whistle-like cry used to summon the *jecula*.

"*Ble, ble, ble*," he began to chant. "Come to me, come down now."

His actions were deliberate. Raising his hands, he pointed down to Jemoshawä, showing him to his *jecula*. They began to swirl around him. These were not the ones that were to be given to Jemoshawä, but they helped in the initiation by helping Guajaribo find and bring in the young *jecula* that still lived free in the rocks of the jungle. One of the assistants prepared the blow tube again. The end was inserted once again into Jemoshawä's nostril even though he was still almost unconscious; the second assistant sat behind him supporting him and making sure his legs were still open in line with the trail. He was given two more shots up each nostril before they decided he had had enough. The only reason he had not fallen over was because he was being supported. Guajaribo continued to dance, as he implored Sloth spirit to find as many adolescent *jecula* as he could and bring them down the trail to Jemoshawä.

As he danced, he chanted to his own spirits, asking them for help in summoning only the good spirits that would endow his student with power to heal and protect. First, though, a dwelling for the spirits had to be constructed in his student's chest. Oriole spirit was the first to be asked for help in making sure the house was built strongly. Anaconda spirit was summoned to tie up the new dwelling, and he and his partner, Boa spirit, raised it high and made sure all the vines were tied tight. *Malashi* and other turkey spirits were called to bring the leaves that would be woven for the roof. Spider Monkey spirit was scolded as he began swinging upon the newly erected dwelling before it was strong enough to support his weight. As the spirits came to him, he began to speak as and mimic the traits of the different *jecula*. First he was Anaconda, twisting the vines with his tail. Then he was Spider Monkey spirit, jumping around on all fours.

The session went on and on. Guajaribo was officiating, but his assistants took turns chanting and imploring their own *jecula* for help. As they chanted, they embodied and imitated the various different spirits they were imploring. They, the *shabolis,* became *jecula*. That is, at that point they were the spirits they were channeling. In their chants, they also told the history of the spirit world, which Jemoshawä was expected not only to listen to, but also to repeat back as the session progressed.

Finally, it was over for the night. Jemoshawä was half-led, half-carried to his hammock. This was a very meager, bare-vine hammock that had been hung from two peeled poles that were dug into the ground away from any contact with the structure of the *shabono*. Jemoshawä was laid down and because of his fatigue and drug-induced state, was almost instantly asleep. He could have no fire during the night, but toward morning, a very small blaze was lit near him, built from carefully selected branches.

It is in his dreams that he first sees his *jecula,* hears their soft chants in his ears, feels their breath on his chest, and smells their sweet, flower-like scent. As the sessions progress, he begins to confuse his sleeping and waking times, never knowing what is real or what is a dream. He can eat almost nothing and can drink very little. The only thing he can do in any quantity is drugs. These are blown up his nostrils at the start of every session until he almost passes out. His world has contracted to consist only of his teachers and the spirits that are becoming more and more clear to him. He has no contact with any other people from his village. During this time, and even long after he has become *shaboli* (a shaman), he can have no sexual contact with his wife (or, for that matter, with any woman). To do so would cause his *jecula* to leave him. Only after he has had the *jecula* for a long time can they stand for him to have this kind of intimate contact with anything else.

Day after day the sessions go on. Jemoshawä is in such a continuously drugged state that he has no idea of whether it is even day or night. Guajaribo and his assistants take turns calling and chanting. Many times the chanting has to stop momentarily when

Jemoshawä briefly passes out and has to be revived. The chanting has to be repeated and answered by Jemoshawä. Sometimes the chanting is stopped and the initiate is scolded for repeating incorrectly or misspeaking his piece. The scolding comes directly from the *jecula* through the *shabolis*, and many times the *jecula* actually threaten not to stay around if Jemoshawä does not concentrate more. When the witch doctor/*shaboli* is under the influence of drugs and his *jecula,* he *is jecula.* Slowly Jemoshawä makes progress, and by the sixth or seventh day he is answering chant for chant.

To show his progress, he is crowned with the *wadoshe,* the symbol of the *jecula.* In Jemoshawä's case, it is a headdress made of a jaguar skin that is decorated with the down of birds of prey, with a long string hanging down his back and holding the skins of many brightly colored birds. This headdress symbolizes the Jaguar spirit. Sometimes the *wadoshe* is made out of the tail of the black wooly monkey, or it can even be made of woven palm. In the case of the real *jecula,* the part hanging down the back and right in front of the *wadoshe* (crown) is always made from something alive, like small birds, bees, or butterflies. As the *jecula* moves, this swirling head covering is in constant motion around it.

By using a *wadoshe* of jaguar skin, the shamans are trying to convince Jaguar spirit that Jemoshawä is where he should make his home. Guajaribo is convinced this is the spirit that is coming to make its permanent dwelling in Jemoshawä's chest. Jaguar spirit is his own personal *jecula* and he has controlled it for a long time and now desires it for his son. Jaguar spirit is one of the most prized spirits, as he bestows much power and prestige. All shamans want him, but he is hard to control, and once a shaman has this spirit, if not careful, instead of healing his people, this spirit will actually cause him to start stealing the souls of his own village's children, thereby killing them to satisfy the bloodlust of Jaguar and other cannibal spirits.

Finally the day comes when Guajaribo decides his apprentice is ready. While Jemoshawä is sleeping after another all-night ordeal, Guajaribo and his three helpers head out into the jungle looking for a certain type of tree. When they find it, they clear all the underbrush and debris away from the base of the small tree, which is about the size of a man's arm.

After preparing the site, they take small branches and beat the tree, the air, and the surrounding jungle to dislodge any evil spirits or enemy shamans that have come in the spirit world and are lurking there to destroy what they are trying to do. They begin to chant to call their own spirits; this is done quietly, almost to themselves, as they rub the tree with their hands to remove any moss or other debris. They also shake the tree gently to dislodge any debris that might be caught in its leaves. They then peel the bark off, cutting the bark right at the base of the tree where it goes into the ground and peeling it up the tree. Guajaribo then cuts the tree all around the base, being very careful not to cut it all the way down. All the men then grab the tree and shake it back and forth until it breaks through. They lay it down, and after much heated debate decide where it should be cut to length. They cut it to about the same length as one of their six-foot-long arrows. Finally, it is taken back to the village, where it is turned over to other men to further prepare it for the ceremony. This pole will serve as a replica of *bei cä macö,* the rock where the spirits live. The young free spirits will leave their home in the rocks and make their way to the replica and from this symbolic replica of their home into the chest of the initiate.

The men prepare it by sharpening the top end of the pole. The pole goes into the ground inverted, with the small end in the ground and the big end up top. They rub it with *nana* until the entire pole is red. Wavy black lines are drawn on it. Then, on top of this, they cover the entire length of the pole with bird-of-prey down. The entire pole is almost totally white from this down. One of the men gets busy weaving a headdress for the top of the mast, the big end. This is the mast's *wadoshe.* He weaves this one of an immature, still-furled palm leaf and decorates it with *moi* bird skins and more bird-of-prey down.

Meanwhile, Guajaribo and his assistants have finished their own preparations. They look splendid in all their feathers and paint. Again, each man has painted on his body his own interpretation of the look of his particular *jecula.* The assistants have *wisha* (black wooly monkey) tails around their heads, each with a long string down the back with many different *moi* bird skins tied on. Guajaribo has his usual jaguar skin around his head; this time it too is decorated with the snow-white bird-of-prey down. When they are finished, they go out to retrieve the pole. They bring it in with great fanfare, walking slowly. They are *jecula,* each shaman emulating his own special spirit. Guajaribo is Jaguar spirit and you can almost see the jaguar in his sinuous steps and contorted, snarling face. Guajaribo has the *bei cä macö,* holding it above his head. With great ceremony it is brought in and a hole is dug between Jemoshawä's outstretched legs. Before the pole is planted in the hole, Guajaribo orders a fresh batch of drugs blasted into Jemoshawä's nostrils. Jemoshawä looks terrible: skinny as a rail and even now barely conscious. Once the drugs hit him, he can no longer even support himself, but has to be supported by one of the assistants. It seems the entire male population of the village has gotten involved now. They are all in their feathered finery and are sitting in a half-circle both to the left and right of Jemoshawä. All the witch doctors of the village are also here—and are on their guard, as this is the most critical time of the entire process. This is when enemy shamans will try to disrupt the process by stealing the *wadoshe* off the planted spirit pole.

By this time all the men have taken drugs, and the ones that are *shabolis* are on guard in the spirit world. The *shabolis* are all *jecula* now. Monkey spirit is there, gazing off into the distance with his hands shielding his eyes. Hawk spirit waves his arms, simulating flight, as he peers down at the ground on the look-out for enemy *jecula.* Buzzard spirit and Moon spirit are also represented by mimicry of the *shabolis* as they attempt to guard the mast from attack. This is when enemy shamans with their spirits will try to infiltrate the village, to attack and wreck the *bei cä macö.* If they are successful in their attack, all the work and effort, all the pain and sacrifice, will be for nothing, and the entire process will have to be repeated from day one.

This time no enemy spirits are detected, and the ceremony proceeds. As the officiating shaman, Guajaribo directs the placement of the decorated mast, which is planted like a flagpole between the outstretched legs of the initiate. The palm-and-feather headdress, similar to the one Jemoshawä is wearing, is placed atop the pole. Now it is time for the *jecula* to arrive. Guajaribo is in turn Moon spirit, Sloth spirit, Toucan spirit, Caiman spirit, and the myriad of other spirits that are summoned for this occasion. As the adolescent spirits come again, Guajaribo mimics each one in turn. Either he is truly possessed and each spirit is demonstrating itself through him, or he is an incredible actor. His movements totally capture the essence of each animal or natural spirit he is at the time.

Finally, it is over. Jemoshawä is helped back to his normal hammock to sleep off the drugs. The mast is removed and, along with the *wadoshe* that he was wearing, is taken out to the jungle and tied to the largest tree the men can find. The place is then avoided for a long time.

Jemoshawä continues to have weekly sessions with his mentors, although now he is getting his own chants from the *jecula.* His *jecula* are now teaching him the chants he needs both to summon them and also to begin to heal. Each witch doctor receives his chants from his own *jecula,* and everyone's chants are different.

Although other witch doctors and even others who are not *shabo-lis* will chant these songs sometimes, everyone knows who they belong to.

Speaking of their chants, I had known that each song was given by the *jecula,* but I guess I had forgotten, because an odd thing did happen to me. While I was going to Bible school, I listened as seasoned missionaries from other fields told how, instead of translating Western music into the Indian languages, they used the songs and chants of the native peoples, just putting Christian words to the tunes. Wow, I thought, this is great! I can try that. So as soon as I returned to Cosh, I sat down with a few friends and we put Bible verses to the tunes of the chants I had learned as a kid.

I couldn't wait for Sunday to wow the church with these new songs praising our Lord. *They will really appreciate this, I remember thinking. This will finally be their own expression of their love and praise for our Lord.* Yacuwä and I got up and announced that we had translated some new songs that we wanted to teach them. They listened intently as we launched into the first chant, to which we had set John 3:16. As I watched their faces, my heart sank, because instead of smiles, their faces showed gathering frowns. Thinking they might not have really gotten the gist of what we had done, we went right into the second chant, hoping to salvage a bad situation. To be honest, I couldn't understand why I was not seeing smiles. We had worked hard on this, and the words fit well. Why the frowns?

Bautista clued me in as he stopped me before I could start on the third chant. "What are you doing?" he asked me.

"I am giving you songs that you can sing that are really yours. This way you don't have to just sing our songs," I told him. He shook his head.

"No, you can't do that."

"Bautista, listen to me. These songs will be yours. Do you only want to have something that we take from our country and bring you? Why don't you understand what we are doing here?" I was frustrated and I am sure it showed in my voice.

Thankfully, Bautista had more patience than I did. "No, Maikiwä, *you* don't understand. Do you think just because you change the words that now it is OK to sing those old chants? Don't you know that not only do the words come from the *jecula*, but the entire chant is theirs? They even give the way it goes and sounds. Who do you think is smiling right now? I don't think it is God that is happy with hearing *jecula* songs in His house. But I will tell you, I believe that the *jecula* are enjoying this. Well, not in my church. We will never sing those songs in our worship services."

Quickly recovering, I realized what a mistake I had made. I promptly apologized, not only to Bautista but to the entire church family as well. It was a good lesson for me as a new missionary beginning work, a lesson I really needed to learn. The Yanomamö believers had a lot they could teach a green missionary—namely, *me.* I needed to listen to these men. They knew an awful lot more about the spirit world than I did, and if I wanted to avoid a bunch of different pitfalls, I needed to listen. Praise God, I learned it right off! I can't tell you how many times I have been grateful that Bautista felt comfortable enough to stand up and correct me, instead of just quietly going along. What a shame that would have been!

Now, I am not making a statement or passing judgment on missionaries who have used native chants with their own tribes, but I am saying that one needs to exercise real wisdom, and have a clear understanding of the culture and beliefs of the peoples one is dealing with. I sure do know, it did not work for us with the Yanomamö!

As I mentioned, I never saw Jemoshawä again. He never returned to Cosh; in fact, he goes to no other village. Despite the many times I have gone to his village, even spending days up there teaching other believers, I never see him. His people say that while our boat is still coming up the river, he gets agitated and takes off into the jungle. He cannot stand our presence. They tell me that shortly after becoming a witch doctor and getting his own spirits, he was lured and deceived by Deer spirit. His father and mentor, Guajaribo, after repeated effort and campaigns in the spirit world to free his son from this frightening spirit, at last gave up. There was nothing more he could do. His son, in whom Guajaribo had placed such great hope, had the deer spirit. Thereafter he startled at every sound and was gone like the fleet-footed deer.

Of course, I was not present during my friend's initiation. I was getting my own training, at the New Tribes Bible Institute in Jackson, Michigan. I received the account of his ceremony from his brothers and other friends of mine from his village after I returned. When my friend received the deer spirit, I was saddened beyond words: first of all, to hear that he had become a witch doctor; and second, that he now had the deer spirit. I knew I would never be able to see or talk to him again. Still, I have always prayed that one day something we told him in our youth would come back to him and he might cry out to the Lord for his salvation, but so far this has not happened.

Guajaribo, now an old man, lay in his hammock thinking back on his life. As he pondered what he had and did not have, he realized that his spirits had deceived him. They had lied to him. He did not have power; it was all an illusion. Instead of making people well, his once large village had been decimated by bouts of sickness after sickness, until of the formerly large village there were only enough families that he could count them on his fingers without using his toes—and very few of his families had any children left. They had all died. Even his own fine young son Seduwä was gone! Seduwä had been killed in a chest-pounding duel. Guajaribo still mourned this death: he had tried everything in his power to heal his son but had had to watch Seduwä die. He had not even been able to avenge his son's death; the coward had escaped. His village was dying out! His son Bali Bali was sick all the time, tired and constantly out of breath. He could not even garden, and nothing that Guajaribo did in the spirit world helped. Guajaribo knew that his son was slowly dying and there was nothing he could do to help.

What had the spirits done for him? How had they helped him? Why, instead of healing his children, he himself had even eaten the souls of many of them to satisfy the cannibal spirits that resided in him. These spirits were getting louder and louder in their ever-insistent demands for more blood. It was so bad that he could no longer control them, and in spite of his desire to heal the children of his village, the very spirits that had been given him to heal had turned against him. In an unwary minute, instead of showing him how to heal the child, they would sink their long talons and beaks into the small soul, killing it and the child. He was sick with depression as he lay there thinking about his life.

In his despondent state, he even wondered when *his* time would come. He knew the only way most spirits leave a shaman is for them to kill him. He had always believed that he was above this—that he enjoyed such a relationship with his *jecula* that they would never kill him—but now he was having doubts. When will it happen? Will I know which one comes to kill me? How will I know when my time comes? He thought about his relatives in Cosh: Bautista, Yacuwä, and so many others. They were so happy in comparison to how he felt. Could it be true that they were right and he was wrong? This spirit that they had, they called Him *Yai Bada.* Supreme Being. Guajaribo had always called Him *Yai Wanonabälewä* (the Enemy Spirit).

He remembered again the different times he had followed the beings who had captured the soul of an infant and were trying to get back to the Supreme Being's land. If they made it, it would cause the death of the infant. As the leading shaman, it was up to him to decipher what had happened and figure out the best way to give chase and try and retrieve the soul of the child before the beings got to that land and the soul was eaten.

How many times had he taken his *ebena* and gone into the spirit world to try and retrieve the soul? So many times he had not been successful. The beings made it to *Yai Wanonabälewä's* land and the child died. The times he had actually seen this land from far away haunted him still. It was such a beautiful land. Even from a distance he could see the body of water that was so clear, it was like there was not even anything there. He also heard the noise of the incessant singing of the *aiboshokoli* (angels) of this Supreme Being. He saw the light coming from the place where this Being sat and the *aiboshokoli* sang to Him. It was so beautiful. When he was by himself, and allowed himself to think about it, he wondered. Could He really be the enemy the *jecula* said He was and still live in such a beautiful land? It never made much sense to Guajaribo, but to be honest, he had never allowed himself to think much about it until now, because down deep he was afraid of what he might find. He enjoyed the power of the spirit world too much to want to give it up. But now, with his son Jemoshawä having the deer spirit and basically worthless to him, and himself getting to the age where he knew the spirits would try to kill him sooner rather than later, he could not help but begin to wonder about this spirit he had thought he knew so much about. Now, because of his age, he began to doubt everything his *jecula* had told him. He now knew that his spirits *had* lied to him in many other areas, so why would they be telling the truth now?

The next day his morbid thoughts were still with him as he retrieved his small roll of fishing line and his plug of tobacco.

Picking up his machete, he told his wife he was going fishing. He was not even taking his paddle, as he was just going to walk along the stream downriver and fish from the shore. As he walked along he enjoyed the coolness under the jungle canopy. Although his mind was far off, he was still aware of all that went on around him, but in a subconscious kind of way. He was not really thinking much about the jungle right now, but habit dictated that he be aware of everything around him, even the land along the small creek that was squishy underfoot; the osprey flying by, diving into the water with barely a break; the splash causing the water to splash up, the droplets catching the sun and sparkling like diamonds. He chuckled as the bird went all the way into the water after its elusive prey, but came back up to the surface empty-beaked. He watched a family of otters frolicking around ahead of him. And he was constantly on the lookout for the *alowamö* snake, the type of snake that the *shabolis* used most often to kill. He was on his guard, but he did not think the *jecula* would come at him with a snake. They would know he would be on watch for that kind of an attack. But while part of his mind was busy cataloging all the different ways they might try to kill him, he kept coming back to what his brother-in-law had told him on his last visit.

> "Brother-in-law, why have you resisted my words for so long? You are old now and suffer, you know the fate that is waiting for you. You know your *jecula* can only be released by your death, and they are going to cause your death so they can be free from your old body. Why don't you listen to this message of peace and love that I want to tell you?" He had paused to judge my reaction, and I had answered the same way I have answered him for so long.
>
> I clicked my tongue to show my displeasure. "No, no, no, don't tell me that any more. Don't dirty my ears! I am unwilling to hear that! I have told you so many times that I have

no intention of getting rid of my *jecula*." I shook my head emphatically and frowned. I was hoping to make my brother-in-law angry, but this time, instead of taking the bait, he smiled at me.

"Brother-in-law, I have known you all my life. I used to carry your game as you took me hunting before I even had my first arrows. But my heart is sad that I cannot make you at least listen to this great story. *Yai Bada* loved you so much that He sent His only Son to become a Yanomamö. His Son lived a life where He never sinned, although *Omawä* tempted him with every sin. But He was killed, not for His bad doings, but for yours and mine. He took all the bad we have done, and gave us, in turn, all the good He had done so that we could one day go to live with Him in the beautiful land that you have seen only from far away. You cannot approach any closer than you have, because of His light. You cannot approach the light coming from the Supreme Being because of our sin and bad doing. Well, this Supreme Being loved you enough that His Son left this light and beautiful land and became a man so that He could make a path to His land. A path that any can walk who will put their heart's desire on Him."

Before he could say any more I abruptly stood up, ending the conversation. Quickly untying my hammock, I tied it up and, slinging it over my shoulder, started out the door telling my wife to come on, I was heading home. Seeing my determined face, she cut short her own conversation and hurried after me. My mind was in turmoil and my heart was racing. Why did talk of *Yai Bada's* Son always bother me so much? Not only myself either, my *jecula* were even more agitated than I was, if that could be possible. But even while I assured them I had no intention of listening to this talk and I would never throw them away, my mind kept hearing his words: "*Yai Bada* loves you enough that He sent his only Son to become a Yanomamö to show you how to get to His land . . . "

My heart just was not in fishing, and they weren't biting anyway, so I finally decided to turn around and head home. I was tired and feeling my age. As I started home, out of the corner of my eye I caught sight of Jaguar spirit swinging a huge machete at me. Along with him were many other of my spirits that I had followed for so long. It was so like them, I could see it clearly now. My best friends in all the world, although they were spirits, were the ones to come to kill me. Some friends! They did not look as handsome and as beautiful as they had before, either. They were snarling and clawing to get at me. Before I could even react, I felt his machete slash through the back of my head. A bigger horde of *jecula* had now joined the attack and they were laughing and shouting at the sight of my blood. The lust to kill was in their eyes, and now I also realized this lust to kill and destroy was a look I had seen and even participated in many times. I think for the first time I saw myself!

All these thoughts ran through my mind even as I was trying to defend myself. I needed to put distance between us, so I made a mad dash into the jungle. I was running all out when I tripped on a vine and fell headlong. They were on me, pounding me, their hard fists smashing into my body. The hordes were biting and scratching me and my struggles became weaker. In my mind I called out to the Spirit my brother-in-law had told me about.

"Yai Bada, help me," I breathed.

I really did not think He could or would help me; at this point I knew no one could. But I just had nothing else to do. I was losing ground fast. I was finished. But suddenly, even though my eyes were closed I sensed a tremendously bright light. I opened my eyes, surprised. What was this? I could not believe it. The *jecula* that had been punching me were lying all around me on the ground. They were still snarling and snapping, but the fight was gone from them. I felt different than I have ever felt in my life. My pain and stiffness because of old age were gone. I felt renewed and young again. I clearly heard a voice coming from the Light: "Leave him alone, he is mine now!" They ran in droves away from me.

About this time, my son and his *shaboli* friends came running up. They had sensed in the spirit world that I was under attack and was going to be killed. By this time I was sitting up. They were surprised to see me alive. They had thought they would find me already dead. But I was fine.

"No, I'm fine. The fight is over. Let's go home." Standing up, I brushed away their offers of help and walked home. I felt good.

My son insisted on sending someone down and calling our family from Cosh. They arrived expecting to see me on my deathbed. I was glad to see my brother-in-law Bautista.

"Now I know what you were saying. I know for myself the love and concern that *Yai Bada* has for us. He saved me and broke the bondage that I lived in all my life. I regret that I wasted so much of my life. I wish I had listened to you earlier. But *Yai Bada* is not the enemy god. He loves us Yanomamö," I told him.

[Bautista] listened with a big smile. "Yes, yes, now you see. I am so happy that you now are a child of His. His Spirit is so full of peace. I used to be angry all the time, I would lay in my hammock and only want to kill or destroy. But after I accepted God's gift, then I had His Spirit and my heart was at peace. I don't want to kill now. This is what you are talking about. God's Spirit is so different than all the other spirits we have known."

I nodded as I listened. I felt so alive, so new. I was truly happy, possibly for the first time in my life.

8

A Shaman's Story

I am called Mayebö. I am a Yanomamö of the Shamatari group. I am a headman of the village of Sejal on the Orinoco River. I grew up way inland and my village was called *Mömaliböwei-teli*. My father was a very powerful shaman and at an early age I was chosen by the spirits to be trained in the ways of the shaman.

I can vividly remember how it all began. As a young boy, I had made myself a set of *lujumasi* (young boy's bow and arrows). I went out into the village gardens to shoot lizards with all of the other children. We would get together as children, boys and girls, and pretend to be adults. We would shoot lizards, small birds, and small rodents. We would pretend that they were the same wild game that our fathers killed for food. We boys would bring the game back to where we had built our small imitation village and the girls that were pretending to be our wives would clean the animals and cook them, and then we would all eat together. In times of peace, which were very rare, this was one of our favorite games.

One day I was aiming at a big blue-tailed lizard when it turned its head toward me and said, "Why are you shooting at me?"

I was terrified and I ran back to the village as fast as I could. I didn't tell anyone about what had happened because I thought everyone would make fun of me. But not long after that, I was getting ready to shoot a small *loja nasi* (smooth-tailed jungle rat) when it looked at me and said, "Older brother, don't shoot me." I fled for the village again. I was quite a ways from the village and I ran out of breath, so I sat down on a log to rest. All at once I heard a voice under me saying, "You're heavy, get off of me. Just because I'm lying across the trail doesn't mean you can just sit on me."

Once again I fled in terror. When I got home my mother saw how frightened I was and she asked me what had happened. She asked me if I had seen a *boleana* (ghost). I told her no, but that animals and trees were talking to me and that I was fearful to leave the village anymore because as soon as I was alone, things that could not talk would begin to talk to me.

My mother was not surprised; she smiled and said, "Don't be afraid. The *jecula* are coming to you. They are choosing you; you will become a powerful shaman because they have chosen you."

After that I was no longer fearful and I listened to the *jecula* talk through the trees, the animals, and the birds. It wasn't long before everyone in the village realized that I had a special power with the *jecula* and everyone knew that I would become a very powerful shaman.

As I became a young man, my days were filled with taking *ebena* and chanting to the spirits. After many days of fasting and chanting and taking drugs, the spirits began to come to me. They were beautiful, human-like creatures, each having distinctive characteristics of the animals they represented. Each one, as he hung his hammock within my chest, promised me unbelievable power. They told me I would be a great healer, a great hunter, and that I would have many wives, and that I would be virile enough to satisfy all of my wives and any other women fortunate enough to receive my desire. But most important of all, they promised me power as a warrior. I would become fierce. Everyone would fear me. Even my own village would fear me. A darkness that one cannot describe completely took over my life. I was so controlled by this dark power that I no longer needed the drugs to make the *jecula* visible to me. They were right there with me all the time.

One day I was coming back from a hunt and a young girl from our village who had just reached puberty was down at the river alone getting water. A powerful feeling rushed over me as never before. Uncontrollable lust that I could not divert completely took me over. Through my mouth I heard *Howashiliwä* speak. Not being able to control what I was doing, I rushed like a killing jaguar on top of this unsuspecting girl. My hands closed around her throat and, roaring like a jaguar, I threw her to the ground and raped her; all the time my inner being was appalled at the stream of dirty words coming from my mouth in the voice of *Howashiliwä*. Leaving the girl unconscious, I fled back to the village, dreading what all of my people would say when they found out what I had done. It was not long before I heard women wailing and they came carrying the girl into the village, crying that she had been attacked and raped by a spirit jaguar. All she remembered was being thrown to the ground by a huge, roaring animal.

In spite of my fear of being recognized, I went over to look at her. She had been terribly mauled and when she looked at me there was no recognition in her eyes. I then knew that somehow the spirits within me had used me to do this horrible deed and had kept her from knowing it was me. I was the shaman that was called to bring her back to health, with no one suspecting that I was the guilty one. As all shamans could tell you, I had a double life pretending to care for my people and at the same time destroying all that I could in secret. Many horrible acts of violence would follow wherever I would go because the beings within me were far more powerful than I, and more than anything else they enjoyed inflicting terror.

Not long after this, my village went to war again (it seemed like it had always been that way) with *Iwa Jicolobateli* (caged alligator village). True to the promise of the *jecula,* I became my village's fiercest warrior. My skill at killing others with the bow and arrow was only surpassed by my skill at killing others through my dark power in the spirit world. I had the ability to leave my body and go to the village of my enemies and destroy their children. In the spirit form of some dangerous animal, I would leave my body and go to another village and kill their children in the spirit world. Because of the damage inflicted on his or her spirit, the child would then get physically sick and die. A shaman that can obtain this kind of power is then known by the terrifying name of *child eater.*

In the spirit world, I could shoot my enemies and hear a few days later that the person got sick and died. I became so powerful that I could tell my people I had killed someone even before he died. The more powerful I became, the more I had to kill. The more I killed, the more my enemies revenged themselves by killing my people. But sadly, I became guilty of killing people in my own village to satisfy the dark power within me. I no longer tried to heal. To satisfy my killing lust, I killed my own patients by strangling many of them. My people would believe that I was in a terrible fight with the spirits that caused the sickness, but in reality I was killing my patient. I had become such a master of deception that I could kill someone right in front of them and they wouldn't even know it. I would then blame the death on enemy shamans. They in turn blamed me for all of the deaths in their villages.

Our warfare became so terrible that my father decided to move our village closer to the *nabä cäbä* (foreigners). What a terrible ordeal for our village as we set our faces toward TamaTama. Day after day, we trudged in the direction that we knew TamaTama to be. Over endless mountains and rivers we crossed. All the food we had carried from our gardens was long gone. All of us became gaunt with hunger and many of our children died. But, for some reason that none of us seemed to know, we pressed relentlessly toward TamaTama. Maybe we all remembered the strange Yanomamö man who had once been a shaman, who was now filled with the spirit of peace. He seemed so happy and satisfied with life, when he visited us that I desired to be like him. I was not able to talk much with him because the spirits within me feared and hated him. Whenever he would come around me, they would clamor so loudly that I could not think. He only stayed a few days, but he told my people that a *nabä* from TamaTama had moved to his village and had shown them the way of peace. I believe that was the reason my father wanted to go there. He had been a powerful shaman and a fierce warrior, but now he was just a tired old man full of sorrow and tired of all the constant killing. He wanted peace.

After many moons we finally arrived on the bank of the Casiquiare River. We were excited, as we had no way of knowing that TamaTama was still many days' travel upriver. After days of walking along the river bank, some of our young men caught a ride on a motorboat going upriver to TamaTama. There they met a *nabä* called Pablo [Paul Dye] who spoke our language.

Pablo, we found out right away, loved the Yanomamö. Even I, a person so full of hate, could see his love and I desired to know what it was like to love. Pablo began to help us get to TamaTama, but because we were still so far away it took many days to get all of us there. Pablo purchased land from the Piaroa tribe and helped us settle in one of their deserted villages called Sejal. We are still there today.

When we first moved to Sejal, two Yanomamö men from the village of Honey came to visit us. They were from the village of the strange Yanomamö that had come to our village many years before. I saw right away that they both had been shamans, but their chests were now empty of all of the spirits that fill a shaman. The spirit that they now had within them caused my chest to be filled with terror. I learned they were called Alejandro and his older brother, Luis, names they had taken from the *nabä*. Even though I tried not to listen to what they said as they talked to my people, my inner desires were drawn of their own selves to the message of peace. They talked about *Yai Bada,* the enemy spirit who lives way up in heaven. All of us shamans knew about him. We knew that His is a beautiful land, a land of plenty. We knew that the *Walalai* river flows there; a river that is crystal clear, that if you could just drink of it you wouldn't die. No sickness or death and no hunger, a land of complete light. He is the greatest of all spirits, but my spirits feared and hated Him. They told me as they have told all shamans that He is the enemy spirit, and that the Yanomamö are not welcomed to His place. But these men were telling us that He was not our enemy. He wanted to bring peace to the Yanomamö. That He could help us end our fighting and killing. But the greatest wonder of all, He could drive out all of the spirits from the chest of a shaman: The spirits that so controlled me, the spirits that desired to kill so much that they made me kill people of my own village!

I truly had become just like *Alowä,* our ancestral legend and hero, who was a Yanomamö who had become so violent and

Reneé with (*left to right*) Ryan Daniel, Stephen Ruben, and Joshua Michael; in Reneé's parents' home, Cicero, Illinois; 1990.

Michael standing; (*front row, left to right*) Joshua Michael, Stephen Ruben, and Ryan Daniel; 1993.

Keila and Michael; 1995. Life was good again.

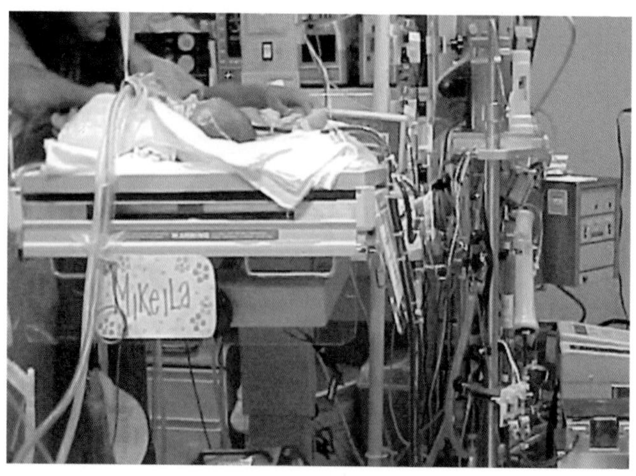

Mikeila on the ECMO machine, University of Virginia Hospital NICU unit; March 2000.

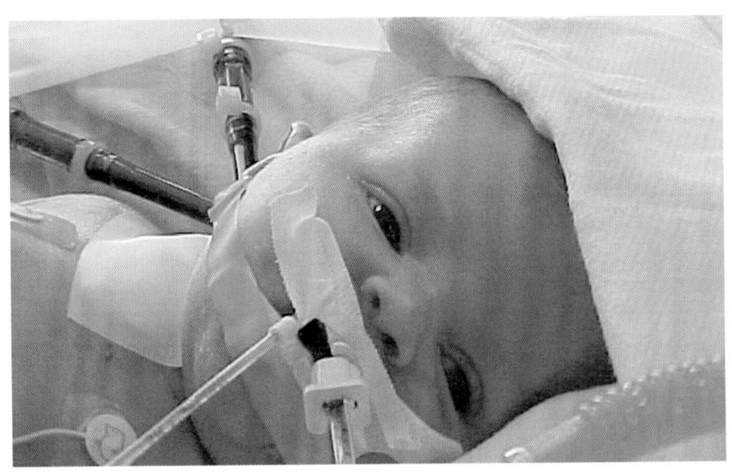

Mikeila Reneé Dawson

I remember the day you were born
we were so scared you weren't going to make it . . .
but you were a fighter . . .
God heard our prayers . . .

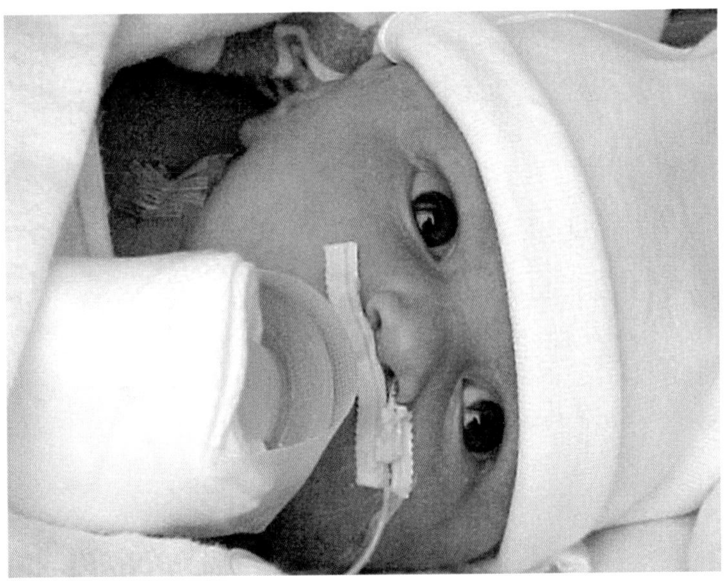

how happy we were to get the call saying you were better . . .
our miracle girl we called you . . .
yes . . . I remember . . . !

I remember how you loved music . . .
dancing . . .
singing . . .
Once when you were crying
wouldn't be comforted,
I picked you up
began to sing.
You leaned your little head way back so
you could look me in the eye.
Before long your tears dried
you were humming along with me.
Together we danced around the room,
singing . . .
humming . . .
"Jesus loves me"
and "See the moon beams."

Yes . . . you loved music . . .
you loved dancing . . .
you loved singing . . .
I remember . . . !

I remember when your mom went in to have your little sister
I babysat you . . .

I remember . . .
the only thing that would keep you content
was to let you watch a movie your big brothers had made.

Hour after hour
you watched, squealing with delight and
pointing out to me over
and over again
Josh
then RyRy
and then Stephen.
By the end of the day the rest of us were so fed up
with that movie—
Still you insisted on watching it . . .
I remember . . . !

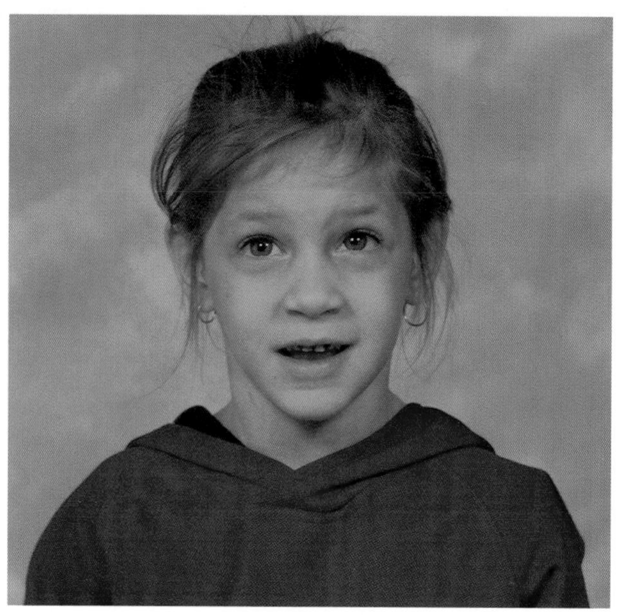

And . . .
I remember meeting your family in Caracas
when you had come back from the States.
You had gotten taller . . .
but your eyes were just as blue
and . . .
your smile,
just as beautiful.
Your mother had given me a bag of trail mix;
You sat on my lap on the way to the hotel and together we ate it.
Me eating the nuts
You picking the M&Ms one by one from the palm of my hand.

I remember how excited you and Mia were
because "we were gonna go eat at McDonalds."
You both jumped up and down, screaming in delight.

And then how disappointed you were when we got there and
discovered the play area was closed.
I had to hide a smile when you crossed your
skinny little arms across your chest
and with head tossed back you informed the world . . .
I'm mad!

Oh happy
beautiful
little girl
there is so much I remember about you . . .
Your beautiful smile . . .
your blue blue eyes . . .
your wild and carefree spirit . . .
I'll always remember . . . !

—Sandy Dawson Jank

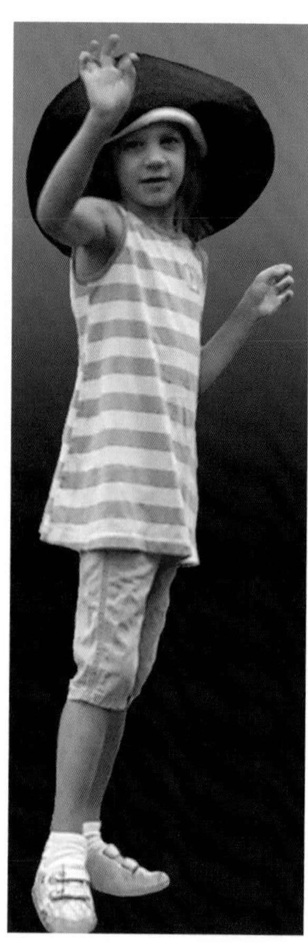

I was feeling so bad
'Cause I couldn't get the awfulness
of that day
Out of my head

I was lying in bed
And I was praying
Telling the Lord how badly I felt . . .
We had so wanted Him to heal you
You were so young
So full of life . . .

Then I don't know if I fell asleep
and dreamed
Or what?
But all of sudden I saw you, Mikeila.
You were skipping along
Clapping your hands
And looking over your shoulder at me
your big blue eyes
Crinkled up in laughter
Your face full of wonder and
excitement
you were so alive!
And I noticed that under your feet
You were skipping on a pavement
of gold . . .

I sat up in bed
As the image faded . . .
The beauty of what I had just seen
or dreamed
(Either way, it was real!)
Still held my heart in awe.

And now I am filled with that wonder
And I know that you are still
so full of life
Capturing all of heaven
With your laughter
As you skip on the pavements of gold.

—Faith Dawson

(*Left to right*) Joshua, Stephen, Michael holding Mia, Ryan, and Keila holding Mikeila; 2003.

Michael, Mia, Mikeila, and Keila; October 2005.

Last family picture taken with Mikeila; January 2006.

The ten of us with Dad and Mom (the family gathered in Cosh due to Dad's health); April 2008. *Back row:* Gary, Michael, Steve, Joe, and Jerald. *Middle row:* Faith, Joe, Millie, and Sharon. *Front row:* Sandy, Velma, and Susan.

Fran Cochran driving, with Ramon and Octavio's mother; Ocamo River (Aratateli contact); 1974.

Michael driving by the Mawedi Mountains on the Ocamo River (Aratateli contact); 1974.

Our experimental Zenith Aircraft CH 801; 2002.
Top: Flying by Duida mountain. *Bottom:* CH 801 in Jalalusiteli.

Bautista (Shoefoot); 2005.

Shamans dancing and chanting to the spirits. (Photo by Pastor Von; http://www.pastorvon.com)

Yacuwä; missionary trip on the Buta River; 2004.

Girl from Bashobäcateli; 2004.

Girls are given in arranged marriage at a very young age. Girls as old as this little girl would already have a husband. She might be one of many wives. (Photo by Pastor Von; http://www.pastorvon.com)

Boys are trained early to shoot and dodge arrows. (Photo by Pastor Von; http://www.pastorvon.com)

Nando. (Photo by Joshua Dawson.)

Yacuwä teaching in Aweiteli on the Buta River; 2003. (Photo by Rick Johnson.)

The New Testament was printed and given to the people in 1984, portions of the Old Testament have also been translated, but much of it still remains to be finished. So the work continues. It is always a blessing to see the Yanomamö reading the Word. (Photo by Pastor Von; http://www.pastorvon.com)

killed so many of his own village that they finally ambushed and killed him. One of the stories I remember well about *Alowä* was that one night his small child kept crying. He told his wife to shut up the child, but she was not able to stop the child from crying. In a terrible rage *Alowä* got up and chopped the child's head off with his machete. No one in the village dared to do anything about it. This was the man that all of us warriors wanted to be like. All of us claimed that he was our personal ancestor.

Finally I went to these two Yanomamö and told them I wanted to listen and I wanted them to tell me more about *Yai Bada's* Son who they said had come to earth to bring a way of peace to the Yanomamö. I wanted them to show me the trail that *Yai Bada's* Son had made for all of us to be able to go to *Yai Bada's* land. Many, many days they taught me. As I listened to their teaching, the clamor within my chest grew less and less. My mind was cleared and I began to talk to *Yai Bada* and knew that He was listening to me. My new friends were asking *Yai Bada* to set me free from all the spirits that lived within me. They warned me not to take any more *ebena.* They told me the *jecula* would use it to once again cloud my mind. I still had not hung my desires on *Yai Bada,* and whenever the spirits within me had the opportunity to get me alone, they would cry and beg me not to allow *Yai Bada* to come to me or they would be expelled and forced to leave me.

One day they convinced me to take *ebena* and chant to them again. I didn't want my new friends from Honey to see what I was doing, so I sent the children to go and see where they were in the village at that time. The children came back and told me that Alejandro and Luis were asleep on the other side of the village. I got down my old *ebena* tube, filled it full of *ebena,* put it into my nostril, and had my younger brother blow the *ebena* into my head with all of his force. As the *ebena* entered my head, I felt the old thrill and my spirits whirled into focus. Suddenly one of the most powerful of all grabbed up his spear. "Try to leave us, will you?" he yelled and thrust his spear through my head. The spear passed through my ear on one side and out my other ear and drove into the ground. I could see my body on the ground, blood coming from my ears, mouth, and nose. My family began to wail as the other shamans sprang into action to try to save me. They were yelling that my spirits were killing me and they began to battle for my life. I knew that I was dying. I could no longer move and darkness began to cover me.

All at once I heard Alejandro and Luis running up to where I was lying on the ground. "Move away from him and let us ask *Yai Bada* to save him," I could hear them telling the other shaman. They moved away from me and Luis and his brother began to pray for me, sitting down there in the dirt beside me. They begged *Yai Bada* to spare my life and to give me another chance to experience *Yai Bada's* love. All at once I felt safe and my spirits fled in terror. I felt the spear pulled from my head and a presence of absolute power and peace like I had never known. I opened my eyes and saw my two friends praying for me. I saw relief in the faces of my family. All at once I realized I was free, the evil spirits were gone and my chest was full of light. I was at peace for the first time in my life. Right then I asked *Yai Bada* to make me His own and to keep me free of the spirits.

Oh, how that day changed my life when Jesus, *Yai Bada's* Son, stepped in and set me free! I desired to see all of my village turn to Jesus and I was so happy when Pablo began to come every day and teach us from *Yai Bada's* book. My friends went back home to Honey, but Pablo continued to teach us and help us. The future looked so bright and hopeful. Many of my village turned to *Yai Bada* and we were on the road to peace and happiness.

But then one day Pablo came and told us he was leaving TamaTama. My desires filled with sorrow and I feared what would happen to us when he left. I asked him, "Who is going to teach us from *Yai Bada's* book when you are gone?" He reminded me that there were many other missionaries in TamaTama.

Pablo has been gone many years now. Many other *nabä* have come to my village now and we are in a turmoil of so many evil *nabä* now trying to seduce our young people out to the towns and cities of the outside world. The only thing that has stayed constant in my life are my Yanomamö friends from Honey, even though my good friend Alejandro has now gone on to *Yai Bada's* land, where I am sure he is sitting at the base of the eternal tree enjoying the fruit that constantly falls there. They continue to encourage and help me in my spiritual quest. I go to their village often where Pepiwä lives. Pepiwä went there with his wife when they were both young. They have become old now, but the village of Honey has grown both physically and spiritually as they have been taught fully in the ways of *Yai Bada.* I have grown to love Pepiwä's sons, and they have taken the time to teach me more from *Yai Bada's* book.

9

Docudico

After more than twenty years of visiting villages up and down the rivers in our area, we paused and studied our efforts and their results. They were disappointing. In spite of all our efforts and sacrifices, we had very little to show for it. In every village we visited, although there were a few Christians, they were, for the most part, defeated Christians. This was discouraging for us as well: We so desired to see our believers grow! We believe Christ's statement of "I came to give life, and that more abundantly" was also speaking of our lives here on this earth, not just once we get to heaven—but we were not seeing an abundant life for our Yanomamö believers. And we knew the reason. There were so many villages, and to be honest, so few of us, that the best we could do was get into each village once, twice, at the most three times a year. Well, this is just not enough time to really do much with lasting effects. We knew the problem, but what could be the answer?

After much prayer, we decided that instead of us going to each village, we would bring key people from each village to us. We decided to hold two weeks of concentrated teaching every eight weeks. Looking at our discouraged believers, we figured there were about twenty men who would fit our criteria. We set the date and with great anticipation sent out our boats to pick them up.

After the first two-week session ended and we had taken our students home, we began to receive word from other villages up and down the river that they also wanted to come to our Bible course.

"Just wait," we told them. "This is not for you yet. Once we finish with these students, then we will open the course up for more."

The next course went even better than the first one and the requests to join the course really picked up. Finally, my dad spoke up. He has allowed us to pretty much run the work, and only speaks up if he feels strongly about something. Well, he felt strongly about this. "Listen, we have been praying for a breakthrough with the Yanomamö for over fifty years. I can't believe we are telling people 'no.' We should not try and play God like this with them. Who knows how much more time they have? With so many of them dying, who is to say one of the guys who wants to come now will still be alive when we finally get around to letting him come? I say, let's open the course up to any who want to come, and let's trust God to meet the needs and supply what is needed."

We stared at him, realizing that he was so right!

I remember the thrill I felt when I wrote the following update to my prayer partners back in the USA:

> The last couple of evenings some of the guys from way up the Ocamo river told the whole class that while they had heard about a God who loves them, they finally had come to the place where they were realizing that they were sinners, and that they had never had the new birth that the other students were talking about. I had tears in my eyes as Gary led them through the sinner's prayer. Then last night, a good friend from way up the Mavaca River, whom we have been working with for a long time, confessed that although he has known about God for a long time, during the course of this seminar, he had come to realize that he was still living in darkness. He asked that we pray with him. Right after him, two other guys also confessed to the Holy Spirit working in their lives convicting them of their sin. They too wanted to put their trust in the sacrifice that God has provided. Wow! Folks, God is really working, and we are truly excited about how God is answering prayer! Please keep praying!
>
> We ask for prayer for them as they head back up to their villages and confront all the challenges that await them, from hostile witch doctors, to skeptics, mockers, and just the difficulties of living for the Lord in a pagan village. Also, please pray for safety for all the guys involved in taking them home. Boats are heading up the Ocamo, Mavaca, Orinoco, Juluta, Cuntinamo, and Padamo rivers. Thank you all for being faithful to pray! We had an incredible time with them! As most of you all know, it has been difficult for the Yanomamö people to see their own need of a Savior. They have for the most part, never seen themselves as sinners. Years and years of labor and tears have been expended in trying to get this foundational truth across to them. But now it is obvious that the Lord

is really working in hearts. In this seminar we had 48 students. We had planned on 37, but many of the students brought either a son, or a brother, or some other relative with them that also wanted to hear more. As we spoke on who God is, creation, the fall and the sacrifice that God provided, it seemed finally that God's Word was really penetrating. During the two weeks of studying, first one and then another asked that we help them pray the sinner's prayer. What a thrill it was to be able to watch the truth of God's Word take root in hearts.

One of the guys asked if he could be baptized, so we took the last day's session and taught what baptism was for, and what it meant to follow the Lord in this way. While we were doing this class, most of the first-time students that had come with the other students asked if they could get saved as they wanted to go home knowing that they were covered by the blood of Jesus. They then also asked if they could be baptized. Then some of the wives of the students asked if they too could get saved and be baptized. I have to confess, that in the excitement of the time, I lost count at how many actually did get saved, but I know it was more than twenty. One of our guys was writing everything down, so I will get the info later on today, but rejoice with us! The Bible says there is rejoicing in heaven when a sinner repents, and down through the years, there has not been a lot of cause for rejoicing over the Yanomamö. Just one here and there. Well, this last two weeks made up a bit for that! and we want to tell you all thanks, because of your partnering together with us, we were able to see a great victory!

Then, in my update six weeks later, I wrote:

We currently have 105 students here, and we know of people from at least two villages that have not gotten here yet. When we dreamed of this, we figured we would get about thirty students. But God had so much more planned for this. The amazing thing is that so many of them are coming from areas where we have not gone before. They have heard from their relatives in different villages so they have come to see for themselves what is happening. It reminds me of Andrew, after he found the Christ, he went and called his brother Simon, because so many of the new ones we have here now are brothers, uncles, nephews, cousins or fathers of many of the students that got saved last time, and they have come because of the testimony of their relatives saying, "We have found the truth, come with us and hear it for yourselves." This has been the prayer of so many different people both working with and praying for the Yanomamö that as they heard, they would tell their own people, and we are seeing this prayer answered. God has promised that His Word would not return void, but it would accomplish what He had for it to do. A lot of the people at the seminar this time are from villages that thirty years ago turned their backs on the Gospel and the mission pulled out of that entire area. But God's Word they had heard so long ago has come back to their minds and they realize the truth in it and are getting saved. God's word does not return void! Now the Lord gave the harvest. We are in awe realizing that over 87 people got saved! I am not positive of the exact amount, but what I was able to get written down was 40 men and 47 women, and I know I missed a few. Gary, Steve, and I will get together after the students leave and really compare notes, but suffice it to say, we are rejoicing. By the way, six of these men were witch doctors! A number of the men are guys that we have spent years praying for! I know one old witch doctor is a man that Dad and Mom first met when they arrived, and they have prayed and witnessed to him for years, and he has never wanted anything to do with the Gospel. So it brought tears to my eyes listening to him pray asking God to free him from the bondage of Satan, and to chase the demons out of his heart. He told us his heart was dark with demons. Now the old guy has such a huge smile on his face! Another witch doctor told us that when his brother came back from the last seminar and began to tell him what he had learned, he got very excited. He went out into the jungle and tried talking to God like he had seen his brother do. He admitted he even tried to sing the songs that he heard his brother singing. But he confided, "I only did that way out there, where I was sure no one could hear me, I don't know the words, so I just sing what I think they were, and besides, my voice doesn't sound that good." He told us that finally out there in the jungle, he told God, "I believe what I am hearing about you, that you are the only one who can save, please clean my heart out. I am so full of demons, and in such bondage I can't help myself. Please untie me if you can." He said while he was still praying, such a bright light came into his heart lighting up the furthest corners! Demons were thrown violently out of his heart, and they fell like dead from the power of God! Now I am all clean inside." He told us with a huge smile.

Thanks again for your continued prayers for all these new ones in Christ.

In a later seminar session, on our first night of allowing our students to speak, Benito stood up. He had gotten saved during one of the first seminars after we had opened the course up to anyone, and the change in his heart was evident from the large smile continually breaking across his face. I wrote the following account to our prayer partners:

"I went right into the middle of the war and picked him up," Benito pointed at the man from Washäwä and smiled, waiting for our reaction. After sitting through almost three hours of, dare I say, longwinded testimonies, it took a while for his comment to get the response he was waiting for. Finally enough heads had straightened up, and glazed eyes slowly focused on him to make him continue. "Yes, I went right into the middle of the war to pick him up, but only because God directed my steps." By this time he truly did have all of our attention. "I had gone up the Mavaca River to pick him up as you all had asked," he said, talking to Gary and me, "but then the river got too shallow, and a huge tree was across the way. I could not go any further by boat, and yet their trail was still a long way upriver. So I prayed asking God what I should do. I felt God would have me go on up and try and find him, but their village had moved because of the war. They were now living way inland. I decided to just get out and start walking. 'Maybe I will find their trail,' I thought. Because of the war, we felt it would be safer for us to leave our guns in the boat. And every so often I would stop and yell. I was hoping to find some hunters out from their village who we could go in with, which would be safer for us, but at the same time I was nervous, because what if the hunters thought we were raiders? So every time I would yell, I would also add. 'I am sent from God to get the student from up here. Don't shoot me, I am not a raider, but am sent from God.'"

We all laughed with him, and he said, "Well, you all surely would not have wanted me to get shot, would you? So I had to say something. Anyway, I walked and walked. We were worried we would not find a trail, or a hunting party, when finally off in the distance we heard someone answer. We made our way that way, now wishing we had brought our own weapons, as we sure felt naked out there. We kept walking until all of a sudden I heard 'nk, nk, nk.' I froze. Slowly I turned my head. There were four warriors with their arrows drawn on us. 'Brother-in-law, I am not one of your enemies,' I assured them. 'Look at my hands. I am empty. I am looking for our student. The missionaries sent me to get him. God led me to you.' I kept talking really fast so they would put their arrows up. Finally one of the guys looked at me and told the others, 'Yes, he is from Modolema. I know him. He is my brother-in-law.'

Boy, I breathed a sigh of relief. I was afraid I was going to get shot, and since I had left my own weapons would not be able to avenge myself, but now I at least had someone to talk for me. Anyway, I looked around. 'Are we close to your village?' I asked, 'I left meat in the boat. Send someone to backtrack me and get the meat.' They looked at each other, and I got nervous again. 'No, we are really far from home; we were just sent out to scout,' my brother-in-law told me. 'We were out with a group, let us call them to come on in, and we can decide who will get the meat.' He began to call, but no one answered him. I had felt like there were people watching me, and now I was really nervous. I kept looking behind me, and yet I still never heard the guy until he spoke up right behind me. 'What are you doing up here, when I am expecting shooting enemies?' I jumped a bit at the sound of his voice. I quickly looked at the guy who called me brother-in-law. Thankfully he spoke up for me. Slowly five more guys came out of the jungle where they had surrounded us. I thanked the Lord for His protection. To make a long story short, they finally escorted me into the village, and I was able to pick up Camillo here for the seminars. But do not send me up there again, because it is a long way up there, and next time the wrong people might catch me."

He sat down with a smile, and I marveled at what he had gone through to get one guy to the seminar. Would I have gone to that much trouble? Wow!

Thanks for your prayers for us and for our guys. We don't ask for safety for them lightly.

The next night, one of the guys from Caravana stood up and addressed us. Using the formal speech that they use when addressing matters of great importance, he pointed to the man from Washäwa and began to tell us of all the atrocities the people of Washäwa had committed against them. I glanced at Gary to make sure we could get between them if it came to that, but the man from Washäwa stared stoically off into the distance and didn't say a word.

The next night then, he was the first to his feet. "Now my friends," he said, "our brother from Caravana forgot to mention a few facts. Let me set the record straight for you all." This time it was the man from Caravana who sat staring off into the distance, but it must have been good for each of them to get it off their chests, because over the next two weeks of seminar they spent time together laughing and joking and comparing notes, so to speak. They left today in the same boat heading back up to their villages. Please pray especially hard for Antonio and QueQue as they take them home. They will be stopping at Caravana first to let the three guys from there get out. I asked them if it would be dangerous for our friend from Washäwä to be in the boat. They both looked at me as if I were crazy and said, "Oh no, we are friends now and brothers in the Lord."

Human that I am, I still worry, so pray.

In our current courses, we now average more than 150 students, and we could have many more if we had the boats to bring them, and the housing capacity to sleep them. God has honored our efforts above our wildest dreams. We have classes every day from 8:00 a.m. to 12:00 noon, then from 2:00 p.m. to 4:30 p.m., and then from 7:00 p.m. to 9:00 p.m. The day classes are for us to teach them, and then every evening we meet for two hours with the students and just let them share. As we listen to how the Lord is working in their hearts, it is refreshing to realize that He has promised to build His church, and we are being allowed the privilege of watching part of it happen.

One of the big unforeseen benefits of these seminars has been that the believers from all the villages are beginning to bond together as one body of believers. For so many years, each little group of two or three believers in the different villages has thought they were basically the only Christians there were. In their minds, every one else had rejected the Gospel and only they had not. This made it very difficult for them to really live for the Lord, as there was no one that they could look up to, or that they, as believers, could be held accountable to as believers. Now with the seminars, as they meet and begin to bond with other believers from so many different villages, they realize that they are not alone, there are many Christians and in spite of difficulties there are men who are standing for the Lord. This has given a real resolve to the men who have been Christians for years, but have never taken a stand. While I was beginning to sense this momentous shift in thinking, it really was brought home to me listening to Docudico's testimony one night:

> You all know me. I am Docudico from Alata. For many years I lived a horrible life of killing, raids to steal women and was very controlled by the demons of hate and revenge. My life was a constant pit of suffering and there was no peace for me. But now, Jesus found me and He cleansed me. He gave me a new heart and He took away all my hate for others.
>
> But this is what I have been learning as I have been trying to live for God. I am still a person in need of God's continual cleansing because from my old way of life there are many things that are habit with me that are displeasing to God; for example, I was still doing all of the old feast[s] and drinking of the bones of the dead calling on friends and relatives to come to the feast to join me in revelry and sexual immorality. But one day in my heart, God told me "Docudico, these feast[s] displease me. They are sinful. To cleanse you of that sin is why I had to die in your place. So I don't want you to have any part of that any longer." So I quit doing the feast[s]. When the nonbelievers in my village have a feast, I leave for the jungle for a few days until it is over. You know what has happened because I have stood up for my belief? All of the young men and women who have professed Christ go with

> me and we have a good time fellowshipping in the Lord. Let us all listen to God's Spirit and let us learn from His word. Let's all of us determine to obey God! This is all I have to say.

As I listened to him talk, I looked again at his curly hair that caused him to stand apart from the other Yanomamö—but to be honest, it was not just his hair that had caused him to stand out. He was a very feared warrior, both with his long six-foot bow and arrows, and also in the spirit world before he had the change of his new birth. My mind went back to the first time I met him . . . .

He had his bow bent all the way back and a curare poison-tipped arrow aimed right at my gut. Because he was standing hardly fifteen feet away from me, there was no way he could miss. I tore my attention away from the tip of his arrow, and looked into a set of very cold eyes. His mouth was drawn in a tight line from the exertion of holding his long bow bent so far, but his poison arrow was rock-steady. Along with him were five other warriors, all with their bows bent as well and aimed at our small group. Suddenly—and I don't know why it seemed important—I noticed that he had really curly hair. Now, why that should suddenly seem important, I have no idea. But I noticed he had curly hair. *This is it,* I thought, *I am going to be shot in the gut by the only Yanomamö I have ever met with curly hair! What in the heck are we doing up here anyway?* Well, it was a long story that had started about five days before in the village of Cosh, when Octavio had run into our house.

"Pepiwä, you all have to help us. My mother's people are dying! They sent word to bring help." Octavio's face was all contorted from his sense of urgency. Runners had brought word that there was some form of epidemic in the village of Alata, where his mother was from. She had been stolen as a young girl and was the wife of the head man of Cosh, Octavio's father.

Dad and Mom were in the middle of the long process of trying to translate the New Testament into Yanomamö. I'm sure, by that time, that Dad would just as soon have gone and gotten away from all the desk work, but their own sense of urgency to finish this most important job just would not allow them to take any time off. He, Mom, and Bautista had been spending about ten hours a day on this project for the past two years and the job still stretched on into eternity for them.

Hearing the commotion, I walked into the room to see what all the fuss was about. "Mike, why don't you run down and pick up Frannie [my friend Fran Cochran] and run on up there and see what is going on?" Dad asked me.

I was only too happy to oblige. If there was one thing I truly enjoyed doing, it was heading off to some unknown village—and brother, the people of Alata were unknown to us! Cosh had pursued an on-again/off-again war against them since before we arrived, and the situation had never improved nor relations normalized enough that visits could be exchanged, not to mention that they were just a long ways away. Our trip would take us up the Ocamo River as far as it was navigable and from there we would have to find their trail and walk about two days over the Alata mountain range to their village. We started to plan immediately.

The first concern was fuel for such a long trip. We didn't have enough gasoline on the base, so the first thing I would have to do would be to head down to TamaTama and pick up some gasoline. This was not bad, as Cochran was down there at his parents' place and I could kill two birds with one stone, so to speak: pick up the fuel *and* Cochran. The next morning, before it was truly light, found Nando, Yacuwä, and me heading downriver. It was a cold rainy morning and yet I was filled with an exuberance that wouldn't quit. In my mind I kept going over the trip, reviewing the myriad little details that have to be addressed, such as how much fuel and food we would need to take us all the way up there, and then all the way back out again. The fuel was easy, the food more difficult. We struggled with figuring out how to handle the food situation, because if we weren't careful, we could very quickly find ourselves feeding entire villages while we were there. Caesar's Roman legions could not carry enough food to feed a hungry Yanomamö village for very long, so we always ended up trying to find ways to keep our meager food supplies hidden.

They say the night always gets darkest before the dawn, and boy, this night was sure fulfilling that prophecy. To make matters worse, there was a fog on the river so thick I couldn't even begin to see through it, and our light only made matters worse. We finally made it down to the mouth of the Padamo and turned onto the mighty Orinoco River. The loud cavitational sounds coming from my 20-horsepower Mercury outboard meant I had leaves trapped on the lower unit of the engine, so I slowed down, put the engine in neutral, and pressed the stop button. Lifting the engine, I made sure the leaves did in fact fall free. We floated in the darkness, enjoying the sounds of silence there in the middle of the Amazon rainforest.

Commenting on how thick the fog was, I told Nando and Yacuwä, "Keep your eyes open, I can't see a thing, and I sure don't want to run into the bank or worse." They both laughed and assured me they were doing their best. I knew they were both more asleep than awake, and that as soon as we got underway again, they would give in entirely to the seductive sounds of the motor and the water rushing by the boat and would be asleep before I got around the next bend. I didn't really care: This was a well-known river and we had no problem driving it at night, but boy, I sure wished I could see further than six inches in front of my face.

Starting the engine, I paused before putting the motor in gear. I strained to see the skyline through the fog. Through breaks in the swirling mist, I was able to get a glimpse once in a while that did allow me to see a indistinct darker tree line against the lighter dark of the sky, so I kept going in the night, down a river I thought I knew—not realizing that my boat had gotten turned around in the fog when we stopped to clear the prop, and I was now heading upstream instead of downstream like I thought!

After about an hour, I myself was beginning to give in to the seductive sounds of the motor and rushing water, but I was suddenly jerked to wakefulness by some indefinite blur in the misty fog. I stared hard. Yes! I caught the sense of something more substantial than fog right in our path. I panicked and stopped the motor, and the boat settled down. Nando and Yacuwä both jumped up to show that they were diligently watching the river, but because they both had been lost in sleep, they were more confused than I was.

"Why did you stop so hard?" they both demanded.

"Look there," I told them, pointing. "What is that?" We strained to see through the damp fog. The hair on the back of my neck stood up in fright as I realized that the swirling fog had been concealing something even more substantial than I had thought. Huge rocks loomed up over us, bigger than houses. If we had kept going, we would have crashed full speed into them. I shook my head; something was definitely not right. "Where are we? There should not be any rocks on the Orinoco like this!"

Even in the poor visibility of the fog it was obvious that the rocks were huge and stretched all the way across the river. There simply was not a stretch like this on the Orinoco where we should be. I kept looking, trying to figure out where we were, looking at the little tiny patches of tree line I could see as the fog began to clear a bit. Something was terribly wrong. This did not match up to any stretch of the Orinoco that I knew. The rocks looked familiar, however, and in the clearing fog, as I started to be able to see a bit more of them, I got the haunting feeling that I should know them. I had traveled the section of river we were on too many times to count, and considered myself almost an expert on it, rain or shine, day or night, but I just could not come up with where we were. I knew, based on how long I had traveled from the mouth, we should be down by Chiwide, but there were no rocks like this anywhere around Chiwide. So where in the heck were we? All of a sudden I knew! We were back on the Padamo, and not just back on the Padamo, but *way back* on the Padamo. Halfway back to Cosh on the Padamo!

"Hey, you guys, this is Tedicaiyaji," I told them.

"But we passed that long ago," Nando argued. "How did we get all the way back up to here?"

"Well, if you all had been awake and watching, you might have seen that we somehow got turned around and headed back upriver instead of going down." I threw that out quickly before they could get around to this whole mix-up being my fault (which it was; I was the driver, after all). The Yanomamö love to throw blame, and I knew I was going to have a hard time defending myself tomorrow, but more than being worried about the blame, I was disappointed: this would set us back by at least two hours. So now, instead of getting down to TamaTama in time to get our fuel and start back upriver, we would have to sleep down there, which would further delay our heading up the Ocamo to Alata. Still, what was there to do but start the long way back downriver, retracing the route we had already done twice that same morning before light?

As I drove back downriver, I wondered how I had ever stayed in the channel for that long. When traveling the river at night, you know where you are by the tree line. This gives you references for rocks, what side of the river you should be on, and so on, but the entire last hour I had thought I was heading *down* the Orinoco, when in reality I had been heading back up the Padamo. So, as I judged turns and about where I was by time and vague visuals through the fog, somehow I had managed to stay on the river without running into anything, even though I was totally off about where I thought I was. I chuckled to myself, wondering what my guardian angel looked like then. Bet he was mad!

We finally made it down to TamaTama and purchased the amount of fuel we would need for the round trip up to the headwaters of the Ocamo River. Frannie was as excited as I was to be heading back out. Both of us really enjoyed the adventures that always seemed to be waiting for us, and had even gotten used to the fact that many times our adventures turned into full-blown crises. We loved the work we were doing, but almost more than that we enjoyed coming home and telling about all our fine escapades.

Three days later, we made camp at the rapids on the Ocamo called *Alata Bola;* the mountain we were going to have to climb over was called Alata Mountain, and the village we were trying to find was Alatateli. *Well, with a history of wars like they have had, I guess it didn't give them much time to get fancy with what they named stuff,* I thought to myself. Either that, or they have an awful lot of macaw parrots around here: *ala* is a scarlet macaw in Yanomamö. Regardless of what they name stuff, I sure hoped they would be friendly now.

We ate well there in our camp by the rapids. The fish were biting furiously, and both Frannie and I loved to fish, so in no time at all we had a mess of peacock bass and some *maloja* (*bocon* in Spanish). These are a large game fish, and the only reason they are not more sought after is that they are only found up in the headwaters of the jungle rivers and very few sport fishermen know about them. But fighters! Mercy! Enough to make a grown man sit right up and cry! And a very good eating fish, I'll tell you. We breaded the fish and fried up some; the rest we wrapped in leaves and nested them in the red-hot coals. Nando kept watch on the bundles and turned them enough so that the leaves did not catch fire, while the leaves and the smoke and open fire cooked the fish with a flavor that is just unreal. Eaten with some roasted plantains and yucca, we had a feast fit for a king. We ate long into the night, realizing that tomorrow was going to be a long day and we wouldn't be able to stop and cook anything. Traveling with Indians, one quickly adjusts to the feast-or-famine method. When food was available, you feasted, because as surely as you took your next breath, the famine was coming.

The next day, as we were drudging up one more mountain in a long day of climbing up and down mountains, the tension was so high I could feel the hair on the back of my neck standing straight out. Along with the tension, I was hungry! I was wishing we could stop and eat something, as the feast of the night before was just a distant memory by then. But because everyone thought we were being watched or followed, no one wanted to stop and start a fire.

We thought we could make it to Alatateli before nightfall, but no one was really sure, as no one in our party had ever actually been there. We were going on hearsay. The people of Wabutawäteli had pointed the trail out to us, but had declined to come with us, as there were bad feelings between the villages. To be honest, we really did not need the distraction of traveling with a group the Alatateli might not want to see. Being strangers here was dangerous enough, as any strangers could be classified as enemies, whereas if you were caught *with* an enemy, you were for sure one! So I was glad it was just our group quietly hurrying down the trail.

I wondered if we would make it home to tell about this adventure. It was obvious we were getting closer to where people were living, because the trail all of a sudden had gotten more traveled. I kept glancing over my shoulder, and noticed others in our group doing the same. As I mentioned, we all felt like there were eyes watching us from the depths of the jungle. I didn't see anyone, but of course the jungle is so thick and dense that an army could have been hidden just a stone's throw from where we were walking and we would never have seen them. The Yanomamö are masters of ambush and have the patience of a hunting jaguar, so I figured we probably would not see them before it was too late, but that didn't keep us from constantly swiveling our heads around trying to spot them.

As a strategic move, we had placed Octavio's old mother in the front of the line walking through the jungle. No, not that we thought we could escape while they slaughtered her, but even though she had been stolen as a young woman, we figured someone might recognize her and her presence might avert a disaster, an arrow-in-the-gut type of disaster, which we were all in favor of averting, I can tell you. Octavio kept up a lively dialogue with his mom (well, it was more a monologue, since his mother wasn't saying much), making sure he called her name loudly and just basically going over the reason for this trip: in essence, that we were peaceful, his mother was from Alata, and we were hoping to arrive at the village to help them with medicines. It was obvious that his monologue was not for his mom's benefit, but rather for anyone hidden behind the dark depths of the impenetrable jungle who might be listening to us.

Suddenly the familiar "nk, nk, nk" sound cut his monologue off. We all froze, recognizing it for what it was. We had blundered into an ambush and they had us dead to rights. I was not sure whether I should turn toward the sound. I heard Octavio pick up his monologue again: "Yes, I am traveling up here to visit my uncles. I am with my mother, she has assured me that my uncles will be happy to see us and will welcome us into their village. Now is the time of ripe plantains and they will feed us and treat us with respect and dignity."

Deciding it might be OK to turn, I first turned my head slowly toward the sound. There were at least six men with arrows drawn back aimed at our party. My eyes were drawn first of all to the arrow points. They looked wickedly sharp and glistened with the shine of new poison. We were close enough that I could even see the little grooves cut into the points to cause them to break off inside whoever had the misfortune to be shot with one of them. I hoped it would not be me. My eyes slid up along the arrow shaft to look into the cold eyes of the warrior who was standing there with his long bow bent all the way back. His face was set hard and his muscles looked as if they had been carved in granite, tight with the exertion of holding his long bow bent, but his arrow was rock-steady. Suddenly I noticed his hair. He had curly hair! It just did not seem right to be shot by a Yanomamö with curly hair. I found my tongue and moistened my lips.

"We are friends," I was quick to explain.

The curly-haired guy chuckled, "With this many arrows aimed at them, that is what everyone says."

I smiled my relief; he sounded friendly. After another minute or so, the guys suddenly let their arrows down and they surged to where the old lady was standing. What a family reunion! She was their mother's sister and they had not seen her for years and years. Because the Yanomamö don't keep track of time, it was difficult to know for sure how long it had been, but everyone had told me she had been captured as a young adolescent girl, and she looked about as old as Moses now. However long it had been, I sure was happy that the old lady was with us and that they had recognized her. The tension was gone and now everyone was happy and full of good will.

Suddenly, without a sound, another bunch of warriors melted out of the depths of the jungle behind us and joined the group. I realized again what masters of ambush the Yanomamö are. We had been deftly caught in a crossfire scenario and had not even known it. It was only after the first group showed themselves, and it became obvious what our intentions were, that the second group showed themselves. By that time, I was doubly happy that we had the old lady with us.

I was pleased to learn that the warrior with the curly head was one of the old lady's nephews. He was obviously the leader of the group. He was tall for a Yanomamö and his wavy head of hair caused him to stand out from the rest of the Yanomamö with their straight black hair. He looked over at Fran and me and it was apparent he was a man of quick humor. His eyes crinkled at the corners and he smiled broadly.

"Yes, yes, yes, this is good that you have come! I am pleased that you have come to visit me. Long I have said I wanted you *nabä* to come and see me. I knew once you were here, you would know that I am a worthy opponent in warfare, but a good friend if not bothered. We have been following you for a long time today. We watched you cross the creek back at the foot of the mountain, and we followed you as you crossed toward the peak. Many times we could have taken you out, but we just followed you. It would have gone bad for you, but I recognized my aunt who was stolen from us so many years ago. It is good that you have brought her back to me." I nodded again to show how friendly we were. I felt that Octavio was the real spokesman and I did not want to say too much. Tension was still high, even though we all felt a lot better. I hadn't really acknowledged how much stress we were all under, but I sure felt better now that we had met them.

After the reacquaintances were made, the village warriors led off and we quickly moved into position to follow them. Octavio was now walking with his cousin/brothers and Fran and I found ourselves hurrying along trying to keep up. Ramon was walking right ahead of me.

"Who is that curly-haired man?" I whispered to him.

He lowered his voice so he could not be overheard. "That is Docudico," he whispered. "He is Alata. He is their main warrior." In calling him by the name of the village, Ramon was letting me know that Docudico was the headman of Alata. I had heard of him . . . and not much of it good. Rumor said he had killed many men and was a fierce warrior. I knew he was the scourge of Yoblobäteli and Yeisibäweiteli. Funny thing was, he looked like such a nice guy. I would have thought someone with his reputation would have been much bigger, uglier, and older.

After about an hour of following them through the jungle, the trees started thinning out and we found ourselves walking out onto a savanna (grassland). The trail led on up to a ridge that towered above us. We continued walking at the same brisk pace—actually more like a half-run—that the Alata guys had set when they took the lead, and we quickly began to climb. My chest was heaving and my tongue was hanging as we kept climbing. How I wished one of our Alatateli hosts and now guides would stub a toe enough to make them slow down! None of us Padamo River guys was doing very well. We were not used to running up mountains like the Alata guys were. Even Ramon was panting a bit.

Finally we came to the top of the ridge. Turning on the trail, I looked behind me. What a sight! The grassland stretched out below me with the jungle forming a border further away. Looking carefully, I could even see where our trail had come out of the jungle onto the grasslands. In the distance I saw more mountains rising up. Turning, I looked for the guys in the lead, and saw that they were disappearing down a slight dip in the trail. Wishing for a longer break, we hurried to catch up. Coming around a turn in the trail, I caught sight of the village. It was sitting right on the edge of the cliff! *Boy, I would hate to be the one going for water!* I thought.

Catching up to everyone where they had stopped to let us overtake them, I noticed that only the guys who had come with us were panting. The Alata guys looked like they had hardly even exerted themselves. As soon as everyone caught up, Docudico led off again, heading straight for the small opening in the *shabono.* Ducking down, I went in behind Ramon. Fran, Nando, and Juaquin were behind me. I flinched as the villagers yelled and shrilled their welcoming cries. We were immediately engulfed in a mass of yelling, dancing, shrieking people.

Docudico and his guys had kept walking to their hearths without a backward glance, but Octavio, Tito, and Ramon had stopped right in the middle of the *shabono* and assumed a dignified pose as befits important visitors. I stopped beside Ramon while Frannie and Nando took up positions beside me. I was holding my gun across my chest just as Ramon was holding his arrows, and I tried to look as disinterested as he did in all the shouting, yelling warriors. The fact that the warriors were armed to the teeth and looked like they were ready to use their weapons made me want to keep at least a wary eye on them, but, knowing how important it was to appear totally calm and unworried, I looked off into the distance and waited for someone to direct us to where we could hang our hammocks. Because of Octavio's kinship relationship with Docudico, we were shown to his hearth. Quickly hanging our hammocks, we laid down, still pretending to stare far off into space. I grinned as I heard orders given to prepare us a meal. I was hungry, as we had not eaten anything all day, but because of the long day's walk, I was actually more thankful that the culture and customs demanded that we lie there quietly until they fed us. *I hope they take their time,* I thought to myself. I was tired! And the hammock felt so good.

Soon our food was brought to us: a huge gourd of banana drink. Squatting down by my hammock, I took the small gourd that was floating on top of the banana drink. I briefly wondered if the person who had squished the bananas between their fingers had washed their hands before squishing, but it was too late to ask, so I scooped up some of the contents of the gourd and drank it. Once you got past the initial thought of how it was made, it was really good. Now, one time up the Ocamo, that was something else. I almost could not get that stuff down, but we had to . . .

We had been traveling for two hard days when we finally arrived at the village of Aweiteli. This was before there was much traffic up there and most of the village people had never seen a white person. A white person who could speak Yanomamö was even better, is what I guess they were thinking, because they sure were excited to see me. I was with four Yanomamö friends: Timoteo, Yacuwä, Julio, and Dädöwä. We were standing around waiting to be shown where to hang our hammocks. After an exuberant welcome, the people acted friendly and curious about who we were, and stood around laughing and talking.

As I mentioned, this was before there was much traffic up there. I don't think there were more than two or three pieces of cast-off clothes amongst the entire village. A few of the men did have loincloths, but most of them wore just the string around the waist and had themselves tied up.

While a few of the women and girls did have on the tiny string aprons they make, most of them only wore a single string around the waist. Their bodies fairly glistened with the shine of red paint. They wore beads around their ankles and below their knees, bright red string crisscrossed across their chests, and sticks in the corners of each side of their mouths and lower lips and through their nasal septums; combined with sweet-smelling jungle flowers and leaves stuck in the holes through the earlobes, they are a very beautiful people.

The headman was so excited to have visitors, especially his white visitor, that he forgot protocol. We should have been shown a place to hang our hammocks first, then fed, but he forgot or ignored the custom, and began to yell at the women because they were so slow in making us food.

The women ignored him because they were gawking as hard as anyone, and the old man became even more agitated. Grabbing up an old battered drinking gourd, he banged it against his naked leg to dislodge any cockroaches that might be clinging to the inside surface. Satisfied, he poured some water into it from a calabash that was sitting beside him on the ground.

Old man, please wash that gourd out first, I thought to myself.

He didn't. Next he grabbed a hand of ripe bananas and, peeling them, began throwing them one at a time into the open gourd.

After he had more than a dozen large, peeled, ripe bananas in the gourd, he looked around for the pronged stick they use for mixing this drink. Not finding one handy, he looked down at his hands to ascertain their cleanliness. I also looked at his hands, with a more critical eye than he did, obviously. Looking at the crusted residue of countless other meals dried on his hands (if I had wanted to take the time needed, I'm almost positive I could have given you his previous week's menu, but I digress); anyway, looking at his hands, I thought to myself, *Old man, please wash your hands!*

He didn't. He began to squeeze the bananas into a watery pulp with gusto, every so often picking out a rather hard lump that would not squeeze down. Rather than throwing it away, he plopped it into his mouth, giving his fingers each a good lick. The large cud of tobacco in his mouth took up so much room that he barely had room for his fingers, but he expertly moved his cud around enough to allow him to lick each finger in turn.

Oh, no, not back into the drink, I groaned to myself. Looking over at Timi and the rest of the guys, I saw they were watching the old man with as much horrified fascination as I was.

An old mangy dog—and I mean really mangy, with great big globs of the dog's hair gone, exposing large sores all over its emaciated body—came walking by to see if the old man might share some of his food. Hardly missing a beat in his mixing and his running diatribe directed to the lazy women, the old man pushed the dog away without sharing the food. After having watched him mix it up for us, I would surely have preferred him to have given the entire gourdful to the dog.

No, don't put that hand you just pushed the dog with back into our soup! I thought to myself.

He did. One of the young ladies who was watching the proceedings, and who had taken the brunt of the old man's harsh tongue, spoke up. "Old man, with you licking your fingers and slobbering all over yourself, who is going to want to drink that stuff?" she scoffed at him.

I quickly looked at Yacuwä and Timi. "This lady just gave us a great out! Tell him we are not hungry any longer," I begged with my eyes. They ignored me, mesmerized as they were with the drama of the banana drink unfolding before us.

The old man finally finished his preparation of our drink and, after wiping his hands through his coarse black hair to clean them, handed me the gourd with a huge smile. He was so excited to be feeding us that I didn't have the heart to turn it down. Praying for the Lord's protection while I drank it, I drank a polite share and handed the gourd to Yacuwä. They all drank in turn and finally handed the empty gourd back to the still-beaming man.

Well, it hasn't killed us yet, but that brew gave us a case of the "quickies" that you would never believe. It took us forever to get back down the river, as every couple of minutes another one of us would frantically wave us over to shore and make a mad scramble up the bank to take care of business.

Anyway, at least I did not watch the person who had made this drink that I was now drinking in Alatateli, so I could assume she had either washed her hands really well or had used the stirring stick.

After I drank my share, I passed the gourd to Frannie and lay back in my hammock. I looked around. The *shabono* at Alata was a really nice structure. The roof was beautifully made and curved gently around to form one continuous construction. The Yanomamö make their *shabonos* to reflect their view of heaven. The *shabono* is a replica of heaven, with the open space in the center representing their view of the celestial disk, the roof and how it slopes down being the physical heavens, and where the roof meets the ground is the corresponding horizon. Thought of in this way, it gives the witch doctors their bearings when they have "out of body" experiences. For instance, if a witch doctor has to journey to the highest heaven, to the land of *Yai Wanonabälewä* (the Enemy God), he climbs one of the structure poles of the roof, the tallest poles. This allows him direct access to the celestial disk and, once there, he is perfectly oriented because it is just like the *shabono* he left. He can move freely, either vertically or horizontally, to any place without leaving the central plaza of his *shabono.* Also, because of his orientation, he has no problem getting home. Of course, the entire time he is having his out-of-body experience, either going up to the furthest heaven or to other locations far removed from his physical location, his physical body is there in the central plaza, but I have had *shabolis* describe places that I know they could never have been to in person, yet they can describe it perfectly. They can speak of people and places in ways that make you wonder how in the heck they have ever been there. So when the *shabolis* speak of the spirit world, it is better not to try and explain it, as many things are truly unexplainable.

While Octavio and the rest of our guys were talking with our hosts, Frannie and I quietly talked over our trip. I was also keeping an ear on the proceedings at Docudico's hearth, scant feet from where I was lying in my hammock.

Hearing a small rustle outside the sloping roof of the *shabono,* I turned to look at where I heard the sound coming from. I got Frannie's attention and we both were looking right at the spot, when suddenly—almost as if by magic, so quiet and smooth were his movements—there was a Yanomamö warrior crouched there. His long bow was bent fully back and I noticed the sweat gleaming on his taut muscles. He was sighting down his long arrow shaft at us. The tip of his arrow was utterly still. This man was serious!

Keeping my voice as close to a normal conversational tone as I could under the circumstances, I said (this was harder than you might think!), "I hope your fingers aren't sweaty, I sure would hate for your fingers to slip off your bowstring. It would not look good for our host to have me shot right here at his fire. It would ruin both our days for sure!" I smiled to show that we were legitimate guests. Docudico jumped up.

"Ma, ma, ma, Jamayä bä yabäca dijä!" (No, no, no, don't bother my guest!)

Slowly the long bow unbent and our friend stood up from where he was crouched near the small hole he had worked in the palm. He grinned and, taking his plug of tobacco from where it was placed between his hip and his g-string, he placed it in his mouth. I might add his g-string was the only clothing he wore, if a string tied around your waist can be classified as clothing.

I grinned back—it's much easier to grin without an arrow trained on me, I'll tell you.

"Too bad you weren't an enemy, my *lajaca* is thirsty." He turned his back, and without another word, stalked across the *shabono*.

Later on, as Frannie and I made our way around the *shabono*, visiting and chatting with the different family groups as they relaxed in their hammocks, we came to the hearth of the man who had had the arrow trained on us. I greeted him.

He was unperturbed and talkative. "I heard the uproar in the village when I was still a long way off," he said, "so I ran as hard as I could thinking if it were raiders, I could avenge ourselves before the raiders got very far away. The noise died down before I arrived at the village, so I crept around to where I heard strange voices and came in to make sure you all were friendly," he told me.

Cochran and I stood there talking with him for a while longer. His young wife was roasting plantains in the coals of the fire and he invited us to have one. We accepted his gift and continued on our way around the circular village on our way back to our hammocks. I was still tired from the long walk.

Over the next couple of days, we spent many hours talking and sharing the Gospel with the villagers of Alata. They were great hosts and we were continually being brought gourdful after gourdful of banana drink and roasted plantains. We even went out and shot some turkeys to supplement the food we were being offered. We had a great time with Docudico and his village. Frannie was able to treat the sick people and after a couple of days, we began to make plans to return to Cosh. Docudico begged us to come back.

"Don't be strangers now, you have eaten my food, you know me now. You know I am your friend, don't be gone for too long," he told us.

"We would love to return, but our *bata cäbä* [leaders] are telling us that we have to go back to our father's country and *libromou* [do books]." There just was no other way I could tell them we were going back to go to Bible school so we could learn how to be real missionaries.

It would be many years before I saw Docudico again. Shortly after that first trip to Alata, Fran and I both headed back to the USA for Bible school, and it was five years before I returned to Venezuela. But my thoughts went back many times to all the friends we had made during the two years we worked up on the Ocamo.

10

Docudico Comes Visiting

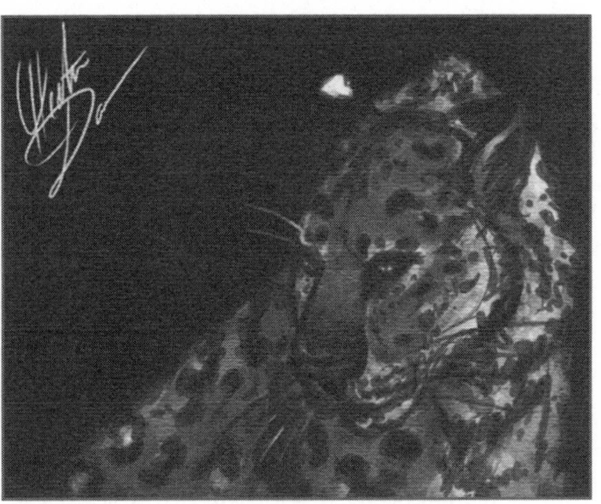

One day in 1981, shortly after Reneé and I returned to Cosh from the USA, while the village was sweltering under the mercilessly hot tropical sun, the afternoon stupor was shattered by the yells and whistles that heralded the arrival of visitors. This was too much noise to have been just someone visiting from one of the villages we get to often, or that come visiting us frequently, so we ran out knowing that someone special was coming. They were still coming downriver in their bark canoes when we arrived at the riverbank to see who it was. As the two canoes nudged their way into port, it was hard to tell who they were in all their paint and feathered finery. The men's heads were all in white bird-of-prey down, and their bodies were painted red with black lines or dots as the mood took the painter. Their faces were bright red, and with the feathered earplugs and their large wads of tobacco, I could not recognize a single person. I had been to about every village that was accessible from our village, as had Gary, so we stood there wondering who this was.

Suddenly we noticed the curly hair, and about this time one of our local Yanomamö must have noticed it also, because a quick whisper went through the crowd, "This is Alata! It is Alata!" The shouts became louder as more and more of the gathering throng realized who this was and what village they were from. We had never been visited by Alata before, so this was a great occasion. They solemnly filed past us up the bank and assumed their pose out in the middle of our village. Our people have gotten unaccustomed to this kind of pomp and circumstance, but they quickly rose to the occasion. Octavio hurried up to Docudico and pointed out his house to our visitor. Without a word, Docudico picked up his hammock and marched over to the house and went in. Slowly this was repeated until every man standing out in the village green had been shown a place to stay. The women hurried to make some food for their distinguished guests.

That evening, the whole crowd of visitors pushed their way into Dad's house and their story came out. I noticed, looking at their faces, which I could now see because they had washed the paint off, that their faces were drawn and pinched from hunger.

"My friends, it is good to see you. It is good to have you in my home," my dad told them. They were relaxed and friendly and wide-eyed, looking at everything. I am sure they each had a private vision of the vast amount of treasures, like machetes and axes, they were going to take home.

"Yes, we are glad to be here," Docudico spoke for the entire group. "We traveled many days to come for this visit." He held up all ten fingers of his hands, pressed together to show that in reality it was actually more than the fingers of both hands, and could possibly have been two or three times the amount of his fingers. This was indicated by the way he continued to open and close his hands. "We left our village when the moon was little, and it got big, and died, then has come again."

Wow, he could be talking about over a month of traveling, I thought to myself. Where did they go first? It should not have taken them that long!

Docudico continued his story, "Yes, we traveled and traveled, and finally came to a big river. We knew your village was on the Metaconi River, so we started down. We made a large *tomolocosi* [bark canoe] and began to float down. We came to a huge waterfall and after trying to come around it, we had to abandon our first canoe. Down at the base of the falls, we found another tree and made another canoe. We traveled for days in this canoe until we came to another large waterfall and had to abandon our canoe again. This was not just one waterfall, but an entire section of river and it took us almost a day to walk around this one. Down at the base, we built another canoe and started downriver again."

Gary looked at me, wondering like me where in the world they had come out on the Metaconi. I thought the first falls he came to was Waqueshi, but the second one sounded more like Waqueshi; how much farther upriver had they come out?

We asked Docudico, "How many days did you travel between the two large waterfalls?"

He held up both hands with fingers extended. Showing us the first one, he said, "This was the day we left our village, we slept here," holding up another finger, another day, holding up another finger, and so on, until he had used up six fingers. "This was the day we arrived at the river. We walked along the river for this many days [holding up two fingers], then we built our *tomolocosi.* We floated down river for this many days [holding up five fingers], then we came to the second big waterfall. It was late in the day, so we slept there, and started walking early the next morning and arrived at the base of the falls when the sun was there in the sky [pointing to about where the sun would be at 1:00 p.m.]. We started looking for another *tomolo* tree to peel the bark off to make a *tomolocosi*, so we could continue floating. We found a tree, the next morning we started to peel the bark off and we finished the bark canoe by late that day, and started to float down the river the next day early. With that canoe we arrived at another falls after this many days of traveling [holding up three fingers]. We were able to work our canoe around that set of falls, so we did not have to build another canoe, but we lost time there while we worked the canoe around. After leaving the falls, we floated just until the sun was there [pointing to where the sun would be at about 11:00 a.m.]. We came to another falls. By this time our bark canoe was getting *ujudi* [weak], so we threw it away, and walked down the river for a day looking for another tree large enough to make another *tomolo*. We could not find a big enough one, so we found two smaller trees, and built two *tomolos* instead of one. Then we came down river for this many days [holding up two fingers], and we arrived here late today. It was a long way for us, we ran out of food, and really suffered. It was a long, long way," he said again, his eyes crinkling up with a smile.

Since that time, we have become very good friends with Alatateli. We visit there often and on one of our last trips up to their village we found they had moved out to the banks of the Ocamo River. They were still just camped in temporary shelters while they worked on gardens and a permanent *shabono*. It was so much easier getting to their village that Keila and I decided to go up there for a few days and just live with the people and visit with them as they worked on their village. Mikeila became fast friends with a little Alatateli girl and they were always together while we were there. When it was time to leave, both girls cried so hard we could barely hear ourselves think as we said our goodbyes and assured the people, and especially the little girl, we would be back. Mikeila's big blue eyes were full of tears. "Not go, Daddy," she kept saying. "Not go!"

"Honey, we will come back soon," I assured her. But I could not see the future . . . because we never did go back up there with Mikeila; she went on to be with the Lord before we had a chance to get back up there.

Still, our friendship with Alatateli has continued. They come faithfully to every seminar now and the growth in the lives of the believers is obvious. It seems like another lifetime ago that I stood with Cochran on the trail and looked down that arrow aimed at me and into the cold eyes of the curly-haired leader of the group.

11

A Time to Dance

The closer we got to the sound of the chanting, the slower we began to walk. I wondered what was going on in the big house of the Panare Indians. I felt uneasy as we walked nearer; because I did not know the culture of the people we had only just contacted a few short weeks ago. The first contact had actually been made a couple of months earlier, by Paul Dye and Michael Shaylor and a few others. It was friendly, and the Panare had asked the missionaries to return to their village and live among them and help them. The families that were going to spearhead this work had already been chosen and were excited to get started. As soon as a strategic village had been located, a team was made up to head in and build a simple house so the families could get in and get busy. Well, we had been busy for more than a month and this was the first day we had been given off, so we decided to investigate. Hearing drums and chanting, we headed over for a closer look. I hoped it would not lead us into trouble. I loved being included on contacts, and would never do anything that might make it so they did not want us along any longer. It was hard work, but we sure had some fine adventures.

As I said, we had already been there for a month; although we were very tired, we were still having a lot of fun. Not that fun is what we had all the time—we were working, after all. When Gary Conklin, another MK, and I were asked to help on this second contact, we enthusiastically agreed, and the next week found ourselves grinding over an endless grassland heading to the area where the village had been located. Not only were we going to build a house, we were told that morning, but also we would first build an airstrip so the base could be better supplied than it could be by Jeep.

Building an airstrip and a house sounded like a tall order to me, but of course I was remembering Frannie's and my efforts up the Padamo where we had to chop down huge amounts of jungle to make an airstrip. The clearing of the jungle was fun and exciting, and if you notched the trees right, one huge tree strategically cut could bring down a couple acres of other trees (don't tell tree huggers I said that). As I said, the thunderous crash of the trees, the snapping of vines, and the ground vibrating under our feet for what seemed like an eternity was fulfilling and fun, but once that was over, digging out the stumps was just plain hard work, and I would gladly have avoided it if at all possible.

So, when they mentioned that we were going to make an airstrip *and* a house, I wondered how long Mom and Dad had indentured me for. Airstrips take a long time, I remembered. I also wondered if this might not be the long-anticipated punishment that we had feared was coming for our breaking into Mr. Lee's house. But as I looked around my mood improved. What the heck, this was beautiful country! So what if we had to stay out here for a while? I was sure the missionaries would be carrying more food than old Cochran and I ever carried. Cochran's folks were home on furlough, which was why he was not with us on this trip. I knew he sure would miss the fine adventures we were going to have here.

Anyway, as we bounced over the grassland, and I realized we were going to build an airstrip out here, *on the grassland,* my mood vastly improved. Mercy, we should be able to knock down the termite nests that were scattered around, and the few shrubs that stood in for trees, in less than a morning. Should be a piece of cake, I figured.

We drove all that day and finally, just as the sun was going down, we came to the banks of a little stream and the Jeep finally stopped. Now, I am used to traveling by dugout canoe, and though it's not the most comfortable conveyance in the world, at least it doesn't bounce you around. In this Jeep, I was sore not only on my rear, where I was used to being sore from the dugout canoes, but even on my head, which hurt from where I had bashed it against the roof during some of the more vibrant bumps. I remember deciding that they could keep their Jeeps; I would stick with the dugouts. Right then, though, I was just tickled to death to have stopped moving.

We all piled out. Talk about your motley crew! Along with Gary Conklin, whom I've already mentioned, there was the missionary who was moving into this area, a Piaroa Indian, and me. The other missionary would be joining us as soon as we got the airstrip ready for the plane to land. *Smart man,* I remember thinking. I should have been smart enough to have joined him.

The missionary who was organizing the expedition was already missing his wife, and the only way he could get his wife in here was to first build the airstrip and then get his house up. Well, he took his job seriously, I'll tell you. He had us up the next morning while it was still dark. Breakfast was meager and fast. *This is the first day, surely we will get more to eat next time,* I thought to myself as we shuffled on out to where they had decided the airstrip was going to be built. An airstrip had already been roughed in by the first group that had been in here, I was happy to learn. They had taken a large log and dragged it behind the Jeep, and the strip actually looked pretty good. We took shovels and picks and went out and began to take out the more stubborn trees, roots, and termite nests that were still standing. I was thankful to see that my assessment had been accurate. It was not going to be that difficult to get an airstrip ready.

Perhaps they have decided to bring in more food by airplane, I thought, because, contrary to my first wishful thought, they had not brought more food than Fran and I were used to taking with us—if anything, they had less, which was hard to believe. I kept snooping around trying to figure out where they had more food hidden. (Never did find anything.) A couple of nights, I heard candy wrappers rustling, but I guess that was none of my business. I can tell you one thing, the rustlings were not coming from my section of the sleeping facilities!

After about a week, we had the strip "good enough." Not my words. It still looked pretty short to me, but the guy in charge (the one missing his wife) decided it was long enough. He was also the one in charge of the radio, so that night he called the pilot and told him the strip was ready. The first flight was for the next morning. Not having a tape measure, he had stepped off the strip and came up with the required 330 meters. Because I had been involved in making a few strips already, I thought his stepped-off 330 meters looked pretty short, but we were told that because the approaches were so great (just over the grassland), the strip did not have to be as long as we needed in the jungle. Hey, great! Bring the plane in! *Please bring some food in,* was all I could think.

The next day, bright and early, we were out at the strip finishing up a few last-minute details. The strip really did not look that bad. I was proud of how much work we had gotten done on it. We were tired, but in a good way. We could hear the plane coming, swooping down the valley. There's nothing quite like building an airstrip and then watching the first plane come in for a landing. We were all a bit tense, and I think we were possibly all wishing we could have measured the strip with a tape measure instead of just stepping it out. It still looked short to me. But here came the plane again. The pilot made two or three more low passes, and the last time around he had even rolled his wheels for more than a hundred yards before pulling back up and roaring away. We watched him set up again for a low downwind and then turn base. I knew he was going to land this time. I watched his flaps come all the way down as he turned final. *This is it,* I thought. He was really slowing down.

Walt Mood made his normal beautiful landing and I saw the plane shudder as he hit the brakes, then hit them again. Then the wheels locked and the plane began to slide. We were standing pretty close to the end of the runway, about where we had figured he would stop, but the plane continued past us at a pretty good clip.

Not good, I thought as I saw the look on the pilot's face. *Really bad!* I decided as I looked at the missionary sitting beside the pilot. He was clutching the handle above the door frame and his eyes were big as saucers as he went past us. *He ain't never going to stop in time,* I decided. Everyone arrived at the same conclusion and we took off running after the plane, which came to the end of the strip and continued bouncing across the savanna. Thankfully, there weren't many trees there and the pilot was able to bring the plane to a stop before it damaged anything except his pride. He climbed out, first verifying that his plane was all right, then taking a long look back down the airstrip. The missionary finally climbed out his side of the plane. Personally I think he was massaging his heart, but he stepped down, and without a backward look at the plane, walked out and while he was shaking his partner's hand, asked him if we had anything to measure the strip with. "Well, we don't have a tape measure longer than twenty feet," the missionary told him. Turning to us, he asked Gary and me if we had a roll of fishing line.

"Yes," we told him.

"Well, run get it please, I want to measure that strip. It sure went by fast!"

Gary ran back and brought his roll of fishing line. These rolls were 100 meters long. Taking one end, the missionary who had just arrived walked to the end of the airstrip that his plane had just overshot. He motioned for Gary and me to continue walking and reeling out the line behind us. When we came to the end, we made a mark on the ground and Doug, the missionary, left his place and walked after us. First 100 meters. He got to our mark and when we felt the line go tight, we made another mark and repeated the process. 200 meters. We were already running out of strip. We had told the pilot we had more than 300 meters, but we were coming up very short. When we arrived at the end of the strip, there was still almost half of the fishing line behind us, and we had only stretched it out twice; even with my boarding-school education, I could do the math and realize that we had about 250 meters instead of the 330 we had bragged about. Boy, no wonder that plane used up so much strip! There just hadn't been that much strip to start with! I can tell you, we worked on that strip again. Nothing like someone who has just almost crashed to become an expert on airstrip construction!

The most distressing thing to me was that in all the distraction of almost ruining the plane at the end of the strip, someone forgot to unload all the food off the plane that Gary and I had talked ourselves into believing was sure to be on there. I was getting to have a bad feeling about our food situation. Our meals had gone from boring to bad. Time has since dulled my memory on some issues, but I remember crackers and sardines. Day after day of crackers and sardines! They get old in a hurry—not that crackers and sardines are much to write home about to start with, but day after day it became almost criminal. We would have gone on a hunger strike to protest our poor conditions, but we were about starved as it was. We were finally allowed a Sunday off. By that time we were working hard on a house, and had finished the roof the day before; hence, it was decided we could have a day off before starting on the walls. Gary, the Piaroa, and I decided to go hunting. Since this was a contact with unknown Indians, though, we had left all guns and other weapons behind. We had nothing. No gun, slingshot, nothing; but the Piaroa had been telling us he thought we could trap something. By this time we were desperate enough to try running after something just in our bare feet and hands, but he was pretty confident, so Gary and I, with excitement mounting, went along with him.

First he had to build the trap. We cut a bunch of reeds and helped him split them as he showed us. He then took the reeds and, bending them into a cone shape, tied them with vines until he had a six-foot-long cone that was about ten inches at the larger end and about five inches at the smaller end. I kept looking for where he was going to put the triggering device or the vine that was going to spring shut and trap something, but all it was was a long cone. *Well, this will sure catch nothing,* I thought in disgust.

"Be patient. We were going to eat good tonight," the Piaroa kept telling us.

So we figured, might as well go along with him. Even if we didn't get anything, just the thought of something beat sardines. Finally, it was finished, but to be honest, it sure didn't inspire confidence. Well, at least we were off work for a while. *Who cares if we don't get something?* I told myself, to help dispel the hopeless feeling I had. Gary knew the Piaroa better than I did, as his parents had actually worked with the Piaroa tribe, but even he had never seen a trap like this one. He fussed at the man in his own language. "They make better traps than this worthless thing," he kept telling me. I tried to soothe him—not that I felt much better about the trap than he did, but I hated to see Gary so down.

The Piaroa told Gary and me to carry it along, and he went ahead of us studying the ground. Finally he had us stop and he showed us a large hole. Well, I knew what that was: it was a *lapa* hole (*Agouti paca* for you scientific types), but in Venezuela, they are called *lapa,* and boy, are they good eating. But *lapa* are smart, and always have about a dozen holes leading out from their burrows, most of them well hidden. This old guy was possibly more tired of sardines than we were, and he kept poking around with a diligence that was rewarded by finding hole after hole, all of which he very carefully and quietly plugged up. At last he was sure we had covered all the holes except the main one and one escape hole in the rear. He quietly inserted his cone into the hole, big end first. He made sure it was wedged into the hole in such a way that it could not be dislodged and anything coming out of the hole had to run into the cone. Telling Gary and me to take up strategic positions on either side of the cone, and giving us each a club, he went back to the main hole. Cutting a long vine, he tied a knot at one end. He inserted this end of the vine down the hole. Twisting it between his hands, he made the knot at the end of the vine jump around like something alive. While it was jumping, he pushed it down the hole, and it sounded for all the world like something alive and furious was running down the hole. Well, before we could even catch our breaths, we heard a furious pounding coming toward us underground and before I could even say "lapa," here came the *lapa.*

It was running fast, it jammed itself into the cone trap so hard it could not even budge. Gary gave it one swift hit on the head and we had a very good supper to look forward to, and a proud Piaroa. Gary and I were lavish in our praise of him. He took it in good stride and hardly reminded us of all the mean things we had said to him while he was making the trap. We lugged our prize home, and brother, did we ever eat well. After that, we were given every Sunday off to see what we could find to augment our meager food supplies. By this time, I think even the homesick missionaries were wishing they had brought just a bit more than sardines and crackers. But that is life, after all; we all want to eat well, but sometimes you just have to eat what you brought.

Eventually, we not only got the roof up, but also had most of the walls mudded up. It was looking like a really nice house. Up until then, we had not had much interaction with the Panare people themselves. Sure, some of them had come by and stood around as we worked (the missionary had even hired a few to help on the house), but we had not had any time to visit them in their village. One Sunday, we were given the day off again, and decided to go visiting instead of hunting. I am not sure, but I think that by then we had in fact received a shipment of food. The missionaries told us to be careful; but to be honest; we did not take that to mean "don't go," so off we went with our trusted Piaroa friend.

The large house of the Panare was located at least two or three miles from where the missionary was building his base, so we walked across the savanna toward the house. We had no idea what we would find, but they had always acted really friendly when they showed up at the work site, so we were not worried.

While still a long way off, we heard the sound of drums beating and another low-pitched noise that sounded like an off-tune bass horn or something. As we got closer, we began to hear sounds of chanting in time with the beating drums and the out-of-tune bass horn. We stopped and asked the Piaroa what was going on. He assured us that it was probably just a fiesta. "Indians always make fiesta," he told us with a big grin. He had a huge grin, and because most of his teeth were missing, his wide smile made the few teeth he had left stand out like lonely sentinels, giving him a snaggle-toothed look. He did not seem worried, so we kept walking, but the closer we got to the sound of the chanting, like I said, the slower we walked. I was getting worried, remembering what the missionary had said about being careful.

Walking into some big shindig and getting everyone angry with us would not make the missionaries very happy. Unknown peoples take a lot of wisdom, and it is never very smart to just go blundering in; still, we figured, one look from a distance would not hurt anyone. Well, we hadn't figured on the posted guards! All of a sudden, from a tree about twenty-five yards in front of us, about six or seven guys dropped to the ground.

"They have guns!" Gary shouted.

As if on cue, all of the Panare dropped to one knee and, bringing their old muzzleloaders to their shoulders, took aim at us and fired! As the smoke from the black powder billowed up from the muzzles and breeches of the old guns, I knew this would not make the missionaries back at the base very pleased. Heck, I wasn't feeling very gleeful myself right then!

This is getting really bad, and we were even trying to be very careful, I thought as I followed the Piaroa's lead and dropped to the ground. I was ready to hightail it out of there—carefully, of course.

Suddenly, the Panares shooting at us began to laugh, great big guffaws of laughter. Slowly, sheepishly, we picked ourselves up out of the dirt. It took us a minute before we figured out that they were funning us. They had not had any bullets in their guns, just the primer and powder—but I tell you what, for a minute I wondered how the headlines would look!

The men came rushing up to us and, taking us by the arms, began to lead us toward their big house. Having heard all the shots, the entire village was now standing outside waiting for us. I realized that our guides (a/k/a captors, I was not sure yet) were all drunker than skunks. *This is not good,* I thought to myself again. But we were involved now, and I did not know how to get out of there, carefully or otherwise.

The Panare are a really good-looking people, and because they were having a party, which we had crashed, they were all painted up. On top of a base of red *onoto* paint, they had stamped intricate designs all over their bodies. The women wore short skirts made out of some kind of coarse material that looked like it was handwoven. Except for some beads criss-crossed across their chests, they were topless. They also had beads tied on the legs above the ankles and below the knee. They were, for the most part, very attractive women.

The men wore baggy loincloths with large tassels down the sides, made out of the same coarse material that the women's skirts were made out of. All the men and boys also wore beads and whatnot. The young boys were wearing only string, made of some kind of hair, around their waists. We found out later that it *was* hair—their own, which had been woven into string. The party we crashed, we found out, was a party to honor an adolescent boy: this celebration was held when they took the string off and he put on his first loincloth.

How I wished I could understand them, because I would have loved to laugh at some of the jokes they were telling, which I was sure by this time, were all about us and how we had flopped in the dirt. They were jabbering two-forty, and we could not understand a single word. They were all still laughing, so we were not worried for our lives yet. However, at a command from an old man, three beautiful teenage girls turned and went into the big house. In less time than it took to wonder what they were getting, they were back outside, each of them holding a huge gourd full of some kind of brew. Judging by the drunken guards, and by this time having ascertained that everyone else was equally drunk, I figured it must be powerful stuff.

The old man motioned the girls to bring the stuff over to us, and the gourds were thrust into our hands. I did not have to put it up to my nose to know that this was heavy stuff. I knew it would be bad, and probably go on my record somewhere if we staggered back to the camp drunk, but I honestly did not know what to do. They kept jabbering at us, making motions to drink. All three of us were shaking our heads no, but it was obvious from the faces of the men around us that this was not the response they were looking for. Again the motion for drinking was made, accompanied by more jabbering. Not understanding a word, it was easy to wonder if they were not saying, "Hey guys, you've crashed our party, now drink up or else!"

Even the Piaroa was nervous by now. In a low voice he told us, "They are starting to get ugly, maybe we should *pretend* to drink some."

Holding my gourd to my mouth, I had to force myself not to gag at the smell of the brew. I glanced at the Piaroa. He was drinking; actually, he looked like he was enjoying it a bit. I took a small mouthful and barely got it down. It tried to come back, but I was able to force it to keep going down.

The Piaroa was still drinking his. He was slurping great big gulps of the stuff and a small stream was running down his chin and splattering in the dust. Gary was drinking a bit of his as well, but as soon as I saw the Piaroa finish his gourd, I immediately swapped gourds with him. No one seemed to mind, and they all laughed as the Piaroa started on the second gourdful. I smiled real big and handed *my* empty gourd back to the tall, comely girl who had given it to me. She smiled shyly. Her face was framed by her long straight black hair, and her teeth flashed white in her brief smile.

As I said, the Panare are a very good-looking people, taller than the Yanomamö, and this girl was possibly one of the better looking ones. As I also mentioned, they don't wear much in the way of clothes, and I sure would have hated to practice my first drunk with them as an audience, that is for sure. I nervously looked away. I was not sure what they might be planning for us next.

By this time, Gary realized that we had both finished our gourds, so he asked the Piaroa for help as well. With a resigned look, the Piaroa took Gary's gourd and before we knew it, he had finished his third gourd in short order as well.

I remembered too late that our friend the Piaroa had not been saved that long ago, and his people also drink this brew. I was glad he had drunk my gourdful, and didn't mind him helping Gary, but I hated to be the one responsible for getting him drunk and possibly even getting him re-hooked on drinking the stuff. I knew our missionaries waiting back at the base camp would not think we had been very careful.

As soon as we could, we mumbled our goodbyes and made our escape. I would like to say we were real sly about it, and crept away, but once the excitement of our visit had passed, the people pretty well ignored us and went back to their dancing and chanting. Not to mention the fact that they were so drunk I think we could have walked away from them nude and no one would have noticed, or for that matter have cared.

We took the long way, trying to allow our Piaroa friend to settle down, as he was actually acting a bit tipsy. When we got home, the missionaries were furious! They could not believe we would do something so irresponsible. "What would you all have done if instead of the gourds of drink they brought you, they had brought out some girls and tried to give them to you?" one of them demanded.

I could not speak for Gary or the Piaroa, but since I could still taste that horrible concoction lingering in my mouth, and could still remember the girls who had brought the brew, I decided I would have preferred the girls. But, looking at the missionaries' scowling faces, I decided it would not be in anyone's best interest to voice my opinion. I meekly nodded my head to show him how contrite I was. Gary was nodding, if anything, harder than I was, trying to outdo me in showing how sorry he was. He had drunk more of the brew than I had, after all. The poor Piaroa was nodding as well, but since he spoke no English, I knew he could not understand us; I think he was half drunk and was probably just nodding off to sleep. I'm sure he would just as soon have found a place to sleep it off, but the missionary was not finished with us yet. He went on and on. That was the last Panare party we tried to crash, I can tell you that. Also, since that encounter with the ill-smelling brew, I have never been able to get as much as a can of beer past my nose. That potent Panare brew probably saved me from a lot of trouble and headache!

Looking back on my time with those two missionaries, I am so grateful for all they taught me. It was hard for those two guys out there, week after week, without their wives and kids. For Gary and me, just two teenagers, it was simply one more adventure. We truly loved it, but it was a sacrifice for the older married men, a sacrifice they made without complaining or even calling attention to their sacrifice. I learned that there were much more important things than food. I also learned that when one loves his God, there is no job too difficult. I was proud to have had a small part in bringing the Gospel to the Panare, even if we thought we almost got shot, and then almost had to get drunk before we could get out of harm's way.

12
Lost Again

We drifted slowly into the bank, our eyes scanning the underbrush for signs of recent activity. The river was low and the sloping sandy beach was torn up with tapir tracks. It was about 3:00 p.m. and I desperately wanted to check out a tapir lick that I had heard was in the area, but none of the guys in the boat knew exactly where it was.

"Go ahead and see if you-all can find it," said my brother Gary, from his place back by the motor. "Timoteo and I will stay here and fish. Julio can go with you."

I looked back at Julio. "OK, let's go find it, but let's go real fast so we can be back before dark." He nodded his head and busied himself getting his stuff ready. I had already picked up my .22 caliber rifle and when I was just about ready to climb out of the boat, I remembered another time not so long ago that I had casually walked away from the boat leaving behind anything that could have made my time easier. While not thinking it was possible for Julio to get lost here, I quickly made up my mind and rummaged through my stuff looking for my little mini-mag flashlight. Finding it, I slipped it into my pocket.

Stepping out of the boat, I started up the beach, trying to figure out which of the myriad tapir tracks were the freshest. Julio quickly caught up with me and assumed the lead. There was no trail, but with the tapir tracks all heading in one general direction, we just picked a set of tracks to follow, knowing they would probably bring us right to the salt lick the tapirs were using.

We kept quiet as we walked, hoping to surprise a tapir in the lick. Although most tapirs are nocturnal, it is not uncommon to see them out in the late afternoon. Periodically I gave the shrill whistle that tapirs use to attract and call other tapirs.

We sure could use the meat. My last hunt had not been successful at all—as a matter of fact, I had spent two days and a night trying to get out of it. I might add, it is amazing how many animals you can stumble over once you quit hunting them and are only trying to find your way out of their habitat. I think it is possibly their form of revenge. After we got lost that time, we almost had to chase the animals away from our feet just so we could walk. We had literally almost stumbled over a whole flock of wild curassow birds—very delicious, but, like I said, when we found those birds we were no longer interested in any game whatsoever, and just kept trudging along to try and find the river. Monkeys came down and screamed insults at us and tried to commit indiscretions on us. Thankfully, their aim was not that good, as they had never been taught to lead a moving target, but it still was unnerving to keep hearing the loud thuds as another smelly bomb fell behind us.

The turkeys were hard to not shoot, the monkeys almost impossible for Lucas to ignore, but because we were both so tired already, and the last thing we needed was something else weighing us down, we grimly ignored the game and kept plodding on trying to find the river. All of a sudden, almost from right beside me, sprang a tapir! I about had a major coronary right there, I'll tell you. Out of habit, I gave the shrill whistle and the stupid thing skidded to a stop, stomped his foot, and turning back, looked right at me whistling. I whistled again just to see what it would do, still not believing the thing wasn't galloping out of there. Normally, a frightened tapir is so far gone after the first couple of seconds that it is only a distant memory. This one had its head up and its long trunk extended, trying to get a sniff of whatever had startled it. The breeze was from it to me, so my scent was not giving me away, and because I was whistling like a tapir, it must have figured I was a tapir. Remembering Gary saying if you are really noisy, you can run right up on a tapir, I decided to try it. I whistled again and took off running right at the tapir. This one must have gone a long time in solitary, because suddenly it decided I was right where it wanted to be. With a huge lunge it came running right back at me. Lucas yelled and sprang up into the low-hanging branches of a tree and I stopped, still not thinking there was any danger. I knew that as soon as it got close enough it would either get a good look at me or catch a whiff of my scent and be gone. But it came on, charging like a mad rhino or something.

"Now why in the world can't you do that when I am really hunting you!" I shrieked at it to try and stop its mad rush, but it kept coming. I did not want to kill it, as there was no way we could use its meat. We had no idea where we were, let alone where the boat was, we had been walking almost two days by this time and had no idea of the ground we had covered. But this tapir was getting too close. I raised my rifle and quickly shot, trying really to graze it, and hoping the noise of the shot going off would stop him. Well, it did; he skidded to a halt scant feet from me. About that time, he finally did get a good look at me and turned and was gone. Like I said, when you are lost, the animals come out to taunt and torment you.

And now we were hunting again, and we needed meat more than ever. But no tapir answered us as we whistled, and when we arrived at the lick it was empty and quiet. We stayed there whistling, hoping one would come to it, but while it was obvious from the very fresh tracks and sign around that they were really using this lick, it was just as obvious that if we waited too much longer it would start getting dark on us, and Gary would probably just leave us and go home. So we turned to head back. We were still hunting, so I kept whistling and Julio angled our path slightly so that we would not be retracing our trail in, but still be heading back out to the river. I did notice that the angle of the sun and its direction were not where they would be if we were heading directly back to the boat, but figured Julio had his own way back to the boat laid out in his mind.

After almost two hours, he suddenly turned to me and asked, "Hey, which way is the boat?"

"OK, Julio, I deserve that, since I made you all waste two days looking for us when we were lost, but you don't have to rub it in," I told him with a grin. "The river is that way."

He stared at me with a funny look on his face. "Are you sure?" he asked.

"Come on, Julio, it is not funny any longer, OK? You tell me which way the river is," I told him.

"Maikiwä, I don't know, it is as if I am all mixed up right now. I don't know," he kept repeating.

I still looked at him, not quite believing he was not pulling my leg. The Yanomamö love practical jokes, and I would give Julio a lot to poke fun at if I panicked and began to rush around, so I determined I would just stay calm and nonchalant. Besides, the last time we were lost, panicking probably added a day and a half to our ordeal, so I had had enough of panics, I'll tell you. They were exciting adventures, and yes, even a tiny bit fun in a twisted kind of way, but when it was over, you were left with a lot of ground to try and recover and as the panic subsided you were left jittery and nervous. No, I did not need to panic this evening. Besides, how far could we have come?

Julio kept looking around. He called in the high falsetto voice they use that carries for great distances in the jungle; we both cocked our heads to listen, but heard nothing. Julio made a vine circle for his feet and, leaning his gun against a tree, began to climb. Higher and higher he climbed until he was up above the second canopy and disappeared into the leaves and vines on into the third canopy. I heard him call again, and again I listened, straining my ears to hear anything coming from Gary or Timoteo. I still was not that concerned. My goodness, how far could we have gone in just a couple of hours?

Well, at 11:00 p.m., as we were still following a tiny little stream that Julio and I had finally come to around 7:00 p.m., I again wondered how far we could have come. By the way, when we found the stream, it was barely a wet spot, hardly flowing, but I knew that sooner or later that little stream would get bigger and finally have to dump out into our river. So we had faithfully followed it since then, and while it might finally get to the river, I hoped we would live long enough to appreciate it. It was sure taking its time. Speaking of time, my little mini-mag was starting to show that we had been using it for too long. The batteries were getting very weak.

We twisted and turned to force our way through a section of jungle that was so thick and full of vines that I could barely fit between them. Even with Julio trying to slash his way through with his machete, it was all we could do to slowly inch our way along, and in one particular place we actually had to get down and crawl on our bellies to get past. The area was in low swampy ground and the cold wet leaves left my chest and belly slimy after I stood back up. I knew this was prime snake habitat and I hoped my guardian angel was on his toes tonight. The last thing I wanted was to all of a sudden feel the hot flash of snake fangs on my bare ankle.

By this time the creek we were following had in truth become a real creek. Its waters were dark and brooding. We had, while it was still a baby creek, just waded through it, because it was easier walking, but now it was deep and in the feeble, dimming light of my mini-mag flashlight was black and sinister looking. Every once in a while we would take turns calling in the high-pitched voice that the Yanomamö use when they are in trouble, hoping that our sound would carry to the river and Gary or Timi would hear us and call back. How we wanted to find that boat! I figured that Gary and Timi had gotten tired and had probably gone on home already. I could just imagine them convincing themselves that we had found the tapir lick so fresh that we had decided to sleep there and wait for one to come to the lick so we could get it.

I jumped back as a loud explosion of wings and feathers took off right above us. It landed on a branch a bit further up, and Julio gestured for me to shoot it. It was a curassow bird. I dejectedly shook my head; the last thing I wanted was something else to carry. Julio motioned me to pass him my rifle. I passed it to him, figuring that if he shot it, he could carry it. I did not even want to carry my rifle any longer. Julio took careful aim, barely able to see it in the struggling beam of my dying light. I heard the shot and further up heard the thud of the small round hitting the bird; with a crash of branches, the bird thudded into the ground almost at my feet.

Julio picked it up, pulled one of the many vines growing there, and tied up the bird, leaving a strap that went around his shoulders so that he could carry it and still leave his hands free. Picking up my rifle, I waited for Julio to finish with his preparation and start chopping trail again. I was becoming very concerned about the light, or rather the absence of light, emanating from the end of my mini-mag.

By this time, it was after midnight and Julio called one more time. I felt he was calling more in desperation than anything else, but then, faintly, in the distance, we heard a motor coming up the river in the night. How we hoped they would stop the motor close enough to allow our calls to be heard! Actually, I had no idea where we were. I knew we had covered a lot of ground, and judging by the size of the creek we were following, the only one I thought it could be was the large creek that emptied into the Metaconi up by where Octavio had built a garden. If that were the case, we had covered a *lot* of ground, but there just were not any other creeks on this side of the river. We kept going, hoping our light would last just a bit longer.

We stopped to listen again for the motor. It was still making its slow way upriver. How I hoped that it would stop close enough to our position that we could be heard and picked up. The motor kept coming and I held my breath. Sure enough, we heard it slow down and stop. Julio was quicker than I was, and he immediately started calling. I was tremendously thankful to hear Gary answer, but in spite of the distance, I could hear the exasperation in his voice. "What in the heck are you all doing up here?" he yelled. (Of course he was yelling in Yanomamö, but that's pretty close to the equivalent of what he said.) I yelled back that Julio had gotten us lost. Right from the start I wanted them to know it was Julio to blame and not me. I was afraid I would start getting a reputation for getting lost. Gary came back with, "Well, get out here! I want to get home. It's 2:00 a.m.!"

"Gary, send Timi in with your flashlight," I yelled back. "Our light is dead." Sure enough, I turned the beam to shine it in my face, and I could barely tell it was on.

"Sorry, my bulb died just as we pulled over here. You will have to just come on over in the dark," he told us. I could hear Julio moving around.

"Well, let's go," I told him.

"Maikiwä, it is all thorns, I don't know where we can go without a light." He kept feeling around in the darkness and I joined him, trying to find a break in all the growth around us. Everywhere our groping fingers felt, I felt the sharp points of long, jagged thorns.

"Julio, we could just swim," I suggested, hoping he would say no.

"Gariwä, where is your boat parked?" Julio called. "We might just swim out. Are you parked beside the mouth of the creek?"

I shuddered, visualizing that dark, forbidding waterway. The last thing in the world I wanted to do was start swimming in that water.

"Yes, we are right beside it." They were far enough away that it was hard to make out what he was saying, but there was no mistaking the urgency in his voice. "Hurry, the mosquitoes are eating us alive," Gary called back, swatting another handful of mosquitoes off of his bare arm. He should have saved his energy, as another flock immediately landed and began to gorge themselves on his shuddering flesh.

Julio and I stepped into the water. It was cold and so pitch black I could see absolutely nothing in front of my face. I waited to hear whether Julio was getting in the water with me, as I would have really hated to be in it by myself, and I did hear his sharp intake of breath as the cold water came up to his chest. By that time I was already swimming. The ground had been so soft and squishy underfoot that I had pulled my legs up and just started swimming. The bad thing was, I have hunted these creeks at night, and when you shine a light on the bottom of the creek you always see stingrays, electric eels, and enough anacondas to know they are around. Believe me, there were a lot of places I would have rather been than swimming in that Stygian creek. The arroyo was not that easy to get through, either, as there were vines and logs haphazardly scattered across our path. The only reason we thought the creek offered us the best chance was because we could not see anything—and once we were swimming, it was too late. Limbs in the water kept catching my clothes, scaring me into thinking something was grabbing me. I tried keeping my rifle out of the water, but I was so labored getting past all the obstacles that I finally gave up and just swam with it under water. Slowly we began to make headway, and eventually we got close enough that we could hear Gary and Timi laughing at us in the dark.

"Your light bulb really better be blown," I yelled to them. "If it is still good when we get there, I am going to throw you both in the river and leave you all here."

And we were not out of the woods yet—or should I say, out of the creek. We came to a huge deadfall that we could not see in the dark but had to explore with our hands in the darkness. There are so many things that sting, bite, grab, or even embrace you, like an anaconda's squeeze, that we were not overexuberantly exploring, either. We just wanted to find a way around, over, or under this new obstacle blocking our way. Julio was still carrying his silly curassow bird around his neck and I could picture what we would look like to a casual observer, swimming down this black river in the dead of night.

After an eternity swimming in that creek, we finally made it out to the boat. As I was climbing aboard, I expected one or two things to happen. First of all, I anticipated being grabbed and pulled back into the water by something rising out of the deep, as is so common in movies; second, I expected Gary or Timi to all of a sudden "fix" the headlight they had with them. In fact, neither of those two things happened, and Julio and I managed to find the boat in the darkness and climb aboard.

As we lay in the bottom of the boat getting our breath back, I grinned as I heard Julio trying to explain both how he had gotten lost that close to the river, and how in the world we were coming out way up here from where we had gone in. "Wait a minute," I interrupted him, "the only reason we made it out when we did was because when we came to that creek, I insisted we follow it. If we had kept going the way you were taking us, who knows where we would have come out?"

"You know, Maikiwä is right," he admitted. "I just don't know what happened. But enough of this. Let's go home."

13

Pets and Other Things That Go Bump in the Night

Suddenly I was wide awake. What had awakened me? The night was pitch black. Not a sound could be heard. I lay awake for a few moments trying to figure out what I had heard and trying to make sure it posed no danger to me. I was still half asleep, and after a few minutes of lying there staring into the night without hearing anything more, I settled back into my hammock and slipped back to sleep.

Without warning, a huge claw hooked onto the side of the hammock, jerking me awake once more. I lay there staring into the night wondering if I had just been dreaming. Suddenly, my hammock lurched as another massive claw grabbed the other side of the hammock and I felt the weight of something hanging below me. My heart thudded madly! This was finally for real! I was under attack by something I could not see and had no way of defending myself against. I felt the animal moving under me, attempting to get a better purchase on the hammock. At any moment I expected to feel the claws getting a better purchase on my flesh. I wondered if I could make a mad dash to safety, but which way was safety? And where was I? It was so black, and the animal hanging under me had caused my mind to freeze up so thoroughly, that I had no idea which way was up.

The opposite arm moved and I waited to see what it would do. I was afraid it would swing on up and onto me. I held my breath waiting for the arm to fall, but what seemed a lifetime later, it swung ponderously against the hammock and again I felt the claw grip. Something in the movement suggested a slowness that got my frozen brain moving. Slothful movement? Holy Toledo, I'm under attack by a giant three-toed sloth!

Where in the heck am I anyway? I had assumed, when I was awakened by this vicious animal attack, that I must be sleeping out in the jungle. Slowly my mind spun around until it clicked into place; I remembered that instead of bedding down in my hammock on some hunting trip in the jungle, I was housesitting for my sisters!

I was under attack by their stupid pet sloth! Well, how long was I going to be held hostage by a pet sloth? Not very long, I will tell you. I jumped out of the hammock and fumbled to the place I had left my flashlight. Feeling around in the dark, my trembling hands finally located it. Grabbing it up, I clicked it on, shining it at the hammock—and sure enough, there, hanging under the hammock and wondering what all the commotion was about, was my sister's sloth, Kaily. My heart was still thudding and I wondered how in the world I could convince it to let go of my hammock.

Taking a broom handle, I used it to pry the beast's claws off the one side of the hammock and then, on its own, apparently figuring out what I wanted it to do, the sloth transferred its other claws to the broom handle. I carried it out of the room, holding it at arm's length with the broom handle and put it down.

"And stay out," I told it. "You ain't sleeping with me!" I locked the door and tried to calm down enough to go back to sleep.

Those crazy girls, I thought to myself. One of these days I'm going to have a heart attack and it's going to be *their* fault! They have to be the only people in the world who have sloths for house pets and even train them to use the commode. No, not to drink out of, as do many domestic animals in the USA. My sisters' sloths knew what to do with a commode and did it! Pity the poor person who walks in on one, though. They never have learned to lock the door, and the sight of a full-grown three-toed sloth sitting on a commode (or rather, *in* a commode) is something you have to experience to believe.

As I lay there in the dark trying to go back to sleep, I thought back on all the animals we have had as pets. Well, my sisters had most of them, but since I had to put up with them as well, I don't think it's exaggerating to use the pronoun *we.*

Let's see, from the cat family there were jaguars, cougars, ocelots, and margays. Then there were anteaters, honey bears, deer, armadillos, wolverine-like animals, coatimundis, and even shrews and possums from who-in-the-heck-knows what-all families. There were tapir, pacas, agoutis, wild pigs, water otters, turtles (both water and land), alligators, and fish. Next came the feathered fowl: hawks, eagles, owls, toucans, macaws (both the scarlet and the deep red), blue and gold macaws, green parrots, and miscellaneous parakeets. Additionally, there were doves, woodpeckers, hummingbirds (almost all the species), small quail-like birds, grey trumpeters, cock of the rocks, curassow (birds of the three varieties we have here in Amazonas), and various kinds of egrets and herons, along with different species of orioles. Actually the list goes on and on, with more birds than I care to try to name, as I only know their names in the Yanomamö language.

What a zoo it usually was! I can't believe my poor mom put up with all that, though on some days she put up with them with less patience than on others. There was always something underfoot in our home. We felt badly taking their freedom away and thus never kept anything in cages, so they literally *were* underfoot. Sometimes that was to the humans' disadvantage: with a shrill shriek, our dad or mom would start dancing and high-stepping around the room, much to the amusement of us kids. But our entertainment was always short-lived, because once the dancing stopped, the animal in question was almost always banished from the house until tempers had a chance to subside. And sometimes the shriek was from the animal instead of our parents, especially one of the smaller ones that couldn't move out of the way fast enough and got stomped into the mud of our dirt floor. They sometimes recovered, but more times did not, and were buried out in our yard with the tears and ceremony normally reserved for important dignitaries. In the early days a huge funeral was always called for, and we consoled ourselves with the knowledge that God, knowing how important the pet was to our happiness, would undoubtedly take it to heaven for our continued enjoyment. As we got older, though, we just buried the dead pets out in the yard with barely a prayer.

I might add that today, people probably would find it strange that we would play church instead of cowboys and Indians, or school, or something else. But we were always playing church (when we weren't having an animal funeral, that is). Gary was always the preacher, and he did pretty well. I remember that after one of his sermons, one of our friends, an MK just the same age as I was, went forward and actually got saved! I think it was real, too. For the rest of our growing-up years, she always spoke about that time when we were playing church and Gary was preaching and she got saved.

Back to the pets: Most were good for entertainment, but none more so than the green parrots. These learned to talk like you would not believe and were always good for a laugh. That is, until our resident green parrot, Salty, learned to chant like a witch doctor. He even had the dance down, and Dad, always on the alert for a break in our defenses in the spiritual battle, was beside himself trying to make the parrot stop chanting.

"As much as we sing in this house, why can't the crazy bird learn something like 'How Great Thou Art?'" he wailed.

Well, we had to go out to town, and the parrot went with us. Much to my dad's relief, he finally quit chanting . . . but he picked up some very spicy language from the neighbors that was, if anything, worse than the witch doctor's chants. That vulgar parrot would sit in our yard and screech the filthiest obscenities at the top of his lungs at any and all passers-by. Most would whip their heads around to see who was yelling at whom, but once they saw the parrot they would hurry on by, probably figuring that if the parrot had it down so pat, who knew what the real people would sound like if they were riled up? Needless to say, Salty was a continual embarrassment to my poor dad.

We finally left town for TamaTama where we were supposed to be going to school, but there, to make matters worse (along with swearing, which he never did drop), Salty began to attack other missionaries, one man in particular. He would lie in wait and ambush the poor guy. His aim was very good and he would swoop down and nail the guy right on his bald spot. After he tired of this, he then learned he could fly up behind the poor man and grab ahold of his pants leg. With one claw on each pants leg, hanging behind the guy's rear, Salty could bite him on his derriere with impunity, as the guy went hopping madly around swatting at his rear with his hat and yelling to beat the band. Meanwhile, the parrot was laughing and swearing at the top of his lungs, further adding to the confusion.

"That parrot has got to go! I can't have it attacking my coworkers and swearing like a sailor!" Dad informed us one day. This was after the parrot had once again cornered the missionary and had caused him to so lose his temper that, after finally dislodging the parrot, he had flung his hat to the ground and stomped on it in his frustration and anger. The fact that the parrot sat right above him in the branches, laughing and swearing, did nothing to alleviate his foul mood.

We took Salty back up to Cosh and left him there with some friends while we finished our year of schooling in TamaTama. But even there, the parrot was not on its best behavior. It quickly learned it could make people angry by calling out different names it overheard. Remember, names are very much taboo to the Yanomamö, especially their childhood names; if your name is used, it is cause for much embarrassment and anger. Of course, as is the case in every crowd, there was someone who was all too willing to exacerbate the situation. Finding the parrot in a rare good mood, two boys sat down with it and patiently repeated to him the names of the people they did not like. A short time later, they were gratified to hear the parrot yelling out the names loudly and continuously. Well, this went over real big, I can tell you! Not too long after that, poor Salty, while heading south, ran into a hard-thrown northbound spear, and so Salty was finally and forever shut up. Even now, many years later, he is still good for a chuckle or two. If pressed, even Dad can remember a few nice things about the old bird, though he does have to work at it.

Yes, our pets were always good for a laugh. Well, it depends on who you ask, I guess. Take the case of Pooper, Sandy's little water otter. I might say right off, he was well named—though he could equally well have been named Stinker; mercy! Anyway, while a very young pup, he somehow got it into his head that my sister-in-law Marie's rug was his territory, and no matter how many times she shooed him away, he always came home—home to poop, that is. He could be way out swimming in the river, and all of a sudden he would drop whatever he was doing and make a beeline for Marie's rug. I don't think Marie ever actually swore at Pooper, but I'm sure the words were right on her tongue, because as soon as that otter got to her rug, it would let loose. After a shrill scream from Marie, Pooper would come bombing out their front door, heading for parts unknown, and Marie would once again have to clean another of Pooper's "indiscretions" off her freshly cleaned rug.

Speaking of territory, as he got older, Pooper decided that the entire waterfront was his own: anyone swimming or passing by in a boat was stopped and interrogated. This otter was as bold as any tax collector and would climb into the Yanomamö's dugouts and pick through their fish, selecting the largest one as if he were some kind of short, four-legged tollbooth operator. If anyone tried to talk themselves into a lower tax bracket, they were met with a stern discourse and a large showing of teeth. If they still fussed, the rude tax collector picked up the fish he wanted and just left the boat, with the poor owners yelling and angry.

Thankfully, we found him a good home before anything got really out of hand (well, he did bite a missionary who had come up on a consulting trip about the New Testament, but the guy was a good sport, so I won't count that). Anyway, before things got too bad, we had in town one of the many investigating commissions that were always coming up to investigate us about something, and someone from the governor's staff suggested that we send the otter out as a gift to the governor, as he was trying to start a small zoo. So our playful little Pooper went to a fine life in the city where he could claim all the territory he wanted. It took poor Marie years before she was able to relax, though. She was just sure that single-minded otter would get away from the governor and beeline the 269 nautical miles back up to her rug!

My mind made a huge circle and returned to the sloth as I lay there in the dark. I remembered another time the sloth had about caused me to go into cardiac arrest. My sisters left to head back to the USA for awhile, and Keila and I agreed to watch their sloths. "Well," I told Keila after about a week with the crazy things, "I know why the girls are always so tired. Those sloths don't sleep at night, but are moving all over the place, bumping and knocking stuff over all night long. I never have heard such commotions in the house. Those girls probably never get a good night's sleep! How in the world are we going to last for three months with stuff going bump all night long? I just pray one doesn't get the idea it is going to start sleeping with us!" I whined.

Then, to make matters worse, one morning about 5:30 a.m., Stephen, our youngest son, got up to use the bathroom. His blood-curdling shriek set me bolt upright in bed.

"It's drowned! It's drowned!" he wailed at the top of his lungs. "They ask us to watch their pets, and we had to go and drown one!"

Keila, Josh, Ryan, and I rushed into the bathroom to find out what the commotion was about. There, peeking sleepily out from under the lid of the commode, was one of the stupid sloths! It had gotten up at night to use the toilet, and somehow the lid had fallen on it. Because it wasn't strong enough to lift the lid back up, it had decided to just take a catnap while waiting for the rest of the house to wake up and release it from its precarious and stinky predicament. Well, it was awake now! And boy, were we awake! I just hoped Stephen's wails took the same amount of time off the sloth's life as had been subtracted from my own.

Then there was the oriole, who was named Sherbie. He would perch on your shoulder, literally standing on his tiptoes to lean forward enough that he could turn around and stare at your mouth. If he detected a piece of candy or chewing gum, he waited his chance. When you opened your mouth to move your gum, or if you were one of those whose tendency was to chew with your mouth open, well, you wouldn't keep your gum long, I can tell you that. One day, Jerald decided to play a trick on Sherbie. He got a rubber band and, putting it in his mouth, began to work it around like the best-chewing, juiciest piece of gum he had ever chewed. Sherbie came swooping down and stared at his mouth. If birds could lick their lips, Sherbie would have been having a party just on the saliva he was generating. Finally, Jerald gave him the chance he was waiting for. Seeing his opening—literally—Sherbie jabbed his beak into Jerald's mouth and snatched what he thought was a piece of gum, but really the rubber band. Jerald had a death grip on the other end of the band between his own teeth and the oriole started tugging. Finally, the frantic bird worked his feet to where he had one on each side of Jerald's mouth and was tugging for all he was worth, but the rubber band just kept stretching. Jerald finally let it go and the satisfied bird took off with his prize. To this day, I don't know if the bird realized that Jerald had played a trick on him, or if he went to his grave thinking that Jerald just had bad taste in gum.

That oriole was always good for a lot of laughs. He just flew wild, and when he was in the big mango tree where a family of orioles had their nests, it was impossible to tell him from all the myriad of other similarly colored birds—but Mom could always get him to come down. She would walk outside with a piece of candy and start unwrapping it and before she could even get finished, Sherbie would be sitting on her shoulder begging for a piece.

Space does not allow me to tell all about the turkey that held Ryan hostage. I will say that we finally figured the poor kid was being traumatized too much by this big bully of a bird, so Gary went out and put him out of Ryan's misery. Ry was the happiest boy alive there for awhile, and about four times a day he would go over to Gary's house and ask to look in the freezer. Seeing that big old bird in there was the highlight of his day for a while. Of course, we just about had to put him in counseling when they took the bird out for our Thanksgiving dinner. Ryan just could not understand where the bird had gone and was afraid he was going to be attacked again. He had felt safe as long as it was there where he could check it every day, but once it disappeared, he didn't know what to think.

Then there was the capuchin monkey who had delusions of being a boxer. His sparring partner was an unwilling banty rooster that was never smart enough not to get into the ring with the monkey. Well, there wasn't an actual ring, but anyway, the monkey would come up to the rooster and challenge him to a match. The rooster would do its best to ignore the obnoxious monkey but would finally give in. The monkey would assume his boxing stance, weaving and bobbing. The rooster would try its hardest to keep up with the weaving and darting monkey. Finally, it would grab an opening and lunge at the monkey, but the monkey would fade away until the rooster's neck was extended to its max, and then he would spring in himself. Grabbing the extended neck right behind the head with one hand and the beak of the rooster with the other, the little monkey would rub the rooster's head in the dirt for all he was worth. Timing his rubbing just right, the monkey would fade back away just in time to miss the raking spurs of the humiliated banty. This would go on until the little banty managed to escape the clutches of the monkey and run, always swearing he would never get back in the ring. But the next day, the monkey would somehow talk the rooster back for another round.

And what can I say about Thalami? This was another green parrot who somehow learned from Sharon how to sing "Oh, I wish I were an Oscar Mayer wiener." Crazy thing even had the tune down. We did try to get it on film, but the bird was camera-shy and wouldn't so much as open its beak when it detected a camera, microphone, or anything else. I had dreams of taking his picture as he was singing the song and seeing if the Oscar Mayer

Company might be interested in it, but like I said, just my luck, the parrot was camera-shy.

We learned a lot from our pets. Thinking back on all the fun times we had with each one, I once again realize how absolutely blessed we were to be allowed to grow up on the mission field in the Amazon jungle.

14

To Fly

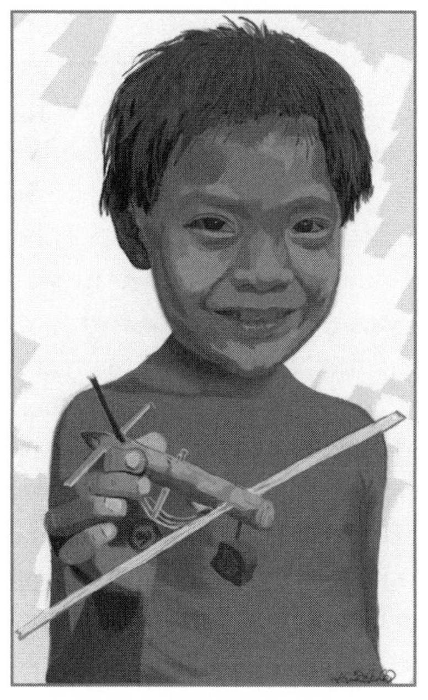

I looked up from pulling yet another rivet . . . one of perhaps millions of rivets. Of course I didn't actually count them; who counts the stars? Suffice to say, there were enough rivets to keep someone foolish enough to start counting busy for a *long* time. These pieces of aluminum and rivets would one day be an airplane; at least, that is what the kit manual said it would be. The demonstration video made it look so simple, and in spite of the difficulties, we were making good progress, mostly because of the help we were receiving from Art Mitchell of Flypass. We were building the plane up in his hangar in Canada, so we were in good hands. When Art heard what we wanted this plane for, he quickly offered his services and his hangar, an offer I was only too glad to take him up on. This little plane would one day be used to take the precious gospel of Jesus Christ to even more faraway villages.

As we worked on this plane, our little Zenith Air CH 801, I couldn't help but remember another attempt at building an "air mobile." Frannie Cochran and I were up in Parima, holding down the base while the missionary couple that worked there went out for the New Tribes annual field conference. When we were not attending to the medical needs of the people, which in this village included doctoring a very badly burned young girl, we had a lot of free time on our hands. As we walked up the open grasslands of the Parima savanna, with the wind blowing our clothes about our bodies on one of our many trips to the *shabono* to tend to the girl again, we began to talk about the wind, and how neat it would be if we could make a hang glider and use it to jump off one of the hills in front of the missionaries' house. How cool would that be? Why, maybe we could even get enough distance that we could just hang-glide into the village, we decided. Wouldn't that be a riot! In our minds we could see the Indians' faces as we swooped down and stalled just feet above the ground, doing a perfect two-point landing in the middle of their village.

The next morning we started collecting the materials needed for this project. Our anticipation was such that neither of us even considered the possible danger we might be putting ourselves in, and never once worried that the materials we were finding and collecting might not be airworthy. First we discovered an old tarp (we figured the missionary would not mind us using it; we could put it back, after all); then dug up some binding twine to tie the tarp to some poles; and then, armed with machetes, we marched out into the surrounding jungle to find three long, straight poles. In the interest of safety, we did choose hardwood poles, not once worrying about weight.

We had seen pictures of hang gliders in books, so we knew the basic shape, but by the time we found and cut the poles, lashed the poles together with some baling wire, and tied our tarp on it, our excitement was such that we didn't notice that the contraption bore little resemblance to the sleek, aerodynamic shape we were trying to copy out of the book. One of the reasons for the lack of aerodynamic form was that, at the last minute, reason prevailed, and we decided we should not cut the tarp. The missionary might forgive us for using it, but we figured it might stretch his grace if we were to cut it in the form of a triangle, as had been our first thought. So we just curled the edges up and tied them up to the pole, not realizing that this huge bump on the leading edge of the wing was going to kill all our lift—not to mention all the parasitic drag it would cause, further compromising our efforts to fly.

This tarp was of the old style and material used by the army, and possibly even *was* an old army surplus canvas tarp (not to be confused with the lightweight tarps sold by stores such as Wal-Mart), so it was heavy! Especially because we were using the complete tarp, the combination of the weight of our hardwood poles and the tarp made our aircraft so heavy we could barely stagger under its weight, let alone run enough to build up the speed we needed to get airborne. This small point did not bother us: we figured we would just jump off the mountain. Once it was all together, though, possibly because it was almost too heavy to get it *up* the mountain, or more likely because our moms were praying for us, we decided we needed to learn how to fly the thing low before just jumping off the mountain, as had been our first thought. The wind blew straight down the airstrip, so that gave us the perfect flat place to learn on, and also provided a good landing area ahead of us, we reasoned.

Well, you should have seen us: first one, then the other galloping up the airstrip against the wind, springing up into the air only to come crashing back down. More times than not, each time we came crashing down, it required a trip back to home base to wire our flying machine back together.

We decided our problem was speed, or rather lack of speed. We enlisted the help of some of the Yanomamö who were continually around offering advice. It made no difference that they had never built a hang glider, nor that they hadn't even ever seen one; they were vocal in their criticism and free with their instructions.

Once again rummaging through the missionaries' stuff, we found a long nylon rope. Tying the rope to Frannie's waist, the Yanomamö and I made ourselves ready on the other end of the rope. As we began to run up the strip towing young Mr. Cochran, he ran behind us with the huge canvas tarp "kite" cocked into the wind. At any minute, I expected him to levitate into the air, and began to imagine how I would brag to our doubting friends. But although Fran was running hard behind us, and ever so often would lunge into the air, he always came back down, hardly getting any lift from the contraption at all. I could tell Frannie was giving up. He was hanging back, causing us to slow down despite our best efforts at sprinting down the airstrip.

I was beginning to doubt our aeronautic abilities myself. Not outwardly, of course, but to myself. To make matters worse, our Yanomamö friends from the village were also doubting our abilities, and they did not have the decency to keep their doubts to themselves; as usual, they were vociferous in their ridicule and laughter.

"How many flying things have you-all built?" I asked, finally letting my irritation show. "My people have been building flying things for a long time. They even flew to the moon! What have you all flown? Don't be so quick to give up! My people did not fly the first day they tried, but they did not give up. We can do this, we just need more wind. Tomorrow there will be more wind and you will see us fly! Come back and run with us tomorrow and you will see!" My logic made sense to some, but others insisted we were never going to fly.

To be honest, we did not fly up there in Parima, but it was not for want of trying. We galloped up and down that airstrip with a determination that would have made the Wright brothers proud, but we just could never get off the ground. Now, looking back at the less-than-aircraft-grade materials we were trying to fly with, and given the benefit of time, how thankful I am that we never did actually get airborne! Still, our Yanomamö friends were disappointed, and Frannie and I were ashamed that we could not pull it off. After trying for two weeks with no success, it came time for us to head on back out to school, and our Yanomamö friends were big-hearted and forgiving. "Well, come back and we will run some more," they told us as we were preparing to board the plane to go home. "One day there will be enough wind."

I smiled and assured them that we would be back and fly with them. I appreciated the fact that they did not rub our noses in our failure, as I knew they could have.

And now, here I was again trying to make a flying machine, and you know what? The skeptics were just as vocal, but this time they were friends and family, not the Yanomamö.

In spite of the skepticism, the plane came together, rivet by rivet, piece by piece. A few flimsy ribs and some sheets of aluminum held together with rivets, and we had a vertical stabilizer, then the rudder. Next came the horizontal stabilizer, and then we started on the wings. To be honest, few things in life can give as much pleasure as we got from watching that little plane come together. We had decided the plane was going to have its final assembly in Venezuela, as I had been told by an official that it would be easier to license it as Venezuelan-built than to fly it in and register it there. Nevertheless, we did put it all together on the weekend before the ship date and held a dedication service for it there at the Flypass hangar. As we formed a circle of friends and family around that little airplane, tears came to my eyes as I dreamed of the great things God was going to do with this unique tool.

The story of this little plane is still being written. We flew it here in the jungle for almost two years. We had many fine adventures with it, but due to an ongoing struggle with the engine, were finally forced to ground it, and the engine was shipped back to the USA. We figured we would sell that engine and use the funds to purchase another engine.

A church in Boston offered to partner with us in raising funds. We made a video showing the contrast between using a boat and the same trip with the little plane. How excited we were when we were told that the special offering for the engine had amounted to $40,500. In one Sunday! We were ecstatic. We had exceeded our goal of $35,000.

I was disappointed when I received a call saying that the church had decided the funds could be used only if we purchased a "certificated" airplane. We discussed this with the base and other close supporters and eventually made the difficult decision to forgo the experimental, home-built airplane in favor of a certificated Cessna 172. I honestly thought this would be the fastest way back into the air for us.

We asked different experts in the field what would be the best modifications to make our 172 the best little bush plane that money could buy. It took a while to get these modifications done, as everything in aviation is very expensive, but finally the plane was ready. The plane *is* ready, but for some reason still unknown to me, it seems the Lord is saying "Wait." We haven't been able to get the necessary documentation to import the plane. We have looked at many options, but so far nothing has worked.

Meanwhile, back to the CH 801. I had loaned two DVDs to a good friend while we were at the air show in Oshkosh and he took them around and showed them to the people of Zenith Air, the company that makes the CH 801 kit plane. They were amazed to see how we had been using their little airplane and were pleased to see it used in a place where it was so obviously needed. When they found out it was still down for lack of an engine, they decided to see what they could do to help. They invited me to their aircraft builder's dinner and once everyone was seated they showed the DVD of the airplane flying in Amazonas. When it was over, they explained to everyone that the little plane was down for a new engine, and anyone who wanted to help could do so. They, as a company, offered to donate all the items needed to complete the engine installation. This was a huge endorsement and commitment. We have been astonished at the response. Along with donations of funds to purchase the engine, friendships have been formed and relationships established.

The engine has been purchased and is now sitting out in Puerto Ayacucho. We have been trying for the past two years now to get permission either to bring the engine up here or to take the fuselage out to town, with no success. These are troubled days in Venezuela and we have been encouraged not to do anything that might cause us to stand out. While chafing at the bit with this, the advice is solid, so we are trying to wait on the Lord for His timing. We desperately need this—or any airplane—flying here! Why, I am so desperate, I am about ready to try a hang glider again!

Since the 12th of February 2006, we have been without air support of any kind. But our confidence is in the power of the Lord and we rest in the knowledge that in His time things will come together. Meanwhile, we continue dreaming of the day we will once again be able to fly over our jungle here, visiting the forgotten little villages that are flung out over the breadth of the land. Meanwhile, it is a lesson in patience for me. Looking back at my life, I see that this has been an area I have struggled with forever. I just wish I would learn it already and move on.

15

An End of an Era

Politically, things in this country have always been more or less like walking a tightrope. There is guaranteed freedom of religion, but there is also a national religion recognized by the government. This has caused us many trips out to town and much wasted money responding to needless government investigations. Protestant missionaries working with the indigenous peoples in Amazonas Venezuela are possibly the most investigated group anywhere. One time we were even investigated by members of the U.S. Embassy, under the Carter administration. Why they were included has always eluded me, but to be honest, of all the people that did come up to the jungle to investigate us, the guy from our own embassy was the rudest and most obnoxious to us. Possibly he felt he had to impress the other members of the investigating team about how impartial he could be even against Americans. Possibly he had forgotten the prime directive of embassies, which is to protect the citizens and the interests of *their own* country. Regardless of the reasons, he was insistent about finding something bad for his hosts.

He soon tired of talking with us. I think he felt like he was so high above us, why should he bother? Whatever the reason, he left us and went out by himself to talk alone with the Yanomamö. He found Pablo Mejias, and since Pablo spoke some Spanish, this guy was soon questioning Pablo to his heart's content.

But he was not getting the information he wanted. "Why have you all allowed these people to come in here and change your culture?" the official demanded. (I'm sure he must have given us his name, but I've failed to remember it.)

"All peoples have the right to adjust their culture to meet the needs of their people," Pablo told him. "Why should the Yanomamö be the only ones that have to stay just the same way we have always lived? My friends here have told us that their ancestors rode horses and their horses even pulled their *carros* [carts] around. But now their descendents don't live like that. I am a school teacher here in this village, and even the Venezuelan history books that we teach from here in the school show Simón Bolívar on a white horse. You all did not come in here riding on horses; you flew here in an airplane. Why is it OK for you to change and better your lives, but my people should stay naked, at war, hungry and sick in the jungle? That does not seem right to me."

The embassy person frowned. He was getting worse feedback from this "savage" than he had gotten from the missionaries. As they continued walking up the village, they came to a large trail that led into the jungle. "What is up that trail?" he asked, finally showing some excitement. "Is that where the mine is located?" (They were convinced that we and the Yanomamö had secretly begun illegal mining somewhere close by.)

"No," Pablo smiled, "this trail goes up to where we have cleared some land for some cows that we are trying to raise for meat for the village. But we can't go up it, because it is flooded this time of the year. If you want to go up there, we have to use this other trail." He pointed to a less-traveled trail that split off heading to the right. "This trail here stays on high ground and we use it now that this other trail is flooded."

The official reluctantly allowed Pablo to lead off on the lesser-traveled trail, but Pablo knew he was unhappy about not taking the large trail. They finally arrived at the cattle field and were greeted not by sights of a working mine, but by twelve head of cattle that came up begging for food. These cows were used to us taking them food and were not too happy that no one had brought them anything. One of the calves began to push and bump the official in a rude way, causing him to cut his visit short, but instead of heading back down the trail he had come up on, he walked around until he once again came to the large trail heading back off into the jungle. This was the other end of the trail that Pablo had told him was flooded. Well, it did not look flooded from this end.

"I am going back to the village this way," he told Pablo. "I want to see what is down this trail that you don't want me to see."

"Well, it's a long way to the water, and once we get there, there will not be enough light to turn around and come all the way back here to this other trail before it gets dark, so if you insist that we are going this way, we are going all the way back this way, even if you have to swim," Pablo told him.

"That is fine with me. I don't believe the trail can be that flooded," Pablo was told.

So off they went, Pablo leading the way while the official phrased and rephrased his questions, trying to trap Pablo into spilling where the alleged mine was. They arrived at a place where the wind had blown down a large tree, leaving a huge hole in the ground where the entire root system had pulled up. The official ran up to the hole with a look of sheer ecstasy on his face, thinking he had finally found his proof of the missionaries' misdeeds. Peering down into the large hole, his face fell. Even in the fading light, it was obvious it went nowhere.

"What is this hole for? Who dug it?" The questions came as fast as the man could frame them.

"No one dug it. Can't you see that tree there? It was standing here, the wind blew it over, it fell, and the hole is where the tree stood. There it lays." Pablo shook his head at the obvious stupidity of this educated man. "But we need to hurry or you will be swimming after dark," he told his disappointed ward.

They took off once again, and before they had gone much further, sure enough, came to a place where the trail dipped down. The black water covering the trail looked foreboding and uninviting. Pablo stepped in and started wading, with the water rapidly covering his knees and then his waist and giving every indication that it would only get deeper. The official hesitated.

"How far does this water go?" It was hard for him to keep the whine out of his voice. "I can't swim that much. I did not think there would really be water. Let's go back."

"I told you once we started down this trail, there would not be enough light to go all the way back around. And you need to hurry now or we will be out here swimming in the dark," Pablo told him. "You are taller than I am, it won't be over your head. I only have to swim a little bit, you will be able to walk the entire way. I just hope the stingrays and anaconda snakes won't be out yet." In the gathering darkness, he was able to hide his smile. *This guy is just too easy,* he thought to himself.

The official quickly waded behind Pablo, but he was not happy. About a half-hour later, it was a much more subdued official who came straggling up the trail behind Pablo. His relief at seeing the airstrip, then the village, was almost palpable, according to Pablo, who later recounted the entire incident to us over a cup of coffee after the visiting officials had retired for the night.

During another investigation, I also had a chance to talk to one of the officials. This time it was to a colonel in the Venezuelan military intelligence service, who smugly told me, "We know you all are secretly mining up here. One day we are going to catch you, and it will be over for you."

I looked at him and decided to try another tack. I was so tired of answering that same accusation over and over again! This time, instead of denying anything, I said, "You know, I am going to take that as a compliment." I smiled. He looked at me with a frown. Seeing his puzzled expression, I continued: "You see, we have been investigated by everyone here in Venezuela. We have been questioned by congressional committees, presidential committees, military personnel, judicial committees—why, anyone who is anyone in Venezuela has investigated us, including our own embassy. Also, for the last fifty years, men, women, and children of the Evangelical Missions working with the Indians have been searched both coming out of and going into the jungle, arriving to and departing from the city of Puerto Ayacucho, and also entering and leaving the country. Our stuff has been laid out on the airstrips in the jungle, and every piece of clothing, every bottle of repellant, perfume, or deodorant has been probed and poked. When that same airplane arrives in Puerto Ayacucho, the same stuff has been strewn all over again and the same bottles opened and probed again. And you know what, not once, not once in all that fifty years, in spite of all the investigations and all the searches, have they ever found one piece of evidence, not one grain of gold or diamonds, not anything illegal has ever been found. To me this means one of two things. Either the people doing the investigations and searches are *all* idiots, or we who are 'hiding' the stuff are so incredibly smart. I prefer to think it is us that are so very smart." I finished with a smile so he would not take offense at me calling him an idiot.

He looked at me for a long moment. I thought he was going to be angry, but then he started to smile. *"Tienes razon!"* he told me. "You're right."

Finally, in 2005, things took a huge turn for the worse. The investigations turned harsher and it was obvious that these were more serious than the problematic surveys of the past. Then a well-known televangelist in the United States blundered on live TV and said the Venezuelan president should just be "taken out." As you can imagine, this went over like a lead balloon down here. Immediately, there were repercussions. Because the televangelist was an evangelical preacher . . . well, all the evangelical missionaries were treated as if they were here for the express purpose of "taking out" the president.

An executive order was issued, giving the New Tribes Mission three months to leave all Indian territory. It was a sad day to see the works closed down. After a long and fruitful ministry, the missionaries began closing their bases down and saying their goodbyes. During this same time, government officials began coming up and acting as if they thought we too would be leaving. We realized that we were mistakenly considered New Tribes Missions. As a mission we decided that, while we would not deliberately lie to anyone, we would not volunteer any information, either. So, even while crews were coming in to measure our houses and divvy up everything on our base, we were polite and only tried to show people God's love.

The mission providing our flight service, although they were not named in the resolution against New Tribes, also began to feel the heat that was being directed against all evangelical missions. We met with them to go over our options.

"We are staying until they actually give us orders to leave," we told them. "God has given us a job and our confidence is in

Him. If God closes the door, we will leave, but we want to know it is God, not man, doing the closing."

"Well, we have to think of our assets. You all don't have much to lose up here in the jungle, but our airplanes are worth a lot of money. So we are going to take them out of the country before the deadline. If, after the deadline is over, it looks like the situation is OK, we will return. Officially, we are going on vacation," the program manager told me.

I was disappointed to hear that. I really felt we needed to stand united, but I also knew this was a choice that each mission and even each missionary had to make for themselves. The deadline for leaving was the 12th of February 2006 and it was coming up fast.

Meanwhile, we were being overrun by more and more "visitors." Each government group was coming in to see what we had, what we planned to sell, and what would be left. With each group, we patiently told them we were not planning on leaving, so we were not abandoning or selling anything. They would look at us as if we were totally crazy and then continue making their plans.

One day, word came up the river that the military was coming in to force us to leave. The Indians all rushed to us to see what our reaction would be and what our plans were, and they were told again that we were staying. As of then, we still had not seen anything official, and we were not going to panic over a rumor. We would cross whatever bridge presented itself when we actually arrived at it. They all seemed relieved to hear that, and we realized again how dear these people were to us—and not only us to them, but how dear we, especially my dad and mom, were to them.

The next morning, our early-morning routine was shattered by the *wap-wap-wap* of a large chopper coming in low. After a few passes, it settled down in front of our houses. Suddenly, from all sides came a horde of black-painted warriors armed to the teeth with axes, machetes, spears, war clubs, bows and arrows, and shotguns. The helicopter was completely surrounded by the mob. The villagers had taken matters into their own hands: they had met together the night before and decided it would be up to them to defend us. They were not going to allow us to be touched. Two warriors, painted so black it was almost impossible to identify them, rushed to Dad and Mom's house where they took up positions. "Don't worry!" one of them told my dad, "no one is getting by my brother and me. We are here to defend your house." Dad looked at their primitive weapons and, knowing the weapons of the military, his heart sank. *What can these people do against modern weapons?* he wondered, but his heart swelled with pride and gratitude at the devotion of these brave men.

Meanwhile, there was still a standoff at the helicopter. The Yanomamö would allow no one off. Finally, in exasperation the general called for my brother Gary to translate for him.

Gary went out to the helicopter and was able to talk to the men enough to get them to stand down and allow the military personnel off the chopper. They walked over to the community dining house and the general assured the people that he was not here to take the missionaries out. One of the men spoke up. Although he did not speak very fluent Spanish, he was able to get his point across.

"General," he said, "when the missionaries came here, there were only thirty-five people left in this village. We were dying out. If Pepiwä would not have come, we would all be gone, and this village would not be here. Now we are a village of over five hundred people. We have a good life here now because of the message of peace they have brought us. But we know we would not be alive today if he would not have come. Now you all want all missionaries to leave Yanomamö lands. What the other people do is up to them, but we are saying here today to you, that our missionaries have only been a help to us, and we want them to stay. General, we are prepared to die to keep them here. Are you prepared to kill to take them out?"

The general was obviously shaken. He assured the people it would not come to that. He talked with Gary for a while longer and then he and his people returned to the chopper and left.

We decided we needed to meet with the village. It had not been our intention to push this to the point where they were fighting and killing and being killed for us. One of the men told us, "Listen, this is for us. We know what life was like without the help that we have received from you. We now know about God and His Word and that we will always have. But there is so much that we still need. Also, what do we do if you all are gone and our babies get sick? We might lose a few people if we fight to keep you here, but if we do nothing and you leave, we will lose many more. We are not willing that you leave!"

Many others in the room voiced their agreement, but we still convinced them that our confidence had to be in the Lord and in His ability to keep us here. "God will not be honored if we break His law," we told them.

Though not real happy with our logic, they finally did agree not to take matters into their own hands again. It was obvious to me, however, that this was one of those times when you are darned if you do and darned if you don't. In the bases, where the other mission was working, the people pretty much stood by at the missionaries' request and did nothing. So, all the reports out in town said, "Well, the people really did not much care if the missionaries stayed or left; there was never a word from the people in the missionaries' defense."

In our case, the word out in town was, "Boy, someone should do something about those missionaries. They incited the people and they almost attacked us!" So, like I said, pretty much darned if we did and darned if we didn't.

The year 2006 dawned with heavy clouds looming—not physical clouds, but political. The deadline was only a month away and the only subject talked about was what was going to happen next. Rumors flew back and forth. Two of our own families decided it would be presuming on the Lord to stay in the jungle without flight service and gave us notification that they would be leaving on the last flights out of the jungle and would not return unless our flight-service providers returned.

Things were looking bleak. While maintaining that they were only going on a two-week vacation to see what the reaction would be, it was obvious that this was long-term, as everything they had in town was up for sale, including houses, hangar, vehicles, and all personal belongings.

"No one goes for a two-week vacation and sells everything!" I said to the program manager—and was basically told to get our heads out of the sand! To be honest, his comment really bothered me. In all this, our only desire was to honor our Lord's command. We just did not feel in our hearts that it was the Lord closing the door. We have repeatedly been told in Scripture to expect persecution, and now it seemed that the "right way" was to avoid persecution at all costs. Anyway, I continued to think about his comment as I lay in bed that night, unable to sleep.

"God," I said, "I want to honor You with my life. I desire that everything I do be what You would have me do. But on the other hand, I don't want to cause shame to Your name by acting stupid. Please give us wisdom to know what You would have us do. Are we truly just closing our eyes and hiding our heads in the sand? Please show me Your will." While I was still praying, all of a sudden I just heard this poem in my mind. I am not a poet, never have been. Normally I can't rhyme anything. But then, here came these words, almost like I saw them written down and I was just reading the lines off in my mind.

It was very late at night, and yet, realizing I would never be able to remember them the next morning, I jumped up and turned on my computer. Sitting down, I began to write the words down as I saw them there in my mind. Here is the poem. Like

I said, I am not a poet, so my sister Sandy cleaned it up for me a bit, but this is pretty much what I saw that night in my mind.

We have been called "too stubborn to leave,"
"too blind to see the dangers at hand."
Some say "like the ostrich,
people who bury their heads in the sand."
but–I prefer to think–
that perhaps we are hearing, as Joshua did
a still small voice that bids us
"Stay . . .
be not afraid, neither be thou dismayed,
for I . . . the Lord thy God . . . Am with thee . . ."

Was this the same voice that Daniel heard on that long-ago day
When he opened his window and knelt down to pray?
He recognized he was breaking the law
and to the lions he would fall
when he prayed to God and not the king.

It's the same still small voice that gave confidence
To Shadrach, Meshach, and Abednego
as they listened to the music flow
around them.
They stood straight
and they stood tall
and did not heed the music's call.
They did not bow their knees. Oh no . . .
when the multitudes all around bowed low.
As the flames roared
higher,
brighter,
hotter,
they stood calmly, trusting their Father,
knowing they had to obey a higher authority.
"Oh king, live forever, our God is able to save
from your fire," they said,
"but even if He does not save, we will not bow!"

I Can See the Shore

And was it perhaps this same small voice
that made Paul and Silas sing and rejoice?
Though they had been beaten, they did not give in;
their faith was strong and they trusted in HIM!
And maybe the most amazing thing that was done,
they convinced hardened criminals to stand and not run
as the jail broke down around them.

I think it is the same still small voice
that Elijah heard one stormy day.
He was tired of running from Jezebel,
so frightened and whining
he hid in a cave.
"There's nobody left . . . there's only me,
and I am so sad and so lonely."
Then amazed, he watched the most awesome thing
as the fiery storms of nature pounded around him.
But it was in the silence after the storm
he heard the whisper . . . gentle . . . warm . . .
speaking to him in loving tone,
"Peace, be still . . . you are not alone!"

And as Daniel had to first go to the lions,
Before he knew his Lord's protection;
And the three Hebrew children,
though they had to go through the fire,
there was a fourth man that walked there beside them,
and not a single hair was burned . . .
And Paul and Silas, by refusing to run,
heard the sweetest words spoken to anyone:
"Sirs, what must I do to be saved?"
So God, help me to stand still and see Your salvation
So that I too might hear with great jubilation
"What must I do to be saved?"
And God, help me please
to bring glory and honor to YOU
in all things . . .
and know you are my God
as these great men of old did.

Finally the big day came: February 12, 2006, the day all evangelical missionaries were to be out of the jungle areas. We waited, knowing it would not be too long before people started coming in to see if we had gone, and if we had not, why not? We were not disappointed. On the 13th, back came the chopper. They circled first and finally landed, not in front of our houses, but way down the airstrip. Avoiding the huge blades windmilling above their heads, a contingent of personnel got off the chopper, and quickly it took back off.

We waited in front of our houses for the people to walk up the 700-meter airstrip. They were sweaty and panting after their long walk in the hot sun. We politely asked them if we could get them something cold to drink, which they readily accepted. The Yanomamö crowded into the house with us and stood there. I noticed that there were quite a few weapons in hand, but none were held in a threatening manner. After drinking something cold and after some polite small talk, one of the guys cleared his throat.

"Ahem, we are wondering when you plan on obeying the resolution and evacuating this base?" he said. It was clear he was hoping he was not going to rile anyone up.

"Oh, we are not leaving," I told him with a smile, "that resolution did not name us."

"What do you mean? It was very clear. 'All New Tribes Missionaries have to be out of Indian areas by the twelfth of February.' That was yesterday." He smiled again.

"Well, you see, we are not New Tribes Missionaries," I told him.

He stared at me. "Well, you know it was aimed at all North American missionaries. But are you sure you are not with New Tribes? We have this base listed as a New Tribes base."

"No, sir, we are not even a North American mission. We are just a Venezuelan mission. We are the Misión Padamo," I told him.

"But like I said, this was really very clear that it was aimed at all North American mission groups," he told me again.

I smiled again. "But we are not North American. I am a Venezuelan."

He looked at me with a bit more hostility on his face. "When did you get nationalized?" he asked. I could tell from the look on his face that he was prepared to tell me the government was not going to accept any last-minute nationalizations.

But I continued smiling. It was not my fault he had not done his homework. "Oh, I was *born* here in Amazonas," I told him. "I was born right out here in the jungle, in TamaTama, not even out in town. My parents have lived here since 1953. My wife is also a Venezuelan, and all my children have been born here except for our daughter, but she is also Venezuelan. Seven of us ten children were born here. I have a nephew who is married to a Yanomamö girl and they have five children, so they are also Yanomamö. So, like I said, we did not feel this resolution was directed at us."

He looked at me very intently, as if seeing me for the first time. "Can you prove that? Can you prove you were actually born out here in the jungle?"

"My birth certificate says TamaTama," I told him.

We talked for a while longer, but he was only killing time. Soon we heard the helicopter returning and they ran back down the strip and boarded and left. We all met over at Dad and Mom's house. "I am not sure what happened, but I don't think they expected that," I said.

For the next month or more, there were choppers in here on almost a daily basis. Finally, the head general came up to speak with us. He was a hard man, but had shown a really soft heart to Mikeila on our last trip out to town. While waiting at the terminal for our flight, she had roamed the entire building, going into all the rooms, as she has done every time we had to wait at the airport. Because we know most of the people there, I knew they did not mind her visiting, and most seemed to enjoy it, so we just let her roam. She went everywhere, even into offices and way back into the kitchen of the restaurant. Mikeila never met a stranger; she could go anywhere and smile and before you knew it had made another friend. Well, on this day we waited longer than normal for our plane to come over to the terminal and Mikeila wandered into the temporary office the military command had set up there. The next thing Keila and I knew, the general was bringing her out to us. It was obvious he had a soft spot for children and he was laughing and joking with her. Although Mikeila could not talk, she had a way of getting her point across. When giving her back to us, the general told Keila. "Here, take care of my little *catire gringa* [blond gringa]." We laughed and Mikeila waved a cheery goodbye to him.

Now this same general was in charge of the entire zone and it was clear that we were an embarrassment to him. When he saw us, it was obvious he recognized us from the airport. He looked at Keila and Mia and then looked around as if searching for someone else. Then, turning to Keila, he asked her, "Where is my little *gringa*?"

With tears running down her cheeks, Keila told him that Mikeila had passed away just a few weeks earlier.

"What happened? Why was she not taken out to the hospital?" he demanded.

"We tried, we called and called. But everyone was so involved in shutting down the flight program and leaving that no one ever answered the radio. We called until she finally died and we never did get anyone on the radio," she told him.

He got a really funny look on his face. Pulling out his card, he handed it to her and addressed us both. "I am very sorry for your loss. She was a lovely little girl. If there is anything I can do for you, don't hesitate to call me." Taking back the card, he wrote another number on the back. "This is my private number. Please don't hesitate to call me," he told us again.

After that visit, we have basically been left alone, but we know the battle still rages. This is the same battle that Paul talked about (Eph. 6:12): "[W]e wrestle not against flesh and blood, but against principalities, against powers, against the rulers of the darkness of this world, against spiritual wickedness in high places." But you know, the battle is the Lord's! The victory is won. We claim this victory in Christ as our own and continue working for His honor and glory. This is a battle for the souls of men, and while it may look like it is just over offended pride, or whatever means Satan chooses to confuse the issue with, let's remain clear that this battle is for the souls of men. God help us to redeem the time!

God continues to do His work in spite of all the opposition Satan has hurled against us. We don't know how much longer the Lord will allow the door to the gospel of Jesus Christ to be kept open, but we do know we want to be found working until either Christ returns for us in person or death takes us to Him. We also know that none of the trials we have gone through have taken God by surprise, and in reality, we really have not suffered anything. We have been inconvenienced, but in light of what other Christians in different parts of the world have had to go through, we have had it good. We are pleased to let you know that God's Word continues to go forth.

In my heart, though, I still wondered if we had done right. The words "stubborn" and "presuming on God" worried me more than I let on, and down deep I found myself still doubting. Finally, something happened that has erased all my doubts like a hot sun taking care of a foggy morning. Here is what happened.

Of all the witch doctors I was familiar with while growing up, possibly the one that impressed me the most was old Yobli (Hot, in English). He was a shaman of renown, but he was mean and irritable. I hated going to his village, as we never knew how he was going to receive us. Because he was the uncle of my best friend, Yacuwä (his father's brother), I called him "father" like Yacuwä did. But he was even mean to Yacuwä. So many times I listened as he told Yacuwä to shut up! He did not want to hear that "sound" and "don't dirty my ears with that name!" Of course, he was speaking about the gospel of Jesus Christ, and the name he did not want to hear was the name of Jesus!

After almost fifty years of being exposed to the Gospel, he seemed as hard as ever. I honestly did not have any hope or illusions that he might one day get saved. But even though I had no idea it was happening, the Holy Spirit kept working on him.

About two months after the other missions left the area, he got very sick, and everyone thought he was dying, including he himself. He told us later he thought he *had* died at one point. The old guy hated to come to Cosh, but because he was so sick, his son and daughter-in-law brought him anyway. He slowly began to recover. While he was still recuperating, we had one of our seminars. We have twelve to sixteen ex-witch doctors as students now during any of our seminars and this was just too good an opportunity for them to pass up. Most of them, while still witch doctors, had battled with or against old Yobli; now they began to take turns visiting him daily. Evidently it was what the old man needed. On one of the last meetings of the seminar, he came and listened intently to all the testimonies of the different students. Finally, slowly, he got to his feet. He walked up toward the front of the church and, to be honest, I wondered what he was going to say. To say I was a bit intimidated by him would be an understatement. He hesitated and stopped. After standing there quietly for a moment, he finally began to speak.

"You all know me," he said. "I have had the *jecula* for a long time. There was not room for one more spirit in my chest. My chest was so dark from the *jecula* that there was no light. I have hated to hear the name of Jesu Christo because my *jecula* hated Him. But when I was sick, I thought I had died. Everyone thought I had died. When I passed on from this life to the next, my feet were on a well-traveled trail. I started down the trail. Suddenly, I was aware of many beings on the trail with me. It sloped down and I began to feel the heat of an as-yet-unseen fire. I could hear screams. Suddenly I did not want to go there. I hesitated, then the beings that were with me began to push me onward. I resisted, but they grabbed me and with some of them pulling and others pushing, I was being drawn irresistibly toward a huge drop-off. I looked at the beings who were tormenting me and was shocked to see they were my *jecula* whom I had served for so long. They began to jeer at me and mock me. I was desperate. I remembered hearing that *Yai Bada* had sent His Son to save me and I had refused to be saved. I screamed in fear and yes, I screamed, '*Yai Bada,* give me another chance. Save me!' Suddenly, I was back in my hammock and the village was crying for me. I realized I was not dead and I asked *Yai Bada* to save me. I did not want to go to that place of fire, that *shobali wacä.* Now, I am here to ask you all to pray for me. I might not have done it right and I want to make sure I am truly untied from the bonds of *omawä.* I don't want to ever go to that place of fire."

A bunch of us went up and, placing our hands on him, we led him through the sinner's prayer. He was ecstatic! The smile on his face was something to see. He went around to everyone and gave them a hug. He hugged Dad and Mom. I am sure it was his way of apologizing for the huge pain he had been to them, and you can believe me when I tell you his smile, as big as it was, was dwarfed by the smiles on my Dad and Mom's faces.

Then, a couple of months ago, he got sick again. We were not even able to visit him, as everything happened so fast; he was dead before we even knew he was sick. In this day of harsh governmental regulation, there is never any gasoline to do any traveling anyway. When I heard he had died, I found myself wondering if the old man had in truth really placed his trust and confidence on the finished work of Christ. I was fearful for him.

But when we did hear what had happened, my heart burst forth in praise to our God. As I have said, after everyone else left, with their words of "stubborn, stubborn, stubborn" still ringing in our ears, we couldn't help but wonder if that was true and they were right: Were we staying because God was not finished yet, or were we just stubborn? I did not know. Well, now I did. It was obvious that God was still calling people to Himself, even cranky old witch doctors.

Here is what happened. When the old guy took sick again, all the witch doctors in his village and in the village right below him got together to make a house call. They came *en masse* and began to prepare themselves for this most heroic fight in the spirit world. Old Yobli was lying in his hammock, more unconscious than not. But when the first chant started up, "*bli, bli, bli,*" he slowly roused himself to a sitting position in his hammock. The mourners around him grouped to hold him. Taking a deep breath, the old guy pointed a weak finger at the head witch doctor.

"What are you doing here? You know I am a believer in Jesus Christ now, why are you here? Go home. I have nothing to do with that stuff any longer. I am a follower of Jesus now."

They began to reason with him, but he was adamant. Finally, amidst yells of derision, they left him. He lay back in his hammock with a contented smile and shortly after this, the angels ushered him into heaven. What sights he is beholding now! Now that I have precious ones in heaven, it has become so much more real to me. I always quoted the verse from 1 Corinthians 2:9: "But as it is written, eye hath not seen, nor ear heard, neither have entered into the heart of man, the things which God hath prepared for them that love him." And I always thought I could not know or even imagine anything about heaven, but then one day I really saw verse 10: "But God hath revealed *them* unto us by his Spirit: for the Spirit searcheth all things, yea, the deep things of God."

As I have said here so many times, "God will build His church, and the gates of hell will not stand against it!"

1 Peter 1: [3]Blessed be the God and Father of our Lord Jesus Christ, which according to his abundant mercy hath begotten

us again unto a lively hope by the resurrection of Jesus Christ
from the dead,

4 To an inheritance incorruptible, and undefiled, and that
fadeth not away, reserved in heaven for you, 5 Who are kept
by the power of God through faith unto salvation ready to be
revealed in the last time.

6 Wherein ye greatly rejoice, though now for a season, if
need be, ye are in heaviness through manifold temptations:
7 That the trial of your faith, being much more precious than
of gold that perisheth, though it be tried with fire, might be
found unto praise and honour and glory at the appearing of
Jesus Christ: 8 Whom having not seen, ye love; in whom, though
now ye see him not, yet believing, ye rejoice with joy unspeak-
able and full of glory.

Part Three

16

A Time to Heal

January 14, 2006

I looked up from my thoughts to realize that we were only a few miles out of Cosh. Could this really be true? How were we going to get through this? What *happened*? Mikeila was so alive when I left just two days ago! I had so many questions and no answers. As the pilot set up for his landing, I looked again at this place in the jungle that has held so much joy and so much sorrow for me. "God, what are You trying to teach me?" I asked in my heart. My eyes filled with tears again as I remembered my takeoff from this strip just two days earlier.

We had just returned to Venezuela in November from Mikeila's five-year check-up in Virginia. We had had a whole battery of tests done on her, not only to see if there were any long-term ill effects from the ECMO process, but also to see if there were other issues that still needed to be addressed. Mikeila had passed every test with flying colors. However, due to all the strong antibiotics and other medications she had been on, her teeth had really begun to decay. It had happened almost overnight. We noticed that her front teeth were getting dark and dead-looking. Her main doctor at the University of Virginia hospital recommended that we just schedule oral surgery, as trying to see a regular dentist would be so traumatic, so we had scheduled the surgery and Mikeila came through it fine. Our last appointment was with her main doctor again, on the first of November, to go over the last test and let him see how she was doing after the surgery.

His words gladdened my heart, because, after greeting us, he said, "I have gone over her tests and Mikeila is really doing well. I see no reason why we should have to see her in 2006. Sometime during the fall of 2006, e-mail me and we will schedule something for 2007. Mikeila is doing great!"

We were so thrilled to hear that. Our little girl had gotten over the hump! We had known that five years was considered a milestone, but I had not realized how much I had been holding my breath. Hearing the doctor say that, I breathed a huge sigh of relief. We had never allowed ourselves to ever forget how sick she had been, and how quickly things could go wrong. Now, finally, she was doing so well. For the first time in her life we did not have a doctor's appointment scheduled for her. We just *always* had appointments pending for her. Wow! I looked at Keila and we both smiled. Mikeila was going to be OK.

Now, not three short months later, Josh, Ryan, and I are descending for a landing on our little jungle airstrip. Keila, Stephen, and Mia are waiting for us there so we can hold our little Mikeila's funeral. "Lord," I prayed, "help us get through this. We don't know why You allowed this, but we do know You do all things well. Give us the strength to get through this next day and then the next. God, we gave Mikeila to You when she almost died there in the hospital in Virginia. We told You if You gave us a day, a week, a year or longer, we would thank You for each day you gave us. Well, God, You gave us almost six beautiful years with our little Mikeila. Just help us all to accept this as from You. Thank you, Jesus." I wiped the tears from my eyes as the plane steepened its descent for a landing at Cosh.

My mom and dad; my brother Gary and his wife, Marie; my brother Steve and his wife, Theda; my sisters Faith, Sharon, and Susan, along with Susan's husband, Jerry: these were my family members who were still here in Venezuela, and they were waiting for us there at the airstrip, as was the whole village of Cosh. There was not a dry eye in the place. It is just impossible to describe the ache and pain in my heart that came from knowing I will never feel those little arms around my neck again, never hear her loud whisper, never feel that wet kiss again. That part of my life is over! She had been the entire focus of our lives for the past almost six years, and now—just like that, with no warning—she was gone. How my heart longed for her. I hugged Keila and Stephen and little Mia. We walked over to Dad's house where the family was gathered. From there we walked to the church for the funeral service. My heart was so full with my grief that I could not think of anything else, until I heard the words, "We don't grieve as others do who have no hope."

We do have hope! I remember thinking. *Thank you, Jesus! We do have hope!*

Job said, "For I know that my redeemer liveth, and that he shall stand at the latter day upon the earth: And though after my skin worms destroy this body, yet in my flesh shall I see God: Whom I shall see for myself, and mine eyes shall behold, and not another; though my veins be consumed within me (Job 19:5–27).

It is *not* over! My first thoughts were wrong. OK, we are separated right now, but we *will* see Mikeila again! Not in some otherworldly body, but in a gloriously resurrected body, totally recognizable for who she is. She *will* hug me again. I *will* feel those arms around my neck and hear her whisper in my ear again, feel that wet kiss again, and you know what? She will be able to talk then! This is the hope that we have. Paul said that without the resurrection, we among all men are most miserable—but praise God, we *do* have the resurrection! We look back at Christ's resurrection and it gives us the confidence of our own!

We will see Jesus! Not as some Spirit, but as our gloriously resurrected Lord and Savior. I *will* see Jesus! I will see Reneé and Mikeila again! With these eyes and with this body; granted, not the corruptible shell I have right now, but as the apostle Paul says, "When this corruptible puts on incorruption," and it will still be me. Granted again, a much grander me than I am right now, but it will be me, and with my memories and feelings of love still intact, I *will* embrace my daughter again. For this is the hope we have! This is the promise of Christ's resurrection!

Our little girl was buried here in the jungle beside my first wife, Reneé, whose name she shared. On her headstone are the words:

Mikeila Reneé Dawson
3-23-2000 to 1-12-2006
Jehovah es mi Pastor;
nada me faltará.
PS. 23:1
A Bible verse she loved.
Our ray of light
Our spark of joy
Dwells now
With the Shepherd above.

Somehow we got through the day. I won't lie and say it was easy. I will say that God has promised us that He is with us when we go through the difficult times. Again, I won't try and act all spiritual and say how much we felt God's presence. I did not so much, not in any big way right off. But as I got the details of everything that had happened in the short days since I had left, I became more aware of the ways that He had been preparing different ones of us.

Keila told me that Mikeila had gotten extremely sick at 1:00 a.m. Finally, at 6:00 Keila hurried up to get my sister Sharon, to give Mikeila a shot to see if they could get her to quit throwing up. As soon as the 6:30 radio time came up, they asked Theda to call for the airplane so they could be med-evaced out. They began trying to call the MAF headquarters out in town two hours away by Cessna 206 airplane. No communication could be established.

Keila could not help but think of something that had happened the day before when she had to go feed the chickens. Mikeila had insisted she wanted to go, so Keila put her up in her stroller and took her and Mia along.

She had thought it odd that Mikeila made a big point of saying goodbye to each chicken. Then, as they were walking home, they ran across Sharon's horse, Snickers. Mikeila told the horse goodbye as well. Keila felt a lump rise in her throat, but refused to allow herself to think anymore of it. They walked back to the house.

When they got home, Mikeila insisted that she be dressed in her favorite dress, even putting on her favorite shoes. She then went into her room and said goodbye to all her dolls, and believe me, a little girl who has spent as much time in the hospital as our little Mikeila has a lot of dolls to say goodbye to. She sat in her bed looking all around. Keila asked her what she was doing, and in her broken speech, she said, "Mimi making memories, Mommy" (she called herself "Mimi"). Again, Keila refused to think what this might mean. Mikeila then came back into our bedroom and, snuggling up to Keila, told her, "Mimi be OK, Mommy, Mimi be OK. Tell Daddy, Mimi be OK." Mia had walked up almost as if she was aware of something momentous happening, and Mikeila told her, "Mia, Mimi be OK. You hear? Mimi be OK." Mia nodded her little head and Mikeila hugged her three-year-old sister. Keila felt the same lump raise back in her throat, and her heart turned cold. *What could be happening? Why is she doing this?* she wondered.

The next day, as she was walking back from Sharon's and Faith's house with Mikeila, suddenly a very sick little girl, Keila remembered these incidents and prayed for God to give her and Mikeila strength. Keila placed her in her little blue rocking chair and my brother Gary walked in to check on her. He felt her forehead and found that she was running a fever again.

"Can Uncle Gary pray with you, honey?" he asked her. At her nod, he knelt down with her and, placing his hands on hers, asked God to intervene and once again do a miracle for this little girl whom the whole family has spent so much time praying for. When he was finished, she then lay back down on the bed. Keila asked her if she thought she could eat something and at a faint nod, walked down to fix her a little breakfast. She brought it up and tried to rouse our little girl. Something in the way she was lying bothered Keila and, bending down over her, she realized that Mikeila was not asleep, but unconscious. She called Stephen and he came running in. Quickly realizing what was happening, he grabbed Mikeila up and they ran as fast as they could go over to Faith's and Sharon's house. The rest of the family was swiftly called, and they began working over Mikeila. This was 9:00 a.m.

Because no communication could be established with MAF by radio, Jody jumped into a speedboat and took off for Las Esmeralda, where there is a government satellite pay phone. The two hours it took to get down there seemed to take an eternity for him. Meanwhile, back at the house, my sister-in-law, Steve's wife Theda, made repeated attempts to contact MAF . . . still in vain. No one answered the radio. Jody finally arrived in Las Esmeralda only to find that the town's generator had failed and the phone was inoperative. He returned to Cosh a little after 1:00 p.m. Remembering that the Yecuana community upriver from us also has a phone, Donny jumped in the boat and drove up there with a sense of urgency that came from watching his mom do CPR on a little girl who had basically stopped breathing at 1:00 p.m. He arrived in Toqui only to find that their phone too was inoperative.

Marie kept doing CPR until about 2:00 p.m., when they felt Mikeila's little heart, which had been beating so hard, finally stop. It was over.

Memory's Dreams

The house is empty
Where rang the sound of her laughter.
The rooms echo the songs she would sing.
The pitter patter of her little feet running,
Now run in the silence through memory's dreams.
Yesterday's laughter is now just an echo
That runs through the hallways deep down in my mind.
I hold to it tightly, I want to remember,
A gift from the past
A gift for all times.
Not willing to let go; Not just for a moment;
Her memory is clear, from me, it won't part;
I still hear her laughter
The sound of her singing
I'll keep them forever; Down deep in my heart.

—SHARON DAWSON

To invest your seed of trust in God in mountains you can't move.
You have risked your life on things you cannot prove.
But to give up things you cannot keep
for what you cannot lose,
now that is the way to find the joy God has for you.

I Can See the Shore

So hold on, my child, joy comes in the morning.
Weeping only lasts for the night . . .
the darkest hour means dawn is just in sight.

—Barbara and John Tubbs
Joy Comes in the Morning

17

I Can See the Shore

In the preface to this book, I mentioned a pastor friend of mine giving me a book called Heaven, and how in this book, author Randy Alcorn tells of a young lady trying to become the first female swimmer to swim from Catalina Island to the mainland of California. The fog hung so thick and low over the ocean that throughout most of the swim she could barely see the escort boats around her. Finally, after more than fifteen hours in the water, she asked to be taken aboard. When she recovered her breath, she was dismayed to find out that she was only half a mile from shore. The next day, at a news conference, she said, "I would have kept swimming if I could have seen the shore. All I could see was the fog."

One of my favorite verses in the Bible is the verse that says: "We walk by faith, not by sight." In spite of my words of bravado, there have been so many times that all I could see was the fog and I felt I could not go on without seeing something. Walking by faith gets hard sometimes, and at those times I desperately wanted and needed to see the shore. Well, it took a little three-year-old to make me look up and over the fog of my grief and see the shore. And when I finally did, it was as if I were seeing the shores of heaven! The Bible speaks highly of the faith of a child, and I long to have my own faith be as the faith of a child. As I said before, I long for the day when my faith shall be sight and I shall see the Lord!

The funeral was over and I sat in my office more in shock than trying to do anything. I sat there wrapped in my thoughts, barely aware that Mia had walked in and was sitting in Mikeila's little blue rocking chair that I had placed right beside my desk. I was suddenly snapped out of my morose thoughts by something Mia was saying, more to herself than to me.

"This is Mikeila's little chair," she said to herself. "Mikeila sat here and Uncle Gary came and prayed for her. Then Jesus sent His people to talk to her and take her home to be with Jesus."

Like I said, she was talking to herself, rocking in Mikeila's little chair. I got down on my knees beside her and asked her, "What did you say, Mia? Who came and took Mikeila to Jesus?" My voice shook as I asked her the questions.

She was not bothered by my questions. "Daddy, Jesus sent people to get Mikeila to take her up to be with Him. She told me goodbye and not to cry, that she was OK now. Why are you crying, Daddy?"

Now, I don't know what Mia saw. But I do know that ever since Mia was old enough to be aware of anything, she and Mikeila had been inseparable. Mia normally took longer naps than Mikeila, but as soon as she woke up, if Mikeila were not in the room, Mia would not rest until she could be reunited with her sister. Her first question was always, "Where is Mikeila?" One of my biggest worries while flying home had been: What do I tell Mia? What can I say to her so she understands and doesn't constantly ask "Where is Mikeila?" I knew it would just be an open sore that would never heal for all of us. I had even prayed, asking God to somehow help Mia to understand, but it was one of those prayers you pray not really—not actually—believing anything can be done. Since that day, though, Mia has never once asked where Mikeila is. She has remained steadfast that Mikeila is in heaven with Jesus.

"I miss my sister very much," she said just the other day. "But she is in Heaven with Jesus now. Daddy, why did Jesus have to take my sister to Heaven?" she asked me.

"I don't know, honey, maybe He needed her for a job," I told her, not sure myself why Jesus would have taken my beautiful little girl.

"Like do you think His room was messy and He needed a little girl to clean it up for Him?" Her little face was so earnest all I could do was smile and hope she did not see my tears.

There continue to be tears, but as we journey through this life, we continue on as the song writer says, "I walk into the unknown trusting all the while." How do we do it? Well, it is because we "walk by faith and not by sight."

I just finished listening to a song by Janet Pascal. The words of the chorus are so beautiful and so true:

It's not about now,
it's not about here.
It's all about then when there's nothing to fear,
it's all about there where the mystery is clear
when then will be now, and there will be here.

And the story continues . . . .

Christian Small Publishers Association Awards – 2010 Biography Book of the Year!

Growing Up Yanomamö: Missionary Adventures in the Amazon Rainforest

by MICHAEL DAWSON

Foreword by Larry M. Brown

$19.95

The New York Times describes *Growing Up Yanomamö* as "Huck Finn with an Amazon twist."

Michael Dawson recounts his adventures growing up and working with the last stone-aged tribe in the world living deep in the Amazon rainforest. The challenges and truths he experiences will equip and encourage you in your faith, even if you've never had the privilege to live in another land.

Michael's sense of humor, wit, and caring come through the pages. It is like sitting down with a good friend who is ready to surprise you with an amazing true story. In this book, you will hear tales of:

- Rainforest and rivers
- Shabonos and shaman
- Tapir, jaguar, cougar, and much more
- Tribal warfare and spreading the Good News
- Literally, life and death
- Over fifty years living with the Yanomamö

Growing Up Yanomamö will expand the mind of even the most experienced traveler. Nothing demands a self-review like a trip through another time and culture. The author provides just this sort of trip in his special book.

Also available from Grace Acres Press:

Life Before Death: A Restored, Regenerated, and Renewed Life

by Ian Leitch

Foreword by Joseph M. Stowell

$14.95

Life Before Death presents a robust basis for living a full life of meaning and purpose. Ian Leitch is both passionate and compassionate as he provides the key to real living.

Engaging, smart, persuasive . . .

—Jerry Jenkins, Author of the *Left Behind* Series

Resources and services for your organization available from Grace Acres Press:

- Author presentations
- Book excerpts for your newsletters
- Fundraising programs
- Writing seminars—elementary school through adults
- Publishing seminars and consulting
- Books, DVDs, and music CDs

Call today 888-700-GRACE (4722) or visit our Web site: www.GraceAcresPress.com

Michael and Keila continue working in the jungles of Venezuela. Because of a lack of air support, they do not have regular mail delivery in Venezuela, but you can reach them via e-mail at:
ulijiflyer@gmail.com.

Or you can reach them via SKYPE.
Please e-mail them for their SKYPE name.

Visit the Web site for more information about the Dawsons and the Yanomamö tribe:
www.missionpadamoaviation.org